THE TASTE OF HEALTH

The BBC Food and Health Campaign

This campaign was launched by BBC Education in Autumn 1985 to give information and practical advice on the established links between diet and health.

TELEVISION SERIES

O'Donnell Investigates: The Food Connection, produced by David Cordingley. Part 1 first transmitted on BBC 1 and 2 from September 1985; Part 2 first transmitted on BBC 2 from February 1986.

The Taste of Health, produced by Jenny Rogers. First transmitted on BBC 2 from September 1985.

You Are What You Eat, produced by Anna Jackson. First transmitted on BBC 1 from January 1986.

RADIO SERIES

Not Another Diet Programme, produced by Sarah Rowlands. First transmitted on Radio 4 early 1986.

BBC PUBLICATIONS

The Food Connection: The BBC Guide to Healthy Eating by Colin Tudge

The Taste of Health: The BBC Guide to Healthy Cooking edited by Jenny Rogers

The Campaign was devised by David Cordingley, BBC Continuing Education Television Department

THE
TASTE
OF HEALTH

THE BBC GUIDE TO HEALTHY COOKING

edited by Jenny Rogers

BRITISH BROADCASTING CORPORATION

The Publishers would like to thank Clare Brigstocke, Elizabeth
Farrar, Alex Laird, Natalie Medd and Maggie Sanderson for their
help in the preparation of this book.

Diagrams: Stan North
Photography: James Jackson
Design: Philip Gilderdale
Home Economist: Carole Handslip
Food Stylist: Alison Williams

Published to accompany a series of programmes prepared in
consultation with the BBC Continuing Education Advisory Council

First published 1985
Published by the British Broadcasting Corporation
35 Marylebone High Street,
London WIM 4AA

ISBN 0563 21136 9 (paperback)
ISBN 0563 21196 2 (hardback)

Typeset in 11/13pt Linotron Baskerville by
Rowland Phototypesetting Ltd, Bury St Edmunds, Suffolk.
Text printing by Jolly and Barber Ltd, Rugby, England.
Cover origination by Bridge Graphics, Hull.
Cover printing and binding by Chorley and Pickersgill,
Leeds, England.

CONTENTS

CONVERSION TABLES

All these are *approximate* conversions, which have either been rounded up or down. In a few recipes it has been necessary to modify them very slightly. Never mix metric and imperial measures in one recipe. Stick to one system or the other.

Weights	
½ oz	10 g
1	25
1½	40
2	50
3	75
4	110
5	150
6	175
7	200
8	225
9	250
10	275
12	350
13	375
14	400
15	425
1 lb	450
1¼	550
1½	700
2	900
3	1·4 kg
4	1·8
5	2·3

Volume	
1 fl oz	25 ml
2	50
3	75
5 (¼ pint)	150
10 (½)	300
15 (¾)	400
1 pint	570
1¼	700
1½	900
1¾	1 litre
2	1·1
2¼	1·3
2½	1·4
2¾	1·6
3	1·7
3¼	1·8
3½	2
3¾	2·1
4	2·3
5	2·8
6	3·4
7	4·0
8 (1 gal)	4·5

Measurements	
¼ inch	0·5 cm
½	1
1	2·5
2	5
3	7·5
4	10
6	15
7	18
8	20·5
9	23
11	28
12	30·5

Oven temperatures		
Mk 1	275°F	140°C
2	300	150
3	325	170
4	350	180
5	375	190
6	400	200
7	425	220
8	450	230
9	475	240

Imperial spoon measures have been used in many recipes. These are *level* spoonfuls unless otherwise stated. If you prefer to work in metric, use the following equivalents:

teaspoon	=	5 ml measuring spoon
dessertspoon	=	10 ml measuring spoon
tablespoon	=	15 ml measuring spoon

INTRODUCTION

by Jenny Rogers

This book is about the joys and pleasures of cooking and eating food which looks wonderful, tastes irresistible . . . and is also good for you.

It is a book about positive health. Much has been written in the last few years about what we must and must not eat. Unfortunately, many such pronouncements tend to have a negative and puritanical tone. Perhaps that is why we so often hear the plaintive cry 'but what *can* I eat? All the food I like seems to be bad for me!'

Happily, there is actually far, far more food that is positively excellent for your general health than there is food that is in any sense 'unhealthy'. Nor does eating prudently mean a life of boring, tasteless meals.

Think, for instance, of this menu. To begin, the startling scarlet of Sweet Red Pepper Soup (page 78) from Mexico, served with freshly baked Irish Soda Bread (page 28). Then, as the main course, Indian-style Chicken and Potato Casserole (page 106), fluffy brown rice (page 59) and a Sprouty Fruit Salad (page 162). Then, finally, a fruit and yoghurt ice (page 223) served with fresh raspberries. This would be an entirely 'healthy' meal as the emphasis is on vegetables, fruit, rice and bread. It contains virtually no fat, very little sugar and has plenty of fibre. It would also look enticing and taste delicious.

In compiling this book we have commissioned cooks with many different backgrounds and interests. Some come from areas like the Mediterranean or the Middle East where the food eaten is already very much of the type now advocated as being good for all of us. Some are top chefs who have adapted their usual recipes along 'healthy' lines. Others are food writers who have been convinced for some time of the need for change. These are people who have already been cooking and eating in the recommended ways for some time and have passed on some of their favourite recipes here.

The result is a uniquely broad-ranging book. It includes traditional recipes from around the world as well as modern adaptations of old friends. There are recipes for children's food, for family eating, for breakfast, for cooking in a hurry or on a restricted budget. At the other end of the scale we include recipes for dinner parties and even for grand celebrations. This book aims to offer you a good selection of recipes for every occasion and to stimulate your own ideas for developing more along the same lines. Bon appetit!

WHY OUR DIET NEEDS TO CHANGE

Some people find it hard to imagine that there is anything seriously wrong with the way we eat now. Furthermore they will say that they actually *like* the foods they are told they must cut down on; they may be able to point to parents or grandparents who have apparently eaten the same diet all their lives and have lived to a ripe old age.

Unfortunately it does look extremely likely that diet is a major factor in causing what are broadly described as 'Western diseases of affluence'; these are the conditions which are rarely seen in societies where the pattern of eating is considerably different. In Britain we are now in the unenviable position of being among the world leaders in these diseases.

Exactly how and why diet contributes to disease is still hotly debated, but links of some kind are pretty clearly established in these cases:

Condition	Dietary Link
Cancer of the colon and large bowel	Too little fibre
Constipation	Too little fibre
Coronary heart disease	Saturated fat
Diabetes	Fat and sugar
Diverticulitis (a painful intestinal disease)	Too little fibre
Gall bladder disease	Too little fibre
Hypertension (raised blood pressure)	Salt
Obesity	Highly refined food; fat, sugar, salt
Osteoporosis (brittle bones)	Too little calcium, too much highly refined food
Stroke	Salt
Tooth decay	Sugar
Vitamin and mineral deficiencies	Highly refined food

Two recent Government documents have backed the need for change. They were the NACNE Report (National Advisory Committee on Nutrition Education) and the COMA Report (Committee on Medical Aspects of Food Policy). These reports follow many others from equally eminent bodies all over the world, for instance the World Health Organisation and the McGovern Committee in America. Taken together, they make broadly the same recommendations: we should cut down on saturated fat from dairy products and meat, reduce our intake of sugar and salt, and increase the amount of fibre and raw, fresh food we eat.

Other countries have already begun making these changes, and perhaps they provide the most dramatic proof of all that the changes are needed in the first place. The number of deaths from heart disease in both America and Australia has recently fallen by about a quarter. Many factors are clearly involved in this – for instance the reduction in smoking and the increase in exercise. But both these countries have also seen substantial changes in what people eat, along the lines described above.

Can we really believe the nutritionists this time?

One reason that some people feel sceptical about dietary advice is that there seems to have been so much of it about. Often it appears that there is a new dietary fashion every few years, which, if you sit it out, will simply pass to be replaced by the next one. Unfortunately, the publicity given to fad slimming diets has sullied the word 'diet' generally, and has led people to think that the reforms now advocated fall in the same category.

One weight-loss diet in particular has been the centre of much confusion. This was the 'low carbohydrate' diet which was at its peak of popularity in the early seventies and was based on the message that eating a lot of high protein food was 'good', and eating carbohydrate was 'bad'. The trouble with this diet is that it involves eating a lot of meat and cheese which have a high saturated fat content. It also lumps all carbohydrates together: refined (eg sugar) and unrefined (eg wholemeal bread). Even now after so much de-bunking publicity, many people still have the idea that 'protein' is 'good' and potatoes, rice, flour and bread are 'bad'. In fact, we should all be increasing the amounts of unrefined, *complex* carbohydrates we eat (such as potatoes), and decreasing the amounts of sugar, red meat and hard cheese. The carbohydrate should have a *complex* chemical structure because, amongst other things, this increases its bulk and prevents us from overeating.

The general shift of emphasis in our diet on which this book is based does not fall into the 'fad diet' category. It is built on the broad consensus which has been emerging the last 20 years from eminent, sober and cautious medical scientists all over the world.

Interpreting the evidence

Another major reason for doubting the 'new' ideas in many people's minds is that a lot of the evidence has been taken from comparative studies of whole populations. To take salt as an example, the Japanese mortality rate from stroke is very high, though their incidence of coronary heart disease is low. Studies which have compared or *correlated* their diet with those of other countries have identified the fact that it is high in salt (although healthy in other respects). Salt *could* therefore be a cause of stroke, but correlation by itself does not *prove* causation. Nor does this kind of study predict what the chances are of any individual Japanese having a stroke. Then, too, there will be many individual exceptions to a general rule. We have all heard of someone who smokes like a chimney, never gets lung cancer and lives to a hale and hearty 90. This does not invalidate the fact that smoking is bad for you and is the main cause of lung cancer.

One other problem is the sheer ordinariness now of heart disease and cancers. We have become so used to them that it is easy to assume they are the norm – for instance, one man in four in Britain has a heart attack before retiring age. Yet a hundred years ago heart disease was virtually unknown. Then, certainly, many people died young, but most died of infections which are now treatable. Their arteries were usually in excellent condition, as indeed they are in countries where, again, general life-expectancy may be shorter than in Britain, but the population does not suffer from heart disease. It is horrifying to discover that in our society arterial disease can now begin even in childhood.

Many people take a shoulder-shrugging and fatalistic view of their own health. They don't feel that making changes in lifestyle and eating is likely to improve their chances of living to a healthy and active old age. As we have already said, the rules can only apply broadly. Just as you may know someone who smoked but never developed lung cancer, so you may know of someone else who was apparently fit, but died young. However, *in general*, the evidence seems to point to a more positive conclusion: you improve your chances of remaining fitter and more active for longer if you stop smoking, take regular exercise and eat prudently.

Research is constantly dotting the i's and crossing the t's of nutritional theory. Sometimes the results of these studies are reported at a popular level in a way that does not do justice to their complexity. For instance, it is undoubtedly 'true' that we should all eat more fibre. However, research has shown that fibre also has the effect of taking minerals out of the body with it. This does not mean that the general fibre theory is suddenly disproved, only that we are constantly increasing our understanding of the effects of food on health. Equally, it is difficult for scientists to provide the direct evidence that fat causes heart disease. There will always be some contrary evidence: that is the nature of scientific enquiry.

Finally, few diseases have a simple cause. Their progress can be accelerated by several factors working together. It is likely, for example, that our general lifestyle is implicated in the development of coronary heart disease as well as our diet. Lack of regular exercise, smoking, and the presence of too much stress can certainly contribute to many of the

'Western' diseases so general in our society. However, diet remains indicted as the most important single cause. Stress by itself is not peculiar to Western societies: it would be foolish to imagine that an Indian peasant plagued by the drought and crop diseases which might destroy his livelihood is any less under stress than an English company director contemplating a difficult shareholders' meeting.

You will find a more detailed explanation of the scientific and medical background to the modern consensus on our diet in the companion volume to this book, *The Food Connection: The BBC Guide to Healthy Eating* by Colin Tudge, also published by BBC Publications (1985).

Our philosophy

The foundation of the recipes in this book is a generous quantity of cereals and grains in the form of bread, pasta, pulses, and grains such as rice. We have also commissioned recipes which make lavish use of all kinds of fruit and vegetables, especially in their raw forms, though there are many recipes for delightful cooked vegetable dishes too. There are some recipes involving the fattier types of meat such as beef, but these always involve 'stretching' the meat in a dish where, with ingenuity, a little goes a very long way. Mostly, the meat dishes emphasise poultry, which has little fat. We have largely excluded bacon, sausages and made-up meats like corned beef and salami because of their high fat and salt content.

Fish in all its forms features strongly, whether it is a delicious (and cheap) mussel stew or a baked, stuffed mackerel. Butter, eggs and cream are used extremely sparingly, or not at all, though we have many recipes using low fat cheeses and skimmed milk. Sauces are thickened by reduction or are based on vegetable purées.

For seasoning, we have emphasised the use of herbs and spices as replacements for salt, though salt still appears in the recipes in modest form, and can, of course, be added at your discretion or left out altogether. We have generally avoided canned or other forms of highly refined food as it is normally so heavily laden with sugar or salt, sometimes both. We have not banished sugar altogether: it appears in some recipes as a 'seasoning', used discreetly to enhance flavour. There are, however, plenty of puddings where sweetness is supplied by the natural flavours of fruit.

We have tried to ensure that most of the ingredients in our recipes are available in a large supermarket. However, for some items you will, inevitably, have to track down a good health or wholefood shop where you will normally be able to find a much wider range of pulses, seasonings and spices. Some foods can only be bought in 'ethnic' shops, though with demand increasing for many of these, they are now becoming much more widely available in supermarkets.

Is 'healthy' food cheaper?

Some people would say that what you save on expensive meat, you spend on buying more fruit and vegetables. However, in theory it should certainly be possible to save substantial amounts of money on everyday eating by putting more emphasis on pulses and grains, which are both cheap and filling, and by only buying cheap seasonal fruit and vegetables.

Moving away from processed and 'convenience' foods saves a great deal of money: ready-mixed sauces, tinned soups and vegetables, crisps, sausages, frozen 'dinners', dehydrated packet meals, biscuits, pickles and instant desserts are phenomenally expensive as well as being full of additives, preservatives, salt and/or sugar. A little extra time spent making or growing things yourself (try growing your own beansprouts or making your own yoghurt) will also save money. Shop-bought yoghurt, for instance, is at least four times more expensive than the home-made variety.

Slimming

The approach to eating we outline is not specifically designed to encourage weight loss and has nothing at all to do with calorie counting. However, if you are overweight, cutting down on fat and sugar in the way this book suggests will almost certainly mean that excess pounds eventually disappear, especially if you also begin taking regular exercise.

Making changes

One recent BBC radio programme involved a 'phone-in about 'healthy eating'. The response took the producers by surprise: a great many hostile letters were sent in by people who had obviously felt personally attacked by any suggestion that their food intake ought to alter in any way.

No-one would pretend that it is easy to alter the eating habits of a lifetime. It takes time to get used to new tastes, new textures or new combinations of food. Yet it can and does happen. In 1950s Britain, few people had ever eaten spaghetti let alone actually cooked it; before the 1960s, Indian food was largely unknown; now every small town in Britain has its Indian take-away. Chinese and Indian dishes even feature in the packs of mass-produced de-hydrated convenience food now available.

This revolution has come about because people have gradually tried out this 'strange' food and found they liked it. Perhaps this is the way to change to a healthier diet, not by trying to make instant major changes, but by gradually altering buying and eating habits until a new pattern is established. Nor does healthier eating mean *never* eating butter, cream or sugar – it just means making very much more occasional use of them than has been customary in our recent past.

HEALTHY COOKING TECHNIQUES

Fat gives food moisture and improves its appearance: fried food, for instance, has a pleasantly browned and glossy look. Cream, butter and egg yolks help emulsify or thicken sauces; salt and sugar intensify flavour. Perhaps it is not surprising that many cooks cannot bear the thought of doing without them.

Fortunately there are many techniques of cooking, some new, some thousands of years old, which are perfectly in line with modern thinking about food and health and which do help preserve the moisture, goodness and flavour of food without too much resort to the frying pan or the salt and sugar pots.

Barbecueing

It is intriguing that the barbecue has recently become so fashionable, as it must be the oldest cookery technique in the world. The word itself comes from Mexico, but we must assume that Stone Age people also 'barbecued' their meat over an open fire.

Like grilling, barbecueing is a healthy way to cook as it preserves flavour, and also allows fat to drip out in the intense heat.

Barbecued food is often marinated first (see page 16) or brushed with a sauce. Most ready-made bought sauces are cloyingly sweet and far too salty. It is simple to make your own and the taste will be much better (see page 210).

It is perfectly possible to cook on an open fire with no more than a green twig to help you retrieve the food from the fire. However, a small investment in some basic equipment will make it all a lot easier. Small barbecues of the solid portable type, are useful. They can cope with a surprising amount of food and can easily be moved about the garden or taken on a picnic or holiday.

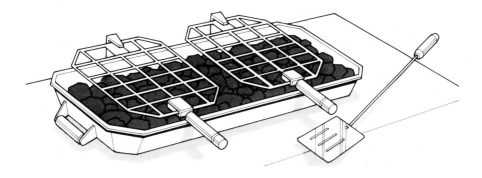

There are many bigger and more expensive barbecues available but if you decide that barbecuing is something that you want to do often, it might be worth building your own using bricks and a couple of door scrapers. When you have perfected the design, you could make it permanent with mortar, but it will work perfectly well with the bricks just piled one on another.

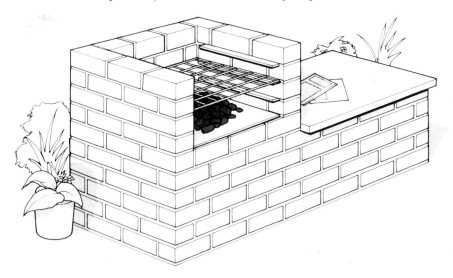

The fuel you use depends on circumstances. Hard lump-wood charcoal is the best, if you can get it. It burns evenly and well without taking as long to reach the right temperature as briquettes. Light the fire using crumpled newspaper and a few pieces of kindling wood rather than spirit or barbeque lighter fuel: these often seem to give an unpleasant taste to the food.

Wood makes a useful alternative to charcoal. Use hardwood for cooking, as pine, other softwood, or wood that has been painted will give the food a taste of turpentine. Fruitwood gives the best results but any slow burning hardwood such as oak will do. While lighting the fire, heap the fuel up in a cone until everything is well alight, then spread out the hot embers and put another layer of fuel on top. When this is all glowing and the flames have died down, there will be a thin layer of white ash over the fire. This is the moment to start cooking.

While you are cooking meat or fish with fat in it, the fire may flare up. You can control this with a little water from a spray bottle.

Special tools

Various grills are available on which to hold the food: the most useful is one shaped like a tennis racket; for whole fish there is a special fish-shaped wire basket with a handle. Greasing the grill with a little oil before you use

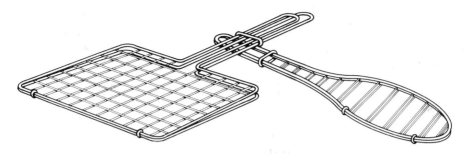

it will stop the food sticking. The easiest way to clean the grill is to use a fine wire brush; you may also need to oil the grill between barbecues to prevent rust.

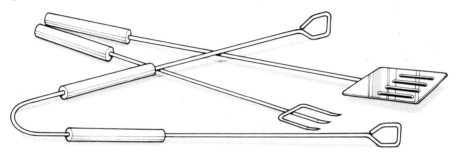

There are various long-handled implements specially designed for barbecue cooking which will help avoid burnt fingers. Of those available, the tongs are probably the most useful. Long forks may be substituted, but be careful not to pierce the meat or juices will be lost. A really good oven cloth is essential.

Skewers should be flat, as the meat or fish will stay in place on these much better than on the round variety.

Blanching

This is a method of cooking vegetables by immersing them in a pan of boiling water – the time will vary according to their size and type and may range from 10 seconds to 2 minutes. They are then usually 'refreshed', ie immediately plunged into cold water (to stop the cooking process) and patted dry. This intensifies their colour, and softens them a little. They can then be served cold with a salad dressing or used in a further cooking process. Brief blanching is also a useful way of removing the tough skins from fruit such as peaches or tomatoes. Dip them into boiling water for a few seconds, then rub or peel off the skins under a cold tap.

Blanching is also used to prepare vegetables for freezing. The heat destroys enzymes which would otherwise lead to loss of flavour and texture during freezing.

Dry-frying

Frying normally involves coating the pan with a generous film of oil or fat and then cooking at a high temperature. In deep-fat frying, the food is totally immersed in hot oil or fat.

Dry-frying means that the pan is only lightly smeared with oil. Apply the oil using a pastry brush or a piece of kitchen paper. Heat the pan for a few seconds on a high flame, then lower it quickly to moderate and put the food in. Turn it over after a few moments if you want the other side browned, then reduce the heat to very low for the remainder of the cooking.

You must have a good quality heavy pan for this method. There are many such pans on the market: heavy-bottomed non-stick pans, cast-iron enamelled pans with a matt black interior. There is a newer non-stick heavy pan which has a grey 'dimpled' bottom, in which the food does not actually sit in the oil, but rests on the dimples.

True frying pans have sloping sides and don't have lids. A sauté pan has straight sides to help keep food under control while it is being stirred or shaken, and a lid. This kind of pan is particularly useful for the dry-frying method. In many recipes, after the initial period of cooking, the lid can then be put on and the food cooked in its own steam.

Grilling

Grilling is a suitable method for cooking tender, evenly sized cuts of meat which are not too thick. The fat runs out and the radiant heat gives a good crisp texture to the top of the food. Grilling is not suitable for tough cuts of meat as the intense heat toughens up the texture of the fibres even more. With fish, grilling is best used for oily fish such as mackerel, herring, sprats and sardines or white fish which have tough enough skins to retain moisture. Delicate white fish can dry out too quickly. Some vegetables can be grilled – for instance tomatoes and mushrooms – as long as they are brushed with oil first and cooked under a medium heat.

Marinating

This is a useful technique with wide applications in healthy cookery. Marinating food reduces the need for prolonged cooking in fat while at the same time providing the opportunity to add all kinds of subtle and interesting flavours.

A marinade typically contains acid liquid ingredients, such as lemon juice, yoghurt, vinegar or wine, and a little oil, herbs and spices. The food is immersed in the liquid, covered tightly and refrigerated for some hours (or even days) during which time the marinade permeates the fish or meat with its flavours. The oil and acid ingredients have a tenderising effect as they start the process of breaking down the fibres of the food. This can be important in certain types of meat or fish which would otherwise be dry or stringy.

Marinades have two main uses:

(i) Fish can be eaten raw after it has been immersed in a marinade for several hours, covered with cling-film and refrigerated. In chemical terms what happens is that the protein in the fish is coagulated so that it becomes tender even though it has not been subjected to heat. This is the method used for Seviche (page 91).

(ii) Meat or fish can be marinated for several hours and then cooked briefly, usually at a high temperature. The marinade softens and moistens the meat so that it does not dry out when it is cooked. This method is often used when food is to be barbecued or grilled. It is also an essential preliminary to most Indian tandoori cooking and to many Chinese stir-fry dishes.

Having done its job, the marinade is often discarded, though it can sometimes be used to make an accompanying sauce. Where the marinade contains a lot of yoghurt, the sauce can usually only be warmed, not boiled, as boiling can make the yoghurt separate and give an unpleasantly curdled look to the sauce.

Microwave

Microwaved food cooks quickly. The food is not subjected to radiant heat, but is cooked through friction when the food particles are agitated at high speed by microwaves. Food is either cooked dry or with a minimal amount of water added (to create steam). Microwaved fish can be ready in five minutes, a baked potato in six minutes, a whole chicken in 30 minutes, and the flavour is superb as there is very little loss of nutrients.

You can use a microwave to dry herbs and make sauces, and it is an excellent way to cook vegetables. For instance, microwaved courgettes can be cooked in three minutes with only a tablespoon of water. They will have a bright green colour and an intense flavour which it is hard to achieve with other methods.

However, microwave ovens do have some disadvantages. Most current models do not brown food successfully, and meat or cheese dishes often need to be completed under a grill. Some foods (for instance rice or pasta) can be just as quickly cooked by conventional methods. Timing can be difficult to get right, as it depends on the depth of the food and the shape of the container. And although microwave cooking is a suitable method for almost any dish that calls for steaming, it is not so successful a substitute for conventional methods of baking.

Oven-cooking

In Britain we typically use our ovens for roasting food and for baking cakes. But the dry heat of oven cookery also provides many other useful techniques:

🌿 *Casseroles:* a familiar method of slow cooking where meat, fish or vegetables are cooked together to produce a rich blend of flavours. Many of the minerals and vitamins leached out during cooking are retained in the sauce. Most casseroles lend themselves well to refrigeration or freezing and then thorough reheating. Doing this also provides you with an opportunity to remove the fat which is inevitably produced during cooking.

🌿 *En papillote* or 'cooking in parcels': originally this term meant oven-cooking meat inside oiled paper cases. Now, however, it has come to mean wrapping individual servings of food inside foil or greaseproof paper where it makes its own miniature steamy environment. It is a specially good way to cook fish, but can also be used for meat and vegetables.

To make a parcel, cut a generous square of foil and place the fish or meat in the centre of it. Normally the recipe will specify a vegetable and herb accompaniment which helps to provide steam and flavour. Roll two opposite edges of the foil together to form the top of the parcel, but make sure it is not too close to the food – you should leave a little dome of air inside. Then fold the two ends neatly and twist them up. Place the parcels on a baking tray in case they leak. The oven temperature for this method of cooking is usually moderate to high.

When the parcels are cooked, slip them from the baking tray on to warmed plates and let people unwrap them at the table.

🌿 Food can also be wrapped in leaves, such as cabbage or lettuce leaves, and baked in the oven, but obviously more moisture is lost than in dishes where the food is completely sealed in foil.

🍂 *Meat or chicken bricks* imitate a primitive clay oven. The long slow cooking in an enclosed environment involves no fat and produces a tender, succulent end product. These bricks can also be used for vegetables.

Pressure cooking

Pressure cooking is an excellent method of cooking food which would otherwise take a long time – for instance, the pulses which are so useful in a healthy diet, or the stocks which form a foundation for tasty sauces. Pressure cooking normally reduces the cooking time to about a third of what it would otherwise be as the food cooks in a much higher temperature. It can also be used to steam vegetables and fish.

There are two main disadvantages with pressure cooking. Firstly, the high pressure can cause a collapse in the texture of food. Secondly, you cannot easily inspect cooking progress, since to do this you must remove the pot from the heat, reduce the pressure with cold water, then take the lid off. With some vegetables, a minute's extra cooking time can make all the difference between crisp tenderness and a soggy mess. Timing is much less important with dishes where texture is not critical, eg pulse purées, stocks and some home-made soups.

Processing

In a few short years, our perception of the food processor has changed. Once food processors were regarded as expensive 'gadgets' with all the derogatory overtones that that word implies, but now many people now see them as an essential part of a modern kitchen. In real terms the price has come down because of increased sales and intense competition between manufacturers. All food processors have a strong metal 'master' blade which will chop and liquidise food. There is usually a variety of other blades and discs for slicing, bread making and so on. The great advantage of food processors over blenders and mixers is that they are so simple to clean and can perform many different operations with such ease and speed in a single goblet: chopping onions, kneading dough, making breadcrumbs, liquidising soup or shredding cabbage. They will be particularly useful for a lot of the recipes in this book. For instance, raw soaked chickpeas can be reduced to a paste in two minutes in a processor; the initial preparation of sauces and marinades can be speeded up enormously. The disadvantage of food processors is the danger of over-processing. Chunky soups, for instance, can easily lose their interesting texture. When you want to preserve the individual colour and texture of vegetables, it is better to use one of the slicing blades on your processor to prepare the vegetables, or to chop them by hand. If you don't have a food processor, a blender is a good substitute for liquidising. Sauces can be sieved, and many raw ingredients can be grated, chopped or pounded instead (eg fresh ginger).

Another useful and very cheap alternative to a food processor is the Mouli sieve which has a rotating handle and three grades of sieving plate. This is easy to use and will produce interesting 'chunky' soups and sauces.

Reduction

Reducing a liquid by evaporation is a useful way of thickening and of concentrating flavour in a sauce without resorting to heavy use of salt, sugar, cream or egg yolks. It is a process which also helps avoid the use of flour to thicken sauces, which can give a raw taste and rather heavy texture.

A large shallow pan will give the quickest result as moisture is then driven off more quickly in the steam. Bring the liquid to the boil and let it bubble vigorously. Skim off any scum. Keep boiling, keep stirring and don't go away to do something else: this process needs your full attention. Remove the pan from the heat when you have the correct quantity of liquid. Add salt and pepper at this stage and not before, otherwise you could end up with an over-seasoned liquid. Hard boiling can reduce the strength of essential oils in some herbs and spices, so when using stock in a dish where the liquid has to be boiled hard, add the required herbs and spices near the end of the cooking time.

Stir-frying

This technique is widely used in all Asian countries and developed out of the need to economise on fuel. It is an excellent way of achieving some of the advantages of deep- and shallow-frying without using anything like the same amount of fat. It is also quick and so preserves a high percentage of both nutrients and flavour.

The secrets of success are:

❧ *The right pan*: Stir-frying is difficult in the conventionally shallow Western frying-pan. The food jumps about too much, and a lot of it is likely to end up all over the floor and the cook. A large deep frying-pan or even a deep saucepan is better, but the ideal pan for stir-frying is the Chinese wok. Its deep, rounded bowl shape means that only a little fat is necessary and the food can be safely and vigorously turned in the pan.

For *gas* cookers look for a round-bottomed wok with one protruding wooden handle. Use it with an open steel stand (not the closed type with a few holes punched in it) for added stability.

For *electric* cookers you must have a flat-bottomed wok as the round-bottomed type may damage the element of your cooker. These woks nearly always come with two D-shaped handles.

In both cases, hunt for a heavy carbon-steel wok. Non-stick or stainless steel will not give such good results. A steaming rack and a lid for the wok extend its versatility considerably.

A new wok always needs 'seasoning' before use. Scrub it well with a cream cleanser and a steel wool pad to remove the machine oil with which it is probably coated; this is the only time a wok should be scrubbed. Rinse it well in clear water and dry it carefully. Now heat a little oil in the wok. Wipe it round the wok thoroughly and leave it on a very low heat for 30 minutes. Wipe it out with kitchen paper. The paper will be black. Keep wiping with new kitchen paper until the kitchen paper wipes clean.

Once seasoned, the wok should only be washed briefly in water after use. Don't use detergent, and don't attempt to scrub away the blackened deposit – this is the treasured *patina* of a well seasoned wok. Pat the wok dry, and oil it lightly to keep rust at bay. If you do allow your wok to go rusty, you will have to scrub the rust off and season it again.

❧ *Evenly sized ingredients*: Stir-fried food cooks so quickly that it is important for the ingredients to be cut into pieces of the same size to ensure that they all cook in the same amount of time.

❧ *Cook the ingredients in the correct order*: Again, the speed of stir-fry cooking makes this essential. The recipe will specify which ingredients need to go in first because they take longer to cook. Before beginning any stir-frying it is vital to have all the ingredients ready-prepared and near to hand.

❧ *Constant turning during cooking*: Stir-frying usually needs the cook's complete attention throughout the cooking period. 'Turning' would be a more accurate word for the action than 'stirring' as the food needs to be constantly lifted and turned against the hot sides of the pan. The ideal implement for this is a shorter solid version of the Western fish slice. Some Chinese cooks say that you should sing loudly while you stir-fry, as this encourages the correct hand and arm action!

Most stir-fried dishes have spices and other flavourings added to flavour the food. Often a little garlic and ginger are added to the oil at the start of cooking. Liquid seasonings (for instance soy sauce and wine) are often added to create additional flavour and moisture later.

Raw food

The simplest 'method' of all. Probably we all ought to be eating a much higher percentage of our food raw: this way the nutrients are not destroyed by immersion in water or by being exposed to heat. Almost all fruit and vegetables can be used raw for salads (see pages 155–162). Fish can also be eaten raw if it is marinated first (page 91). Meat, pulses and many cereals, however, need to be cooked to treat substances which would otherwise be toxic or difficult to digest.

Steaming

There was a time when every British household had its steamer for making sweet and savoury puddings, but the steamer fell out of fashion along with the puddings and many people now have to improvise when they steam food.

Steaming is an especially valuable technique for vegetables, as it dissolves away far less of their flavour, colour and goodness than boiling does. It does take a little longer than boiling, however. Steaming may also be used for fish and grains.

The normal European steamer is a double pan. Water is boiled in the bottom compartment forcing steam through holes in the upper one, which has a lid. (One useful type of modern steamer has three compartments so that, for example, fish and vegetables can be steamed simultaneously but separately in the top two sections.) Other cultures have their own versions of steamers, all of which can now be brought in the UK. The Chinese wok can be used for steaming by fitting a grid inside the pan, and covering that with a domed lid. This is big enough to accommodate a whole fish such as sea bass. The Chinese also use *bamboo steamers*: round baskets with slatted bamboo bases which fit one inside the other over a pan of boiling water. Moroccans have the *couscousier* for their traditional dish, couscous. The grain accompanying the stewed meat sits snugly inside the brim of the pan in which the meat is cooked. There is no lid.

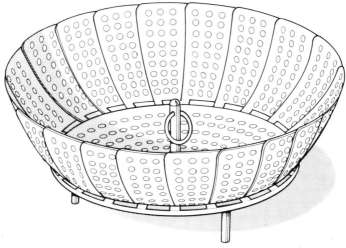

The cheapest, simplest and most widely available steamer comes from Japan. It consists of a metal 'basket' standing on short legs. The basket is made from overlapping steel plates which can expand or contract to fit any saucepan. They are now sold in most kitchen shops and are relatively inexpensive.

Improvised steamers

 Roasting tin and rack: Fill the tin two-thirds full with water. Place the food on the rack, cover with a dome of foil and seal the foil over the edge of the tin. If your roasting tin does not have a rack, you could try using four egg cups to support a heat-proof plate.

 Colander inside a large lidded saucepan: Fill the pan so that the water comes just below the bottom of the colander. Keep replenishing the water as necessary.

 Metal sieve: A sieve propped over a pan and covered with foil is the least satisfactory alternative as it is hard to seal in the steam properly.

Note: When steaming vegetables, you can place them in a bowl or on a plate inside the steamer to collect the juices which would otherwise leach out into the water.

INGREDIENTS

Bread and other cereals

Bread is well named 'the staff of life'. A loaf of wholemeal bread contains vitamins B, C and E, calcium, iron and plenty of fibre. The smell and taste of good home-made bread must be one of the most fundamentally satisfying gastronomic treats there is.

We should all be eating more bread, and more of it should be wholemeal. Bread is not fattening, though it is filling. Its former reputation as the enemy of health and fitness is completely undeserved, and the better bread is, the less likely we are to load it with fat and sugary jam to make it more palatable.

Bread is not difficult to make at home.

The secrets of success are:

&· *Yeast:* Most failures in bread-making can be attributed to dead yeast. Unfortunately, dried yeast often sits around for far too long in shops, especially if it is in a packet. Tins are safer. Reconstitute the yeast with a little hand-hot water and a teaspoon of sugar. The water must be warm but not too hot or it will destroy the yeast. If hand-hot water does not produce an inch of froth within 10 or 15 minutes, the yeast is dead and there is no way it will raise the dough. Buy a new batch and start again. Fresh yeast is usually obtainable from bakers. Use twice the weight given in recipes for dried yeast. Fresh yeast has the advantage of being more reliably 'alive', but there is no difference in final taste between the breads produced by fresh or dried yeast. Work fresh yeast to a paste with a little of the warm bread-making liquid, then proceed as given in the recipe.

&· *Good quality flour:* 'Strong' flour is best for bread-making as it contains more gluten; it may be wholemeal, wheatmeal or white.

Wholemeal/wholewheat flour contains the whole of the wheat grain including the bran and wheatgerm. The wheatgerm gives the bread its flavour and most of its valuable nutrients.

'*Stoneground*' means that the flour has not been subjected to heat during milling, therefore more of the flavour is likely to have been retained. This flour makes an excellent bread, though some people find it heavy as it does not rise as much as other breads.

Wheatmeal flour should be labelled '80% extraction'. It is flour which has had some of the grain removed. It makes bread which is a pleasant compromise between wholemeal and white. If the packet of flour simply says 'brown flour', beware: it could be white flour dyed with caramel.

Granary flour is usually wheatmeal with some malted wheat or rye grains added which give a pleasant flavour and crunchy texture.

Strong white flour has little of the bran or wheatgerm left. However, unbleached white flour makes a crusty springy home-made loaf and usually tastes much better than the shop-bought, wrapped, sliced variety which is steam-baked: this is full of air and moisture and little else.

Kneading: It is important to stretch the dough for most breads by kneading it for about 10 minutes. This produces an elastic dough with a good texture. A food processor or mixer can do the same work in about a minute. Either way, the dough is ready when it has become soft, springy and shiny. Bread made entirely from wholemeal flour, however, is usually better not kneaded.

Rising: Dough is best left to rise slowly in a warm place. The temperature should not be too hot or you may produce a coarse-textured loaf; about an hour at room temperature is ideal. Don't let the dough rise too much: recipes usually specify doubled size. Now punch all the air out of it, put it in its tin or mould and let it rise again, covered with an oiled polythene bag or cling film, or a damp tea towel. Usually it should come just above the top of the tin.

Baking: Bread is always baked in a hot oven – not usually less than gas mark 6, 400°F (200°C). A 1 lb loaf takes 35 minutes at this temperature. Take it out of its tin, turn it upside down and return it to the oven to cook for a further 5 minutes. Cool it on a wire tray to prevent sogginess.

SPEEDY WHOLEMEAL LOAF

No book on healthy eating would be complete without its recipe for a 'Grant' loaf – so called because it was invented by Doris Grant, one of the founders of the wholefood movement 40 years ago. It makes an excellent tasty loaf with a moist close texture. No kneading or second rising is necessary. This bread keeps well and makes good toast.

1 lb (450 g) wholemeal flour
1 teaspoon salt
1 teaspoon sugar
1 teaspoon dried yeast or ½ oz (15 g) fresh yeast

Wipe a 2 lb (1 kg) loaf tin well with butter. Mix the flour and salt together. Reconstitute the dried yeast by adding it, with the sugar, to 4 fl oz (100 ml) of hand-hot water in a large jug. Stir well and leave it to develop a froth – this takes about 10 minutes. If you are using fresh yeast work it to a paste with a little of the warm water and leave to froth.

While the yeast is frothing, warm the flour and the tin in a very low oven. Add another 8 fl oz (200 ml) of hand-hot water to the yeast mixture and mix well. Now put all this liquid into a bowl with the flour. Mix it in thoroughly, using a wooden spoon at first and then your hands. This dough should be soft and floppy – 'slippery' was the word Mrs Grant used for it. Wholemeal flour varies considerably in the amount of water it absorbs so add more warm water if necessary. When a smooth dough has formed, transfer it to the tin, cover it loosely with cling film and leave it to rise for about an hour in a warm room. The dough should reach to just under an inch of the top of the tin. Fifteen minutes before the end of the rising time, heat the oven to gas mark 6, 400°F (200°C).

Sprinkle the top of the loaf with flour. Cook it on a middle shelf for 35–40 minutes. At that stage remove it from the tin, and bake it for a further 5–10 minutes upside down to crisp the bottom. It should then sound hollow when tapped. This recipe does not produce a 'tall' loaf – it never rises above the level of the tin. Place the loaf on a wire rack and let it cool completely before you cut it.

HALF-AND-HALF BREAD

Wheatmeal loaf

This bread is a good basic daily loaf. It will especially appeal to anyone who finds a 100% wholemeal loaf 'too heavy'. Half the flour is white, half wholemeal, so you have some of the advantages of both; the flavour and fibre of wholemeal, with the lightness of white. It produces a well risen, shiny loaf with a good crust and a light texture.

1 dessertspoon dried yeast or 1 oz (30 g) fresh yeast
10–14 fl oz (250–350 ml) hand-hot water
1 teaspoon (5 ml) sugar
12 oz (350 g) strong white flour mixed with 12 oz (350 g) wholemeal flour, or alternatively use 1½ lb (700 g) wheatmeal flour
1½ teaspoons salt
1 teaspoon butter or soft margarine
A little milk for the crust

Reconstitute the dried yeast in 5 fl oz (150 ml) of the water with the sugar (or cream the fresh yeast with a little water and the sugar). Leave it to froth for 10 minutes. Meanwhile, measure the flour into a mixing bowl and set it to warm in the oven on the lowest setting for about 5 minutes. Then add the salt and the butter or margarine and rub the fat into the flour until you have a breadcrumb texture.

When the yeast is frothing well, add it to the flour and start mixing it in. Add more of the water, a little at a time, until you have a smooth dough. It should be pliable and not too wet. Knead the dough for about 7 minutes until it has become soft, elastic and shiny. Alternatively process it in a food processor or mixer for a minute. Put it back into the mixing bowl and cover the surface of the dough loosely with oiled cling-film. Leave it to rise in a warm room for about an hour, by which time it should have doubled in size. Grease a 2 lb (1 kg) loaf tin well.

Remove the cling-film and punch as much air out of the dough as you can. Knead it again for about 4 minutes: it should feel springy and resistant. Fold it into a smooth, fat sausage shape and tuck it neatly into the tin. Cover the top of the dough loosely with oiled cling-film and leave it to rise at room temperature for another 20–30 minutes.

Pre-heat the oven to gas mark 8, 450° (230°C) 15 minutes before the end of the rising time. Then, 10 minutes before the end of the rising time, snip or cut a deep slash along the middle of the loaf. This will give an attractively rough texture to the crust.

The loaf is ready to bake when the top is domed just above the tin and the sides of the dough are level with the top of the tin. Brush the top with a little milk and bake in the centre of the oven for 20 minutes. Then lower the heat to gas mark 6, 400°F (200°C) for 10 minutes. Take it out of the tin and bake it for another 5 minutes upside down to crisp the bottom. The loaf should sound hollow when tapped. Cool on a wire rack.

Variation

This dough can also be used to produce 18 rolls. Knead the dough a second time after the first rising stage as described above. Grease two large baking trays. Divide the dough into 18 equal portions and form each one into a smooth ball. Set them on to the baking sheet, cover them loosely with oiled cling-film, and leave them to rise at room temperature for 20–30 minutes, or until they have doubled in size. Dust them with flour just before putting them in the oven. Bake them in a pre-heated oven at gas mark 8, 450°F (230°C) for 10–15 minutes, then reduce the temperature to gas mark 6, 400°F (200°C) for a further 5–10 minutes. Tap one of the rolls on the bottom to check for the hollow sound that shows they are cooked. Cool them on a wire tray.

IRISH SODA BREAD

PAUL LAURENSON AND ETHEL MINOGUE

Every cook worth her salt in Ireland can knock up a delicious brown soda bread, so-called because bicarbonate of soda combined with buttermilk is used as the raising agent instead of yeast. Its success depends on getting the consistency of the dough right. It must be soft enough to knead *lightly* – too much kneading results in a stiff dry dough and 'heavy bread'. Too wet a dough results in a hard loaf. You can use sour milk as a substitute for buttermilk, but we prefer to use low-fat yoghurt with some water added as this contains less fat. If yoghurt is used, baking powder must be added as well as the bicarbonate of soda.

1 lb (450 g) wholemeal wheat flour
8 oz (225 g) strong white flour (unbleached)
1½ teaspoons bicarbonate of soda
A pinch of salt
1 pint (570 ml) buttermilk or 1 lb (450 g) yoghurt mixed with 5 fl oz (150 ml) water
1 level tablespoon baking powder (if using yoghurt)

Pre-heat oven to gas mark 7, 425°F (220°C). Put the dry ingredients into a large bowl and mix well. Gradually pour in the buttermilk or yoghurt. Knead lightly to get a pliable, moist, but not wet, dough.

Flatten the dough into a round shape and cut a cross in the centre. Bake in the oven for 40–45 minutes. Tap the bottom of the loaf to see if it is ready (it makes a hollow sound if it is done). Wrap in a clean dry cloth to prevent the crust becoming too hard. It can be eaten warm or cold, but do not make huge batches of this bread as it does not keep very well.

GRANARY BAPS

MAKES 8 BAPS   CAROLE HANDSLIP

These baps fill the kitchen with the most wonderful smell. They are made with half milk and half water to keep the crust soft, and the granary flour and malt extract used give them a malty flavour as well as a lighter texture than those made entirely with wholemeal flour.

They are ideal to serve with hamburgers, or for picnics, split and filled with any of your favourite fillings. They also make a good base for pizza: cut them in half, spread them with a home-made tomato sauce, sprinkle on some cheese, then just pop them under the grill to brown.

8 oz (225 g) granary flour
8 oz (225 g) wholemeal flour
1 teaspoon sea salt
½ oz (10 g) fresh yeast
5 fl oz (150 ml) warm water
5 fl oz (150 ml) warm milk
1 tablespoon malt extract
1 tablespoon sunflower oil
Wholemeal flour for dusting

Preheat the oven to gas mark 7, 425°F (220°C). Mix the flours and salt together in a bowl. Cream the yeast with a little of the water and leave it until it has a good frothy head on it. Add it to the flour with the remaining water, milk, malt extract and oil, and mix to a soft dough.

Turn the dough onto a floured surface and knead it for 5 minutes until it is smooth and elastic. Return it to the bowl, cover it with a damp cloth and leave it to rise in a warm place for about 1½ hours until it has doubled in size. The time this takes will vary enormously depending on the room temperature. If you have an airing cupboard this is an ideal place to leave it to rise.

Turn the dough onto a floured surface and knead it again for a few minutes, then divide it into 8 pieces. Knead each piece into a ball then roll it into a 4 inch (10 cm) round and place on a floured baking sheet. Cover the baps with a damp cloth to prevent them from drying out and leave them to rise in a warm place again for about 30 minutes until they have doubled in size. Dust the tops with a little flour. Bake the baps for 10–15 minutes or until they sound hollow when tapped underneath. Place on a wire rack to cool.

Other cereals

Wheat is the best known of our cereals but oats, barley and rye also deserve to be more widely used.

Oats are the basis of all muesli recipes (see page 190) and are also used for porridge. They can be used to replace some of the flour in bread recipes with good results, though the dough will be a little harder to knead. Oats are also useful for cake and biscuit-making (page 183). Oats can be bought in many forms, but all contain the whole grain – they have merely been processed in different forms. 'Porridge oats' are the usual form used for muesli and, of course, porridge. 'Jumbo oats' are the whole grain rolled and flattened so that they look like large flakes. Oats can also be ground and used for thickening stews or in baking: medium-ground oatmeal is best for bread-making; fine oatmeal is best for pancakes and flouring oily fish.

Barley comes either as 'pearl' barley which has had its outer husk removed, or 'pot' barley which is the whole grain and has a much better taste. It makes a substantial addition to soups. Barley flakes are sometimes added to muesli or used for porridge. They are the whole grain rolled flat.

Rye is a dark, rather heavy grain with a strong flavour and is usually used for bread-making. Rye flakes add an interesting texture to muesli.

Dairy products

Dairy products, along with meat and meat products, are the chief sources of saturated fat in our diet. However, they are also good sources of vitamins and minerals – for instance, vitamin B and calcium – so it would not be wise to dispense with them altogether. Instead, a prudent diet will put much more emphasis on the low-fat versions given here.

Butter and butter substitutes

Most of us have grown up with the notion that butter is not only a 'treat' but also a 'necessity' in that, for instance, that bread must always be spread with it. In many parts of the world people have never heard of this idea. Bread (perhaps better bread than ours) is eaten on its own or, typically, is moistened with something else. For example, the pitta bread 'pockets' of the Middle East might be partly filled with a dressed salad as well as a tasty Falafel (page 122). Guacamole from Latin America is a wonderfully spicy avocado dip (page 86) which can be spread on bread instead of butter with a salad lunch. The sticky quality of butter which is so useful for sandwiches may be replicated by curd cheese (page 33).

Nevertheless, bread spread with yellow fat is still very much part of our culture. Toast, for instance, is one of the most commonly eaten breakfast foods, and dry toast is pretty horrible. So some people find butter hard to give up and prefer to look for other ways of reducing the saturated fat in their diet. Others quickly find that they do not miss butter at all: it just becomes an ingredient which adds a pleasant dash to food now and then. If you do manage to reduce the amount of butter you eat, it is probably worth spending a little more on a good quality product when you do buy it. Some of the cheap varieties are heavily salted and also have an unpleasantly oily tang.

Margarine

The bitterly fought public battles of the butter and margarine manufacturers have succeeded in creating thorough confusion in most people's minds about their advantages and disadvantages. The truth is that butter and margarine are equally high in calories, since they are both all-fat. 'Low-calorie spreads' are simply margarine whipped up with water. The calorie content, however, is not the issue in this book. We are concerned with what is 'healthy' and it is true that many margarines contain as much saturated fat as butter. So, if you want a healthier substitute for butter, you should look for a margarine which is labelled *'high in polyunsaturates'*. Some manufacturers are now also producing salt-free polyunsaturated margarines. These products have the added advantage of remaining soft, even when refrigerated, so you are less likely to spread them thickly.

It is difficult to use these soft margarines successfully for sautéing or dry-frying. The taste is not good and the margarine often breaks up when the heat is raised, so use oil instead (see page 51). Soft margarine can, however, be used for baking biscuits and cakes and gives good results.

Buttermilk

This tastes like slightly sour skimmed milk. It is the liquid left over from churning butter, so it has very little fat. It can be used instead of yoghurt in Soda Bread (see page 28), and also in cakes, scones and drinks.

Cheese

There are over a thousand varieties of cheese in the world. Cheese may be made from the milk of cows, buffaloes, goats or ewes; it may be soft, hard, cooked, fresh, matured, blue-veined, low-fat, medium-fat or high-fat. It may be eaten as a snack, a starter, a main course or sweetened as a pudding. From the dietary point of view, cheese can be a source of saturated fat, depending on its type. However, a regime without cheese would be dull indeed: think of soufflés, baked stuffed potatoes, vegetable gratins, soups, Welsh rarebit, pasta, cheesecake . . .

Cheese forms a relatively small percentage of the fat in the British diet – only 4% compared with 14% for milk, for instance. So perhaps many of us are already exercising the prudence and moderation recommended.

Hard cheeses like Cheddar, Lancashire and Stilton are certainly high in saturated fats. Some are also extremely salty, and many distinguished cooks now believe that these cheeses have been used far too liberally in the past. Too much hard cheese may be indigestible in the short term as well as any long-term damage to our health that the saturated fat it contains may produce. However, the flavour of many hard cheeses is irreplaceable; used in small amounts they bring unique qualities to a dish.

Parmesan cheese is especially useful for cooks. This medium-fat, dry Italian cheese has the strong flavour that comes from long maturing. A mere tablespoon of freshly grated Parmesan is enough to give even the simplest pasta dish a touch of class. Buy it in a piece where you can, and grate it yourself. It is cheaper and the flavour is better than the ready-grated type.

Some other cheeses

Some other classic European cheeses such as Brie, Camembert or Emmental appear at first glance to be higher in fat than they actually are. This is because their fat content is calculated on a notional *dry content*, ie as a percentage of the cheese *minus* the water it contains. Since in finished form these cheeses have a high water content, they actually contain less fat than a slice of Cheddar of identical size. So you can enjoy the occasional slice of Brie after a meal with a clear conscience. The Dutch cheese Edam is lowish in fat and is a good melting cheese, excellent in cooking. However, the flavour is bland which means that you may end up using more, thus defeating the object.

Mozzarella is another useful Italian cheese with a medium-low fat content, and it is becoming much more widely available. It is a white, rather rubbery-looking cheese and often comes in a small, roundish shape. It needs to be eaten fresh, though it can be stored refrigerated in a bowl of water for a day or so. Mozzarella is a good melting cheese, excellent for pizza. One of the best simple light meals in the world comes from Italy where a few slices of this cheese are served with a little olive oil, black olives, herbs and tomatoes, all mopped up with crusty bread.

Feta is a crumbly, moist, Greek cheese with a medium fat content made from cow's or ewe's milk. It is excellent cubed in salads.

Low-fat cheeses

Most of these cheeses are soft and look creamy. But remember that *cream cheese* itself is, as the name suggests, *not* a low-fat cheese since it is made from cream or cream with milk. (The label on cheese usually states whether the cheese has been made from skimmed or whole milk, or cream.)

Low-fat Cheddar substitutes taste mild and a little sour, and the texture is rather moist and crumbly. There is now quite a range of these cheeses, which can be used for cooking in the type of recipe that calls for Cheddar, Edam or mozzarella.

Cottage cheese is a familiar low-fat soft cheese with a slightly lumpy texture. It is much better eaten fresh – the 'sell-by' dates are often too generous in the shelf life they allow. It is delicious on its own with tomato salad and Tabbouleth (see page 219) for a simple light lunch. Another happy combination is cottage cheese with a salad made from fresh peaches, apricots and tomatoes lightly sprinkled with a fruit vinegar and oil dressing. Cottage cheese is an excellent filling for baked potatoes and baked savoury flans, and can be used successfully for many puddings too.

Curd cheeses have different percentages of fat depending on the milk from which they are made. Most have much less fat than cream cheese. Use them as an alternative to cottage cheese (see above). Curd cheese is particularly good as a stuffing for pancakes (see page 188) and mixed with carob it makes a pleasant covering for a cake (see page 182).

HOME-MADE LOW-FAT CURD CHEESE

Soft low-fat curd cheese is simple to make at home. It is helpful but not essential to have a cooking thermometer. You will also need a sieve and a piece of muslin, though you can improvise with two layers of kitchen paper. Rennet essence, which coagulates the milk into cheese, can be bought at large chemists' shops and in some supermarkets.

1 pint (570 ml) skimmed fresh milk (or you can reconstitute the same quantity from dried skimmed milk powder)
1 dessertspoon rennet essence

Heat the milk gently until it reaches 98°F (37°C), which is blood heat. If you don't possess a thermometer, dip your finger in. When the milk feels comfortable, ie not hot or cold to your skin, it is just right. Stir in the rennet essence and remove the milk immediately from the heat. Leave it to stand and cool; the milk will set to a wobbly curd. When you can cut it with a knife it is ready for the next stage. Line the sieve with muslin or two layers of kitchen paper and set it over a bowl. Tip in the curd and put the whole thing in the refrigerator to drip overnight. The watery whey will drain off, leaving a pleasant soft cheese in the sieve. Transfer the cheese to a dish, carefully pull away the muslin or paper, and cover the dish with cling-film. It keeps for about four days, refrigerated.

Bought or home-made curd cheeses can be flavoured in a limitless number of ways. They are pleasant with sweet flavours added: for instance, a few drops of rosewater and chopped, soaked dried fruit, or beaten with a little molasses to top puddings. Alternatively, they are delectable mixed with chopped fresh or dried herbs and a sprinkling of ground spices. They can also be flavoured with garlic, chives and finely chopped onions.

Fromage blanc is a low-fat French product rather like yoghurt and is sold in tubs. It has a thick creamy texture and a pleasantly bland taste. Although it is a little less acid than yoghurt, you may find it tastes slightly sour at first. It can be used for flans and pizzas or served instead of cream with fruit (see page 201). It makes a pleasant light pudding mixed with fruit purées. The amount of fat it contains varies. The higher the percentage of 'matière grasse' on the carton, the higher the percentage of fat, so look for the lower-fat varieties. Fromage blanc is now sold in many supermarkets, but you can improvise your own by liquidising cottage cheese with low fat yoghurt. The taste is adequate but not quite so good. Alternatively, substitute quark.

Quark is another low-fat soft cheese, unsalted and closely resembling fromage blanc, though it has a more acid after-taste and a slightly more grainy texture. It is also sold in cartons. Use it in the same ways as fromage blanc. In North European countries it is often eaten spread on bread in place of butter.

Ricotta is a soft low-fat unsalted cheese from Italy which can be made from ewe's, cow's or goat's milk. It is hard to find in supermarkets, so try delicatessens and Italian shops (it looks like a creamy pudding and is sold cut in wedges). This is a truly delicious fresh cheese and can be eaten just as it is with a few spicy olives and a thick slice of wholemeal bread to form the basis of a satisfying lunch. It has a light bland texture and is versatile in cooking. Use it in lasagne instead of meat, combine it with spinach to make flans or stuffings for pancakes and pasta (see page 116). It also lends itself well to puddings and can be successfully used in cheesecakes and soufflés (page 197).

Eggs

The human body manufactures its own cholesterol. A high blood cholesterol level is one of the risk factors in heart disease, and some scientists think that it is dangerous to add to this by eating cholesterol-rich foods. Others feel that the amount gained from food is minimal compared with the amount we ourselves make, especially when we consume a diet high in saturated fat. So it is widely considered more important to reduce your level of saturated fat generally than to cut out cholesterol-rich foods specifically.

Eggs are well known to be a high-cholesterol food, but most people only eat four or five a week anyway. The number usually recommended by nutritionists is just a little lower than that – three. In this book we have used eggs with discretion – they appear in small quantities in a few recipes where they act as binding or raising agents for terrines or cakes.

Milk

Changing to skimmed or semi-skimmed milk is one way of making a substantial and instant reduction in your saturated fat intake.

Fresh pasteurised skimmed milk has a thin, faintly blue look because all the cream (that is to say, all the fat) has been removed. Once they are used to it, most people find the light flavour refreshing, though some still find it watery. Skimmed fresh milk is becoming obtainable from milkmen now and most large supermarket chains sell it in cartons. Fresh pasteurised skimmed milk can be used anywhere you would use full-cream milk: in coffee and tea, for milkshakes, on cereals and muesli, in puddings, sauces, soups, cakes and so on.

Some dairies and supermarkets also sell sterilised and 'long-life' (Ultra Heat Treated) skimmed milk which has a strong flavour of its own because it has been heated to higher temperatures. This treatment means that it will keep, unopened, for several months without refrigeration. Its strong flavour means that UHT and sterilised milk are more acceptable where it is to be incorporated into a hot dish rather than where it is to be drunk on its own, or in coffee and tea.

Some skimmed milk in cartons has had extra skimmed milk powder added to improve the consistency. This does not affect the amount of fat in it, but slightly alters the taste.

Semi-skimmed fresh pasteurised milk. This has had half its fat removed so it is considerably less fatty than full-cream milk. The flavour and consistency are more like ordinary silver-top. This milk can be a good compromise for people who find skimmed milk 'too thin'.

Semi-skimmed fresh pasteurised milk is available in bottles and cartons. It is also possible to buy semi-skimmed milk in sterilised and UHT form (see above).

If you can only obtain silver-top milk, you can approximate your own version of semi-skimmed milk by carefully pouring away the cream.

Powdered skimmed milk. This is available everywhere and is a good store cupboard standby. Reconstituted with water (follow the instructions on the carton – they vary from brand to brand), it can be used in exactly the same way as fresh milk (although few people enjoy drinking it 'neat').

Other milks all contain much larger percentages of fat. These include silver top, green top, Jersey or Channel Island milk and any milk described as homogenised. 'Homogenised' just means that the fat has been distributed throughout the milk so that the cream cannot rise to the top of the bottle.

Powdered coffee whiteners often contain more saturated fat than cream and are better avoided if you are concerned to reduce either the fat or the chemical additives in your diet.

Yoghurt has become so popular that it has lost its 'cranky' image. Unfortunately much of it is now sold heavily sweetened and dosed with synthetic 'fruit flavours' and preservatives. Buy 'natural' low-fat yoghurt instead, which has no added sugar and which is made from skimmed milk. It is easy to add your own fruit – at least this way you will know exactly what it contains.

Some supermarkets now sell 'Greek-style' yoghurt made from full-cream milk. This naturally has more fat, but is still not as fatty as cream if you are using it instead of cream on fruit or puddings. The yoghurt made from cow's milk is a particularly pleasant version. It has a thick, creamy texture and natural sweetness. People who say they detest 'natural' yoghurt often find this one acceptable.

Yoghurt contains lactic acid which is one of the reasons why it is digested so quickly. Other claims for its powers are much harder to prove. However, the ordinary low-fat yoghurt has many uses in a healthy diet. It can be the basis for a refreshing summer drink (page 187), for salad dressings (page 162), or spooned over fresh fruit or muesli (page 190). It is the basis of many dips and salads in Middle Eastern cuisine (page 159). Yoghurt can also be used to thicken sauces, but this needs care. Incorporate it into the hot liquid a tablespoon at a time and stir it in quickly. Alternatively it may be 'stabilised' by whisking in a teaspoon of cornflour. In some sauces it should only be warmed.

HOME-MADE YOGHURT

Home-made yoghurt is much cheaper than the bought variety and is simple to make. A spoonful of any bought plain yoghurt (the fresher the better) is enough to transform milk into yoghurt for the price of the milk.

Ingredients:
1½ pints (900 ml) skimmed milk (or the same amount reconstituted from powdered skimmed milk)
1 teaspoon any plain low-fat yoghurt
Equipment:
A cooking thermometer is a great help as it removes the element of guesswork
You will also need a 3 pint (1·75 litre) pudding basin and a 5 pint (2·8 litre) saucepan, preferably non-stick as the milk burns when it boils

Scald the 3 pint pudding basin with boiling water to sterilise it. Also scald the spoon you will use for measuring and stirring. Set the basin on a tray. This will mean you can move it safely later on.

Bring the milk to the boil in the saucepan and let it continue to boil for a few minutes. This improves the flavour of the finished yoghurt. Pour the milk into the basin and leave it until it has cooled to a temperature of 113°F (45°C). If you don't have a thermometer you can use your finger – the milk should feel slightly hotter than you can comfortably bear but not so hot that you feel you are scalding yourself. When you dip in your finger you should be able to count 5 seconds before snatching it away.

When the milk has reached the correct temperature stir in the teaspoonful of yoghurt. This acts as a 'starter'. Cover the basin tightly with cling-film. Now quickly wrap it up in several layers of insulation – three thick towels, for instance – and put it in a warm place such as an airing cupboard, above a solid fuel cooker or near, but not on top of, a radiator. Alternatively you can put the mixed milk and starter into a wide-necked scalded insulated flask.

After 5 or 6 hours the yoghurt should have set. If it is still runny, wrap it up again and leave it for another hour. There will be a layer of yellowish whey lying on the surface. Carefully pour this off. Then transfer the yoghurt to the refrigerator immediately.

The yoghurt can be thickened by straining it for half an hour or so through a sieve, lined with kitchen paper, or through several layers of muslin tied at the corners and suspended from a tap to drip into a sink.

Keep back some of the yoghurt as a starter for your next batch. Even if you make yoghurt every week you should not need to buy any to use for a new starter for several months.

Everyone encounters the occasional failure in yoghurt-making. Don't let this discourage you. The usual reasons for failure are:

≥ The starter was stale. Use only the freshest yoghurt.

≥ Too much starter results in sour, grainy yoghurt. The teaspoon given in the recipe above is ample for 1½ pints of milk.

≥ The yoghurt was not kept in a warm enough place, or the insulation was not adequate.

≥ The temperature of the milk was too high when the starter was added.

Yoghurt cheese: this simple cheese is produced by extending the straining process described above. Let the yoghurt drip for about 8 hours. This produces a pleasant, slightly more acid cheese than home-made curd cheese (page 33).

Fish

Only a few years ago, it looked as if the wet fish shop was due to disappear altogether, with only a few brave survivors struggling on against all odds. Now, suddenly, the situation is transformed. New fresh fish shops and market stalls are springing up everywhere and the supermarkets, having first cautiously tested customer reaction, now have fresh fish counters too.

Fish is a totally healthy food. White fish has virtually no fat, and the fat it does have is unsaturated. It is easily digested and is full of nutrients. Some oily fish such as mackerel, sprats and herrings are thought to be especially useful for keeping arteries healthy and they are also rich in vitamin D. Although some fish is expensive, much of it is cheap and excellent value with little waste. It cooks quickly and lends itself well to being lightly flavoured with herbs and spices. Red Mullet Orientale (page 133) is a delicious dish where the fish is quickly simmered in a delicately spiced sauce; Grilled Grey Mullet (page 213) is wonderful for outdoor eating and Mackerel in Foil with Herbs (page 125) makes a hearty family meal. On page 174 there is even a recipe for healthy fishcakes for children.

Buying fish

Look for a fish shop which smells of the sea, not of fish. The fish should have bright, shiny, clear eyes and skin. Fresh fish has no 'fishy' smell. Signs of staleness are: fading silveriness, fading blue and green lights, grey, yellow or flabby appearance in white fish, unpleasant smell, sunken opaque eyes.

Frozen fish is an excellent alternative to fresh. Avoid the breadcrumbed variety and look for plain frozen fish. The taste is good, though the texture of fresh fish is probably better.

Preparing fish

Removing scales: You can ask your fishmonger to do this for you, but it is quite easy to do yourself. Scrape scales off from tail to head using a sharp knife. Be gentle otherwise you may tear the skin. In extreme cases dip the fish for a few seconds into boiling water.

The head: Remove this, but save it for stock if you are making a sauce. The head may be left on in some fish – the recipe will specify.

Gutting: Most fishmongers will do this for you if you ask, but it is not always possible if the shop or stall is busy. If you have to do it yourself, start at the tail or vent end. Using a small sharp knife or kitchen scissors slit the belly flesh up to the head. Snip through the spine at the top behind the head and pull sharply at the head. The guts will come free. Rinse the fish in cold running water to remove any remaining blood and slime and pat dry. The liver is regarded as a delicacy in some fish, eg red mullet, but in most fish it is discarded.

Some fish, such as sardines or sprats, are better gutted through the gills. This gives a much neater appearance as the fish are normally cooked with the heads left on. Use a pair of tweezers and handle the fish gently. Insert the tweezers through the gills and reach down inside the fish. Squeeze the body gently, and pull the guts with the tweezers and they should come out. Wash the fish with running water through the mouth.

Filleting and skinning: This is best done by fishmongers unless you know what you are doing since the techniques vary considerably.

Shellfish

Many shellfish can only be obtained pre-cooked and are often also sold frozen. Frozen cooked shellfish such as prawns should only be added to a cooked dish at the last possible moment as they easily shrink and become rubbery with overcooking. Freshly cooked whole shellfish should be eaten as soon as possible.

Mussels: These can be bought live by the pint, or cooked, shelled and frozen. Bottled mussels are not so useful as it is hard to get rid of the vinegary taste. Put live mussels into plenty of cold water as soon as you get home and leave them there until you are ready to start cooking. A handful of oatmeal sprinkled onto the water will feed them and keep them alive if you want to leave them overnight. Throw away any that float to the top or are broken. Look out for the odd unusually heavy one that will be full of mud. Also throw away any that are open and will not close when you tap them sharply. Scrape off any barnacles and all the hairy 'beards'. Rinse the cleaned mussels thoroughly in several changes of cold water to get rid of sand. After cooking (see recipes pages 92 and 108) throw away any that have not opened up.

Crab: This can be surprisingly cheap, especially if you live near the coast. The meat is rich and filling – a little goes a long way. Crabs are usually sold ready-cooked: all they need is 'dressing'.

To dress a crab first twist off the legs and claws. Crack them with a cleaver or hammer and scrape out all the meat with a skewer. Now pull or prise the body away from the shell – use a small, blunt, flexible knife if necessary. There are only two inedible parts of the body: the grey stomach sack with intestine attached, and the white gills which are long, pointed and called 'Devil's fingers'. (These are not poisonous, simply tough and chewy.) Identify and discard these parts, then scrape out all the meat from the shell using a skewer or a thin-bladed knife. The white and dark meats are usually kept separate. Season the meat and moisten it with a little oil and lemon juice.

Crab is sometimes served in its shell. To do this, break away the inner rim from the shell. Dip the shell in boiling water and scrub it well. Pat it dry, then oil it inside and out to make it shine. The brown meat is normally placed in the centre with the white meat piled on either side.

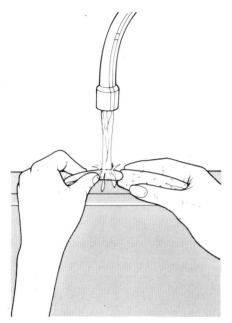

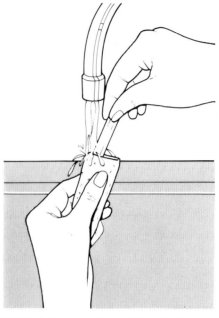

1 Pull head and its attachments out of body.

2 Wash body under cold tap. Pull out and discard transparent quill and all insides to leave a clean tube.

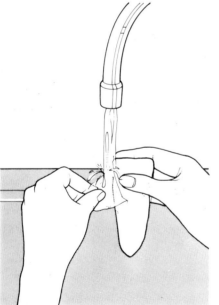

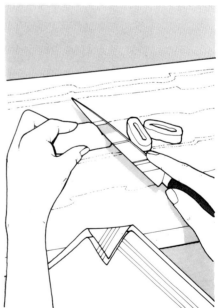

3 Remove and discard mottled pink membrane which covers body.

4 Cut the body into rings.

Scallops: These shellfish are quick and easy to prepare and cook. They are often sold ready opened and cleaned. Look for bright, plump flesh – don't buy anything that looks dull and flabby. Occasionally you may be able to buy whole scallops. Scrub them well and open them with a stout knife. Rinse them free of sand, then cut away the flesh with a pair of kitchen scissors or small, sharp paring knife.

The orange coral cooks in about 10 seconds, and is normally added, sliced or whole, at the very last moment of cooking. The white flesh may be cooked whole, sliced into rounds, or diced. It is easily toughened by prolonged or over-vigorous cooking, so the best way to cook it is by gentle poaching for between 2 and 5 minutes.

Many scallop recipes call for them to be served in their shells. Scrub the shells well in hot water before using them.

Frozen scallops are available in freezer shops. The flavour is reasonable, but the texture is not so good.

Squid: These are very quick to prepare and, if tender, can be cooked in a few minutes. They can be simply poached or sautéed with a garlic and herb dressing or added to richly flavoured stews such as the Sicilian recipe on page 134, Squid with Tomatoes and Capers. The black ink in the inksack below the head is prized for its marvellous flavour and provides the basis of the sauce for the famous Italian dish Spaghetti al Nero. Very often small squid will have lost their inksacks through freezing and tight packing, but the larger squid should still have them.

The best way to prepare squid is under running water, which may help the squeamish too! First pull the head with its tentacles from the body. Then pull out the transparent quill from inside the length of the body, and remove all of the insides to leave a clean tube. Still under running water, rub off the pink-purple membrane covering the body. Dry the squid on kitchen paper, then cut the body into rings about ¼ inch (5 cm) thick. Remove the inksack if it is there, then cut off and reserve the tentacles from the head, just above the eyes, and discard the head. (See diagram opposite.)

Cooking

Fish may be marinated and then eaten raw. Suitable methods of cooking are: smoking, barbecuing, steaming, frying or baking. Grilling is best used for oily rather than white fish.

Fruit and vegetables

The choice of fruit and vegetables in Britain all the year round is now quite staggering. Thanks to the helpfully educative efforts of the women's magazines, the major supermarket chains and the presence of immigrant communities, the range has never been wider or better understood. Kiwi fruit, green peppers, courgettes, red lettuce, mange-tout peas . . . they are all now eaten in British households where they had probably never even been heard of a decade ago.

Fruit and vegetables delight both the eye and the palate, all the way from the bright reds of strawberries and tomatoes, the yellows of peppers and lemons to the clear greens of lettuce and broccoli and the deep shiny purple of aubergines. A meal without fruit or vegetables is almost bound to look and taste dull: a diet without them will be nutritionally deficient.

Increasing the amounts of fruit and vegetables we eat is one of the simplest ways to improve our health. They are full of fibre and are important sources of minerals and vitamins. Vitamin C is critical to healthy skin and bones; folic acid, found in green leafy vegetables, is important for keeping anaemia at bay. However, these vitamins and minerals are fragile and can be destroyed by prolonged storage and lengthy cooking. To keep both flavour and nutrients, the rules are:

୧ Use the freshest vegetables and fruit possible: they begin to deteriorate as soon as they are gathered. Avoid anything limp or tired-looking in shops and markets.

୧ Wash or wipe all vegetables. Most are now sprayed with pesticides.

୧ Don't soak them before cooking as the nutrients will leach out.

୧ Leave skins on wherever possible. Much of the goodness is likely to be on or just under the skin.

୧ Use fruit or vegetables whole wherever possible. Cutting, like soaking and peeling, destroys nutrients. If you do slice vegetables, do it as near as possible to the time you start cooking or eating them. An acid dressing which includes vinegar or lemon juice helps to arrest the loss of nutrients.

୧ Keep the cooking time as brief as possible: 30 seconds is all that is needed for mange-tout peas, 5 minutes for chopped cabbage (less if you stir-fry it). Save any cooking water for stock or gravy. As a general rule, do not start vegetables cooking in cold water. Bring the water to the boil *then* add the vegetables. Potatoes are an exception, as they keep their texture better when they are started in cold water.

୧ Choose cooking methods which use little or no water, eg stir-frying, grilling or steaming.

୧ Raw salads are the ideal way to eat vegetables as this way the nutrients are more likely to be retained. Almost any edible fruit or vegetable can be used in a salad, though some may need to be blanched first (see page 15). It is even possible to eat common garden weeds like young dandelion leaves, chick weed, fat hen or the petals of flowers such as pansies, marigolds and nasturtiums. Some nurseries now also stock seeds for oriental and old English varieties of salad plants, which can extend the range even further. (See pages 284–5 for books and useful addresses.)

Sprouted seeds

You don't even have to have a window box, let alone a garden, to produce a cheap, constant supply of fresh, crunchy salad sprouts.

All sorts of seeds can be used: mung beans (which produce the familiar bean sprout used in Far Eastern cooking), alfalfa, mustard, sesame, aduki, brown lentils, sunflower seeds and many more. Buy them loose from health or wholefood shops – there is no need to buy elaborate packs from seedsmen.

No special 'sprouting kits' are necessary. The equipment could not be simpler: a glass jam jar (wide necked if possible), a piece of muslin (or nylon from an old clean pair of tights) and a rubber band.

Both mung beans and alfalfa seeds sprout easily and are excellent for a first try. Don't mix different varieties in the same jar, as they may germinate at different rates.

Method: Put a heaped tablespoon of the seeds into a sieve and wash them under running water. Remove any which look shrivelled, also any sticks and stones. Put the seeds into the jar, fill it with tepid water and leave it to soak overnight in a warm place, covering the top with the muslin and rubber band. The next day strain this water off through the muslin. Fill the jar with cold water and again strain the water off through the muslin. Repeat this several times. Then leave the jar propped on its side so that the residual water can drain off gradually. Repeat this procedure twice daily. The seeds are best left in a dark warm place for 3 days and should begin to sprout immediately. After about 3 days transfer them to a light windowsill for another day but continue rinsing and draining. If they develop a musty smell at any stage just step up the rinsing. The sprouts are ready to eat when they are a few inches long and have a couple of leaf-tips beginning to develop. One heaped tablespoon of seeds will produce about 6 oz (175 g) of sprouts.

To remove the seed husks, put the sprouts into a large bowl of cold water and swirl them around. The husks will either float to the top or sink to the bottom. Remove the husks and drain the sprouts. They can be refrigerated for up to two weeks in a sealed polythene bag.

Sprouts taste good, their texture is crunchy and they are full of nutrients. For a few pence and very little trouble, they will provide a constant source of fresh salad ingredients all the year round.

Herbs

There was a time, not so long ago, when 'herbs' would have meant a patch of garden mint destined to make a vinegary mint sauce for lamb, a bunch of parsley for decoration only, and a packet of ready-mixed dried stuffing for roast meats. Today all that is changing. There has been a huge surge of interest in growing and using herbs. At the Chelsea Flower Show for the past few years one nursery has displayed a beautiful garden consisting entirely of culinary and medicinal herbs; chain stores now sell herb 'starter packs'; most supermarkets stock a wide range of dried herbs and many even sell fresh tarragon, chives and basil, as well as parsley.

No doubt some of this interest reflects nostalgic interest in the past. However, as with so many fashions, this one also has a core of common sense. Herbs, like spices, were widely used in the past because they are aromatic and therefore able to impart interesting flavours to an otherwise dull and repetitive diet. Today, our diet is astonishingly varied, but if we are to cut down on salt, sugar and fat (all of which intensify the flavour of food) we need to recapture the extensive and imaginative uses to which herbs were put in our own past and to which they still are in other cultures.

Many of the most popular herbs are evergreen or perennial and easily established in British gardens. Others are annuals and must be patiently planted from seed every year. A few, like that most useful herb, basil, are notoriously temperamental and need generous quantities of sun to thrive. Almost all herbs grow best on well drained, peaty soil.

Most herbs have a traditional association with one particular type of food, though constant experimenting will often suggest many more. However, it is normally wise to use herbs with discretion. It is also wise to restrict the use of herbs to one or at the most two together in a dish. Two exceptions to this are:

Fines herbes: this is a mixture of finely chopped fresh herbs. Ideally it will include parsley, chives, tarragon and basil, though the ingredients often vary. Classically this mixture is used to flavour omelettes, and sauces for pasta (see page 113).

Bouquet garni: this is a bunch of fresh herbs typically comprising a sprig of thyme, three or four stems of parsley, a bay leaf and a sprig of marjoram. The herbs are tied loosely together, wrapped in muslin and suspended in the liquid of a dish during cooking and removed later. Any collection of fresh herbs may be used. A bouquet garni is usually considered essential for any of the great European classic dishes which involve the long, slow cooking of meat in a sauce. Dried, ready-prepared 'bouquets' (which look a bit like tea-bags) can be a reasonable substitute for the fresh version.

A small herb garden or even just a well watered box on a sunny windowsill will be an asset to any cook. A useful collection of herbs can also be grown in attractive terracotta 'strawberry' pots. A basic selection might include: basil, chives, tarragon, dill, marjoram, thyme and parsley, but of course there are many many more possibilities – each herb has its own unique flavour.

Basil: There are many varieties of this superb plant, ranging from one with large, juicy, dark green leaves, to a purple-leaved type and a 'bush basil' which has minute leaves. All share the same sweet aroma though in varying strengths. Basil is a tender plant and needs plenty of care in a sunny spot. Pinch out the flowers (which can also be eaten) to encourage vigorous side shooting. Sprinkle the chopped leaves into salads; pound them in a little olive oil and spread them over a tomato salad; or put chopped leaves into tomato sauces for pizza and pasta. Use basil generously as an excellent basis for simple pasta sauces. It is also the foundation of the classic Italian *pesto* sauce, where it is pounded with pine-nuts and Parmesan cheese.

Dried basil is not usually an adequate substitute for the fresh herb, though it may be better than nothing in soups and sauces. If you have a good crop of basil it is better frozen or microwaved (see pages 49 and 50) than dried. Basil is also a good candidate for flavouring oils (see page 50) and vinegars (page 72).

Borage: An easily grown annual – once in your garden it will continue to seed itself and will be hard to discourage. Its uses are rather limited. The leaves are uncomfortably hairy, but have a cucumber-like flavour. The pretty blue flowers are edible and are a well known decorative element in 'Pimms' drinks. They look pleasant and unusual in salads.

Bay: A familiar evergreen garden plant related to the laurel. It is cheap and widely available in dried form. The dried leaves are a perfectly acceptable substitute for fresh, though like all dried herbs, they lose their potency quickly. It can be used in many meat and fish dishes. For a more intense flavour, try pounding half a leaf and sprinkling it into the food. It is an essential part of a bouquet garni (see above) and can also be used in marinades, especially for fish. In Indian cookery it is often sautéed in oil at a high temperature with cinnamon bark, coriander seeds and other whole spices. The heat of the oil is necessary to release the 'essential oil'.

Chervil: An annual with a delicate flavour something like parsley. Use it chopped in omelettes (as part of *fines herbes*), green salads and tomato salads, or as a garnish.

Coriander ('Chinese parsley'): Once a rarely used herb in Britain, the popularity of Indian cookery has made coriander much better known and understood and also more widely available. It looks rather like long-stemmed, flat-leafed parsley, but unlike parsley it is always sold with its fleshy roots attached. The flavour is totally different: strong and lemony, so it is not really interchangeable with parsley except in appearance. Like parsley it is rich in vitamin C. You can grow it in a sunny spot from the seed sold for culinary use, though it is sometimes difficult to establish.

Wash it well to remove grit and chop off the roots. Use it as a main ingredient in chicken dishes; or pound a generous quantity with meat, onions and spices to make meat balls. Used discreetly it enhances many soups and salads, and is a better garnish than parsley in many spiced dishes. It has a particular affinity with lemon, garlic and fresh chillies, hence its value in marinades for tandoori chicken. The seeds (see page 63) taste completely different. Coriander is available fresh all the year round from many supermarkets and specialist food shops.

Chives: These are easily grown in window boxes and pots, though they die back in winter. Their mild flavour is often acceptable to onion-haters. The purple flowers are also edible and look pretty in salads crumbled or whole.

Mix chives with curd or cottage cheeses for a pleasant and not overpowering flavour. Add them at the last moment to omelettes, soups and stuffed baked potatoes. Chives are another useful garnish: snip them over finished dishes using kitchen scissors. Dried chives are tasteless – spring onion tops, finely chopped, make a better substitute in winter. However, chives can be frozen or microwaved (pages 49-50) successfully.

Dill ('Dill Weed'): An annual with pretty yellow flower heads easily grown from seed. The leaves and flowers are excellent in fish dishes, giving a spicy mild fragrance. The dark green feathery leaves make a beautiful garnish, again for fish. The seed can be used for pickles.

Fennel: This resembles dill but it is a perennial and much taller. The bronze variety makes a striking garden plant in its own right. It has a much more overpowering flavour than dill and tastes strongly of aniseed. The seed is used as a spice and the chopped leaves can be added to fish marinades and casseroles.

Lovage: An easily grown perennial, now returning to popularity. The flavour resembles celery but is not quite so strong. Put a handful, chopped, in substantial soups, or add the whole, sharp-toothed leaves to salads.

Marjoram: This is a wonderfully useful perennial herb, and it is worth persevering to grow it in your garden. It will grow well in a window box as long as it has sun and warmth. There are many varieties and, like thyme, marjoram is often grown for its appearance alone. The flavour is delicate and fragrant. It is closely related to oregano, the wild marjoram that grows all over Southern Europe.

Marjoram can be used in casseroles, tomato sauces, or to flavour vegetables that might otherwise have a bland, watery taste, eg courgettes. Add it at the last moment as its flavour is destroyed by long cooking. Dried oregano is an excellent substitute for fresh marjoram.

Mint: Often despised as being too ordinary to be used by a 'serious' cook, mint can be an unmitigated nuisance to gardeners because of its invasive growing habits. However, it is a most useful herb. There are about 25 different varieties, many of them strikingly different in flavour from each other. Apple mint is delicate and juicy, lemon mint is delicious in salads and spearmint is the variety normally grown for mint sauce. Grow mint in a pot or a bucket buried in soil to keep it under control. Mint dies back in winter, but can be frozen or microwaved successfully. Dried mint, however, quickly loses its flavour.

It can be used in stuffings for fish and as a flavouring for cool drinks; use it generously for Middle Eastern dishes like Tabbouleth (see page 219). It is also an important ingredient in the yoghurt dressings and salads so popular in the Middle East.

Parsley: There are two useful varieties of this, the most commonly found herb in Britain. The flat-leaved variety is paler and can withstand cold, drought or even snow. The taste is strong. The darker green, curly parsley is slightly more tender and does not have as strong a flavour, but is better for garnishing. Use in stuffings, sauces and for garnishing.

Rosemary: An evergreen herb which will eventually grow to shrub size. It dislikes cold winters and can therefore be difficult to grow in the North. A few of the spiky leaves are normally enough to give a strong flavour. In Italy it is associated with lamb dishes, but it can also be used successfully with pork.

Sage: This popular perennial herb graces any garden with its pretty silver grey leaves (though there are also purple varieties). It is easily grown from cuttings. Use it in stuffings and sauces, or sprinkle a few well chopped leaves on a bean or pasta salad. However, the raw leaves can be tough, so sage is probably better used cooked in food. And be careful as the strong flavour can be overpowering. It dries well, but if you have a source of fresh leaves, there is little point in drying sage, as it usually retains some of its leaves even in a cold winter.

Savory: Another herb that prefers a warmer climate, but can be grown successfully in Britain. There are two very similar varieties: summer and winter savory. Winter savory is an evergreen perennial, summer savory is an annual. It is a good substitute for thyme, which it resembles in taste. Excellent in pulse dishes and pasta sauces, but use it with care – a little goes a long way.

Tarragon: Like basil and parsley, this is one of the most important and useful of the world's herbs. It likes a sunny spot, but once you have given it some initial care it is easy to grow. The short French tarragon which only grows from cuttings is greatly superior to the large, bushy Russian variety which has little flavour.

The sharp, subtle flavour is particularly good with all kinds of poultry (see page 254), but it is also excellent for fish and a wide variety of sauces. It is the classic herb for making flavoured vinegar and oil (see pages 50 and

72) which is superb in salad dressings. This is the one way of preserving its flavour for the winter, though dried tarragon is a reasonable substitute in a sauce. Tarragon can also be frozen or microwaved.

Thyme: This evergreen, sturdy, creeping herb comes in dozens of different varieties, many of which appeal to gardeners in their own right. The tastes vary considerably. It is a good window box herb and is valued by cooks for its versatility. A sprig is an essential element in a *bouquet garni* (see page 44). Thyme makes a good partner to basil in tomato sauces. Its strength and pungency make it an excellent herb for long, slow casserole cooking, or for any bland food such as pasta or pulses. It dries well.

Storing and preserving herbs

Most professional chefs shudder at the thought of using anything but freshly gathered herbs, and it is true that fresh herbs taste incomparably better than their preserved counterparts. However, not everyone is lucky enough to be able to buy fresh herbs or even to have the means of growing them. Furthermore, in winter many of the best herbs such as basil and tarragon disappear with the first frost. Preserved herbs or no herbs is then the choice, and most of us would rather not be without. If you do have herbs in your garden, it is not normally worth preserving sage, rosemary, thyme, bay or savory, as these plants will continue to provide you with fresh leaves throughout the winter. For those without gardens, buy these herbs when you can or beg them from friends and then preserve them in any of the ways described below.

Storing fresh herbs

A bunch of fresh herbs such as parsley or coriander is best stored in the refrigerator. Half-fill a jam jar with water and put in the bunch of herbs, like a bunch of flowers, so that the water covers the stalks. Now cover the leafy tops loosely with a plastic bag. The bag may be held in place with an elastic band, but this is not essential. Remove the herbs as you need them, and replace the bag. Herbs stored like this will keep for anything up to two weeks. Pick off any yellow or slimy leaves every few days.

Drying herbs

This is the simple traditional way of preserving herbs for the winter. Pick the herbs on a dry day and shake off any dust or grit. It is better not to wash them. Wipe them with kitchen paper if necessary.

Tie the herbs into bunches and wrap them loosely in muslin to keep out dust. Hang the bunches upside down, preferably in a cool, dark, airy place (a garage is ideal) until they feel dry and crumbly. This normally takes between 1 and 3 weeks.

Strip the leaves from the stalks and store them in glass jars. If condensation appears in the jar, this means that the herbs are not quite dry. Spread them out on a tray lined with newspaper for a few more days. A dark glass jar helps preserve colour. Ideally dried herbs should be kept in a cupboard and not exposed to light.

Dried herbs do not keep indefinitely – after about 4 months they often become stale, musty or just flavourless. Many herbs do not dry successfully, notably chives and basil, though the commercially dried types are now much improved.

If you are buying dried herbs, buy small quantities and renew them regularly. Be ruthless with your store cupboard and throw out any dried herbs which have lingered there too long.

Dried herbs have a more concentrated flavour than fresh, so you need use far less. A scant teaspoon of dried herb is normally a reasonable substitute in quantity for a heaped tablespoon of the same herb fresh. Dried herbs can usually only be used in moist, long cooking. They cannot be used for garnishing. Some give better results if they are first reconstituted in warm water then drained – for instance, tarragon and parsley.

Freezing herbs

Freezing is a good way of preserving some of the more delicate herbs which are difficult to dry successfully. Basil, parsley, chives, dill and tarragon are all better frozen than dried.

Pick the herbs on a dry day and wipe them clean. Snip chives, but leave other herbs whole. Fast-freeze them initially on open trays for about 12 hours. When they are stiff, transfer them to small labelled freezer bags in the usual way. Freezing them loose like this makes it easy to pick out small quantities as you need them. The colour and flavour of frozen herbs is usually excellent, but they cannot be used for garnishing or in salads because their texture is too soft.

Another way of freezing herbs is to put small quantities of chopped herbs into ice-cube trays. Cover the herbs with water and freeze. This method is useful for stocks and soups.

Frozen herbs keep for about 6 months – all you need to carry you through the winter months. Use them in the same quantities as fresh herbs.

Microwaving herbs

A microwave oven produces better preserved herbs than traditional drying – both the colour and taste are superior. This method also involves less fuss and bother. Microwave whole or chopped herbs for about 2 minutes – the time will vary with the oven. Store the herbs in glass jars as for conventionally dried herbs.

Herb oils

Like herb vinegars (see page 72) this is a useful way of preserving the flavour of a favourite herb during the winter. These herb oils may be used for salad dressings and for cookery, where they impart an intriguing and subtle aroma to food. Basil and tarragon lend themselves well to this process.

Pick or buy a generous bunch of the herbs. Do not wash them – it is important for them to be completely dry. Wash and then carefully dry a jam jar and place the herbs inside. They may be easier to handle if they have been roughly chopped, but this is not essential. Use any light, good quality oil – safflower is excellent. It is not worth using olive oil as this is expensive and already has a strong flavour of its own. Pour the oil on to the herbs until you have filled the jar to the top. Stir well to disperse any air pockets. Cover the jar with cling-film and leave it on a warm windowsill for about 3 weeks. Give the herbs a stir from time to time and press them down if they have sprung to the top of the jar.

Over the weeks the herbs gradually acquire a blackish and rather unattractive slimy look. This is normal and does not mean that they are decaying.

Prepare a glass bottle (a recycled tonic bottle is ideal) by washing and drying it carefully. You will also need a plastic funnel lined with kitchen paper or a coffee filter paper. Strain the oil into the bottle through the paper. Don't press the herbs, just let the oil drip through in its own time. You may need to repeat this process if too much sediment comes through. The oil will now be a clear green. Top up the bottle with fresh oil if necessary, as this helps to prevent rancidity. Store the oil in the refrigerator where it will keep for several months.

Meat and poultry

Meat is one of the main sources of saturated fat in the British diet. Most reports on diet and health recommend reducing the amount we eat, especially of the most fatty varieties: beef, lamb and pork. 'Made-up' meat products like pies and sausages are also full of fat, especially sausages which can often quite legally consist of rusk, crushed bone and gristle, fat, seasonings and little else.

Poultry and game are far less fatty, so where meat is used for recipes in this book, the majority concentrate on poultry or on small amounts of lean red meat 'stretched' in various imaginative ways by combining it with rice, pulses or vegetables and subtly flavoured with herbs and spices. One of the virtues of this type of eating is that it is also much cheaper than buying chops, steaks and joints.

Where you do buy and cook meat, there are a number of ways in which you can reduce the fat:

🍃 Cut off any visible fat from pork, lamb and beef.

🍃 Where recipes call for chicken to be jointed, remove the skin as this is the fattiest part.

🍃 Roast meat without adding any fat (cover the top with foil if necessary) and stand it on a grid in the roasting pan so that the fat runs out.

🍃 Buy lean cuts. They are more expensive, but there is less waste. If you are eating less meat generally, then the price of the occasional good piece of lean beef will not hurt so much.

🍃 Grill rather than fry.

🍃 Remove the rendered-down fat from roasts and casseroles.

🍃 Minced meat is often made from cheap fatty cuts. If you have time, choose your own lean beef and mince it at home. Never add fat when you are initially frying mince. Put it in a medium-hot pan, stir constantly and let it cook until the fat runs out; then drain it off before using it in your dish.

Nuts

Nuts are an excellent source of fibre, vitamins and minerals. They add flavour in muesli or salads, and can be pounded or processed to make rissoles and stuffings. Crushed nuts and dried fruit can be rolled in carob to make 'sweets' for children or, presented in petit-four cases, as after-dinner treats for adults. Most nuts are low in saturated fat and high in polyunsaturated fats. Salted roasted peanuts should be avoided because of their high salt content. Coconut and Brazil nuts contain a lot of saturated fat.

Nuts can become rancid quickly. Buy them from a shop where the turnover is brisk, and once you find a good source, stick to it.

Oils

There is not necessarily any virtue in using oil instead of hard fat for cooking: some oils are as high in saturated fat as butter or lard. So avoid those anonymous 'blended vegetable oils' and look for named oils instead. The best unsaturated oils for cooking are usually those refined from nuts and seeds. These include:

Corn (maize) oil: This is a fairly cheap oil, good for frying. Its raw taste is less pleasant, so use it for cooking rather than in salad dressings.

Olive oil: The queen of culinary oils with a superb flavour and a deep green colour. Try to avoid the yellow-looking variety sold by chemists.

The best-tasting olive oil is cold-pressed and will say 'Extra-virgin' on the bottle. This means the olives were not subjected to heat in order to extract the oil and it should be the result of the first pressing only. (The residue of each pressing can be pressed again and again, each time producing a poorer quality oil.) Although it costs more initially, olive oil is best purchased in large cans which you can decant into bottles as you like. There is nothing like its wonderful flavour as the basis of a salad dressing. It is also excellent for initial sautéing and 'dry' frying. Unfortunately, the best olive oil is extremely expensive, but if you are only using very little oil altogether, you may consider the expense justified.

Safflower oil: This is a good, light, all-purpose oil. It is high in vitamin E as well as polyunsaturates. It has a pleasant, clean taste and is a good choice for cooking and salad dressings.

Sesame oil: A dark, thick oil used in Chinese cooking, but normally only as a final seasoning and garnish to add gloss to food. It has a nutty flavour which makes an unusual salad dressing. It is not suitable for cooking at high temperatures, however, as it burns too readily. Sesame oil is sold in oriental shops and delicatessens. A refined, colourless version is sometimes sold in supermarkets. This may be used like other oils, but has much less flavour than the dark variety.

Soya oil: This oil is cheap and may be used for high-temperature cooking or for salads. The taste is bland.

Sunflower oil: This is the oil which probably comes nearest to olive oil for flavour in salad dressings, and it can also be used for frying and baking. It has a pleasant but not dominating flavour.

Walnut oil: This strongly flavoured oil is only used for salad dressings. Walnut oil can be difficult to find and is always expensive. It does not keep indefinitely and is better bought in small quantities and refrigerated.

Pasta

Pasta, like potatoes and bread, was once vilified as a wicked, starchy food which caused obesity: it was on the forbidden list for anyone trying to lose weight. Fortunately for all those who adore pasta, the tables have now completely turned. Pasta has been restored to its rightful place as healthy and wholesome. It is not in itself 'fattening' – though of course if you serve it with a fatty sauce it will be. The sauces we have suggested in this book are light and use minimal oil. Pasta can be the centrepiece of a substantial meal (page 116) or a pleasant salad (page 157). It has two other great virtues: cheapness and speed. A pasta meal can be on the table 15 minutes after you first thought of cooking it, and a small quantity of meat, fish or vegetables will go a long way in the sauce.

There are over 100 varieties of pasta and much ingenuity has been expended on devising them:

Tiny pasta shapes (wheels, small shells, twirls) are ideal for soups and salads.

Thin strips or tubes like spaghetti or tagliatelle are the best choice for hot dishes where a sauce is mixed in or served on top.

Sheets or large tubes (eg lasagne, cannelloni and penne) are ideal for stuffing or cooking in layers.

Pasta may come in wholewheat, green (spinach), pink (tomato) or white versions. The taste and texture of the wholewheat variety is heavier and stronger than the others: it is best cooked with a strongly flavoured sauce.

Fresh pasta is now available in many supermarkets. It tastes better and cooks in less than half the time required for dried pasta. You can also make your own pasta without too much difficulty. Fresh pasta is best reserved for simple, light sauces.

Pasta quantities: Use about 1 lb (450 g) of dried pasta for 4 people as a main course, or 8 oz (225 g) as a starter.

HOME-MADE PASTA: VERSION 1

SERVES 2 FOR A MAIN COURSE

This is a basic pasta recipe which uses ordinary strong white flour and an egg. It is very simple to make. The whole process can be speeded up enormously if you have a food processor – about a minute of processing with the master blade will produce a well kneaded dough.

8 oz (225 g) strong white flour
1 large egg
1 dessertspoon olive oil
2 fl oz (50 ml) water

Warm the flour in a low oven for about 5 minutes. Beat the egg and oil lightly and mix them into the flour with a little of the water. Keep adding water until the dough is soft and pliable and then knead it for about 10 minutes until the dough becomes springy and smooth. Cover it with cling film and leave it to rest at room temperature for about an hour.

The rolling out needs some care. Divide the dough into about 5 equal-sized lumps. Lightly flour a board. Roll the pasta lumps out into paper-thin sheets – you should almost be able to see through them. Each sheet should measure about 12 in × 12 in (30 cm × 30 cm). Trim away the uneven edges. Carefully set each sheet aside as you finish rolling it by draping it on a wire cooling tray. Leave the sheets to dry for about 20 minutes. After this they are ready to be cut into whatever shapes you like. Three of the simplest to make without special equipment are:

Ravioli: Spread out one sheet and dot it in rows with teaspoons of your chosen filling (eg ricotta cheese and spinach, or mincemeat in a stiff tomato sauce). Carefully place a second sheet on top and press the two sheets together in the spaces between the fillings. Use a sharp knife to cut out the ravioli. Special ravioli trays and serrated cutters simplify this process and improve the look of the end result.

Tagliatelle: Spread out the sheets of pasta and cut them into narrow strips. Coil up about 10 at a time very loosely into little nests.

Lasagne: Cut each sheet into rectangles about 6 in × 2 in (15 cm × 5 cm).

HOME-MADE PASTA: VERSION 2

Farfale – Pasta butterflies made with semolina

SERVES 4 AS A MAIN COURSE   ANTONIO CARLUCCIO

This version of home-made pasta is easy to make and roll out. You will need fine semolina – obtainable from a good Italian delicatessen. This recipe describes how to make 'butterflies', but you could use this recipe to make other pasta shapes too.

1 lb (450 g) white durum semolina flour
4 egg whites
Water as required

Set aside 2 oz (50 g) of the flour for use while you are working the dough. In a large bowl mix the rest of the flour, the egg whites and a little water to obtain a dough. Work the dough by pressing it with the palms of your hands (dusted with a pinch of flour) on a flat surface until it becomes smooth and still pliable. This may take some time. If it becomes too soft, work in a little of the remaining flour. Now roll out the dough with a rolling pin to form a pasta sheet about ⅛ in (3 mm) thick. If your working surface is small, roll out only part of the dough at a time. With a knife, cut 2 in (5 cm) wide strips down the length of the sheet. Cut the strips into rectangles 2 in × 3 in (5 cm × 7 cm). Now pinch the two long sides together in the middle, using your thumb and index finger, to obtain the shape of a butterfly. Repeat this until you have used all the dough. The pasta shapes are now ready to be cooked. They can be prepared in advance, but should be kept in the refrigerator and used within 5 days.

Pasta-making machines

Various machines are now available which will mix, roll and cut the pasta for you. The more elaborate ones are expensive, but if you make a lot of pasta, you might consider them a worthwhile investment.

Cooking pasta

Use your largest pan and allow about 5 pints (2·5 litres) of water for every 1 lb (450 g) of dried pasta. Add salt and bring the water to a full rolling boil. A little oil may help avoid sticking. Add the pasta and stir it vigorously. Keep the water boiling hard and leave the lid off. Dried pasta takes between 10 and 15 minutes to cook depending on its age and the type of wheat used to make it. The ideal texture of cooked pasta is soft but still with a bite to it. Warm the serving plates. When the pasta is cooked, drain the pasta, then return it to the warm pan and mix in the sauce, reserving a little to spoon on top. If necessary you might heat the whole thing again for a few moments.

Pasta should be served immediately on individual plates as lukewarm pasta is unpleasant. Some people prefer to put the pasta in a large serving dish with the sauce on top; the sauce is then mixed in as the pasta is served. If you do this, it is essential to warm the serving dish and the individual plates very well. Deep dishes are better than flat ones as they help conserve the heat of the food and also make it easier to eat elegantly!

Pulses

Pulses (that is, the edible dried seeds from podded plants) are undergoing a renaissance in Britain. The popularity of Greek and Indian food has also introduced many of us to dishes such as hummus (we have a version on page 87), and dahl, a simple spicy dish made from lentils.

From the health point of view, pulses are a perfect food: high in fibre, full of complex carbohydrates (see page 9), vitamins and minerals, and no fat. Another of their advantages is their extraordinary cheapness. A hearty meal for four based on falafel (little rissoles made from chick peas – page 122) is about one seventh the cost of a meal based on pork chops.

Pulses can be bland, so they need the addition of plenty of herbs and spices. They also have a reputation for causing flatulence because of the gases they produce in the human gut. This effect can be controlled by throwing away the water in which they are soaked and doing the same with the water in which they are first brought to the boil. It also helps to add a few 'digestive' spices to the beans – dill, asafoetida, ginger and caraway are all well known for their ability to prevent or treat colic.

The only real disadvantages with pulses are that they usually need pre-soaking and long cooking. Some pulses, notably lentils, need to be picked over to remove sticks and stones.

You can shorten the soaking time by pouring boiling water over the beans, then leaving them for two hours instead of the usual eight. Don't add salt until the beans have finished cooking as salt delays the softening process of cooking.

A pressure cooker will reduce the amount of cooking time needed. Most pulses can be pressure-cooked from scratch in under an hour, depending on their age and type.

Without either a pressure cooker, or the shortened soaking time, this is how to deal with a selection of pulses:

Aduki beans: soak overnight, boil for 45 minutes.
Black beans: soak for 8 hours, boil for 1 hour.
Black-eye beans: soak for 8 hours, boil for 1½ hours.
Butter beans: soak for 8 hours, boil for 1 hour.
Chick peas: soak for 8 hours. Boil for 1–2 hours. In some recipes chick peas are ground after soaking. They are then formed into rissoles and fried.
Flageolet beans: soak for 8 hours, boil for 1½ hours.
Haricot beans: soak for 8 hours, boil for 1 hour.
Kidney beans: soak overnight, boil for 45 minutes.
Lentils: orange or split lentils can be cooked from scratch in 20 minutes; whole lentils (usually green or brown) take an hour. No soaking is necessary.
Mung beans: boil for 30 minutes. No soaking is necessary.
Split peas: soak for 8 hours, boil for 1 hour.

Note:. Some pulses can have toxic effects if they are not fast-boiled for 10 minutes. It is safer to assume that this rule applies to them all. However, it is not necessary to fast-boil pressure-cooked beans separately as the temperature inside the pressure cooker is high enough to neutralise any toxins.

Pulses lend themselves to an amazingly wide variety of foods: dips and dressings; pancakes and rissoles; stuffings and sauces for pasta; salads, casseroles and soups. They are delicious on their own, and marry well with small quantities of meat, which is no doubt why they are so important in the cuisine of countries where meat has always been a scarce and expensive commodity.

Rice

Rice must be one of the most useful foods there is: cheap, gracefully accommodating to all kinds of other flavours and nothing like so difficult to cook as is sometimes alleged. Even in its white forms it supplies plenty of nourishment, and is another example of a food well designed for 'healthy' eating. For instance, the creamy Green Risotto (page 119) costs little, tastes delicious and contains only entirely wholesome ingredients.

It is claimed by some experts that there are over 10,000 different varieties of rice grown in the world. Perhaps this is not surprising as it is the staple grain of more than half the world's population.

All the main types of rice available in the UK have their own flavours, and each one has a type of dish to which it is particularly suited:

Arborio is a type of Italian rice. The grain is large, round and extremely absorbent; it has an excellent flavour and is ideal for risottos. Unlike other types of rice, arborio is constantly stirred during cooking to produce a creamy texture. It is available from delicatessens, Italian shops and large supermarkets.

Basmati comes from India and Pakistan. It is a thin, delicate rice with a fragrant aroma. It must be picked over for stones, then washed and soaked in cold water for 20 minutes before cooking, and handled carefully. It is available from Asian grocers and now, increasingly, from supermarkets. It is excellent for pilaus and special occasion dishes.

Brown rice is available in many different varieties. It contains the whole grain so has more flavour, more vitamins and minerals and more fibre than white rice. Both the flavour and texture are nutty: some people find this overpowering, others love it. Brown rice takes more water and longer to cook than white rice. However, one of its virtues is that even when accidentally overcooked, the grains usually remain separate. It is a good rice to partner fish or meat casseroles.

Easy-cook rice has already been partially cooked, and is said to be less sticky as a result. It is more expensive than ordinary long-grain rice, takes longer to cook and has a distinctly blander flavour. However, inexperienced cooks often find it easier to handle initially than other varieties. Follow the instructions on the packet as different brands vary.

Patna/long grain rice is one of the cheapest rice varieties and is available everywhere. It is versatile and can be used successfully for a wide range of dishes: salads, pilaus, risottos and so on. The quality varies enormously: some brands can turn into a glutinous mass with dismaying speed. When you find a rice you like, stick to that source.

Pudding or short grain rice is cheap. In Britain it is normally only used for puddings. However, its absorbent, creamy qualities also make it useful for stuffed vegetables (eg peppers) and risottos.

Cooking rice

Some people say that they always find it difficult to cook rice successfully. Finding the type of rice you like and a cooking method which works for you is often a question of trial and error. Each method has its passionate advocates, and many cookery books will allege that theirs is the only reliable one. However, the truth is that there are many different methods which work successfully.

General principles are:

❧ Use the correct rice for the dish – the recipes in this book will specify what type is needed.

❧ Measure both the dry rice and the water in a cup or measuring jug, ie by volume not by weight (although recipes usually give a weight as a basic guideline).

❧ Wash the rice first. This removes the milling and polishing dust and some of the sticky starch. You can wash rice in a fine sieve under running water, or by swishing it around gently in a large bowl in seven or eight changes of water. Do not proceed until the water runs clear. Drain the rice and let it dry a little.

❧ Use a large, heavy pan, the shallower the better. This way the rice cooks more evenly and you avoid the problem of overcooked rice at the bottom with undercooked rice at the top. All methods of cooking rice are helped by having a pan with a really tight-fitting lid which stops steam escaping. It is often wise to drape the pan with kitchen foil to make doubly sure. A heavy pan is more likely to distribute the heat evenly and will help prevent sticking.

The main methods are:

❧ *The open-saucepan method*

This is the best method for cheap rice of unknown quality. Use a large pan and bring a generous quantity of salted water to the boil. Put the washed rice in the water and let it come to the boil again. Now reduce the heat to a brisk simmer and leave the lid off. Keep testing the rice. The length of time it takes to cook may vary from 10 minutes for delicate varieties of white rice to 40 minutes for brown rice. As soon as there is no hard centre left in the rice, drain it in a large sieve. Run cold water through it to remove any traces of starch and to arrest the cooking process. Wash the saucepan and wipe it dry. Put in a little oil or butter and place it over the lowest heat possible. Return the rice to the pan. Drape the top of the pan with foil to prevent any steam escaping and fit the lid on top. Now let the rice cook for another 6–10 minutes so that it becomes dry and soft.

❧ *The steam method*

This method uses very little water as the rice cooks in its own steam. It is the best one to use for basmati and patna rice. It uses one measure of rice to one and one third of water. Sometimes you may even find it possible to use as little as one volume of water to one of rice. The rice must be carefully washed and allowed to dry off before cooking.

Bring the salted water to the boil in a pan with a tight-fitting lid. Put in the rice and allow the water to boil again. Immediately reduce the heat to its lowest possible level and put on the lid (lined with foil if necessary). The lid must be left in place undisturbed for about 15 minutes. Resist any temptation to inspect it before then, as if you do the valuable steam will escape. After 15 minutes the rice will have absorbed all the water and will be cooked, each grain separate.

Variation: for flavoured rice, use a cast iron, lidded casserole and melt a little butter or oil in it. Add chopped onions, and herbs and spices of your choice. Sauté them for a few moments. Now add the washed, dried rice and gently stir it for about a minute. Add the measured volume of boiling water: 1 volume rice to 1⅓ volume of water, bring it back to the boil, then reduce the heat and proceed as before. Alternatively, the lidded casserole may be put into a pre-heated medium oven (gas mark 3, 325°F (170°C)) for 20 minutes.

❧ *The fuel-saver's method*

You must use a flame-proof, heavy, cast-iron, lidded casserole for this method, as this type of pan retains the heat best. The virtue of this method is that it allows you complete freedom to do something else for about half an hour while the rice is cooking.

Gently heat a little oil at the bottom of the pan. Add any seasonings you like, then the rice and sauté it gently for about 2 minutes. Now add boiling salted water: 1 volume of rice to 1½ volume of water. Let the rice simmer gently until the water has evaporated to the level of the grains and the surface is pitted with holes. At this point, quickly remove the pan from the heat and put on the lid lined with a clean tea towel. Wrap the pan completely in several layers of thick towels and leave it for 25–35 minutes or longer if you wish. The insulation retains the heat and the rice cooks on its own. The grains may look a little lumpy at first, but can be gently separated with a fork as you turn them out.

❧ *Special method for brown rice*

This method was perfected by Madhur Jaffrey who, in her book, *Eastern Vegetarian Cookery*, describes experimenting with an enormous bag of brown rice until she achieved a satisfactory result. It works equally well with long- or short-grain brown rice.

Measure out the volume of rice you will need. Wash it thoroughly in cold water and drain it. Put it in a large, heavy, cast-iron casserole or saucepan and add two volumes of water. Now leave it undisturbed to soak for an hour. After this time add a little salt and bring the rice to the boil. Cover it and immediately reduce the heat to its lowest possible setting. Let it cook, without removing the lid at all, for 35 minutes. Take it off the heat with the lid still on and let it stand undisturbed for another 10 minutes. The water should have been completely absorbed. Fork the rice through gently before serving it.

Other grains

Bulgar: this is confusingly called by a variety of other names: burghul, pourgouri or cracked wheat. Popular in the Middle East, it is a good alternative to rice, and could not be easier to deal with, as it has already been partially cooked. It is available from ethnic and wholefood shops and some supermarkets.

Method: Put the bulgar into a basin and add about twice its volume of cold water. Leave it for 20 minutes, by which time it will have swollen in size and absorbed a lot of the water. Line a sieve with kitchen paper and drain the bulgar. Press out as much water as you can. For salad dishes, flavourings and dressings can now be added. In the Middle East these are usually mint and other herbs, lemon juice, oil and spring onions. See pages 155 and 219 for two interesting recipes.

For making pilaus, the method is slightly different. Soak and drain the bulgar as described above. Use a heavy, flame-proof, cast-iron casserole and melt a little oil or butter in it. Sauté a few chopped onions and any other flavourings of your choice, then add the bulgar. Reduce the heat to the lowest possible point for about 5 minutes. Then cover the pan with foil, put the lid on firmly over the pan, and leave the bulgar to steam gently in its own heat for another 10 minutes.

Buckwheat: This may be sold plain or roasted, but the flavour of roasted buckwheat is generally considered to be better. It is another good alternative to rice for pilaus or as an accompaniment to casseroles.

Method: The safest method of cooking this grain is in the oven. Pre-heat the oven to gas mark 4, 350°F (180°C). Melt a little butter or oil in a heavy flame- and oven-proof casserole with a lid and sauté a measured volume of buckwheat. Onions and other flavourings may be included at this stage. Now pour in a measured volume of water: 1 volume of buckwheat to 1¾ volume of water. Bring the water to the boil. Put the lid on, transfer the casserole to the oven and cook for about 40 minutes. It may need to be fluffed gently with a fork.

Couscous: this is a type of semolina popular in North Africa and France.

Traditionally it is cooked in the steam of the stew with which it is to be eaten, and in North Africa it is made in a special double pan called a couscousier. It is possible to improvise a couscousier by using a double-steamer, or a saucepan and metal sieve which must be a tight fit over the pan. Pad it out with a tea-towel if necessary.

Method: The stew is started first in the bottom pan. About an hour before the end of its cooking time, sprinkle the couscous with a little cold water. Put this into the sieve or steamer and gently distribute the grains so that they lie evenly. Leave the pan uncovered – a couscousier does not have a lid. Steam it for 30 minutes then transfer it to a bowl. Sprinkle it again with cold water and gently break up any lumps. Return it to the sieve and steam for the final 30 minutes.

Spices and other flavourings

Like herbs, spices once played an important part in British cookery, when they were much valued for their aromatic powers as flavourings in preserved food.

Today, once again, their use is increasing dramatically. Indian and Chinese restaurants have familiarised a whole new generation of diners with the superb tastes which spices can impart. Television, radio, magazines and books have brought the techniques of using spices to an even wider audience.

As with herbs, spices are important in healthy cookery. They intensify the flavour of food and add stronger subtle flavours of their own. All supermarkets now have well stocked spice racks, and the range is being extended all the time by popular demand. Anything that can't be found in a supermarket can usually be tracked down in Indian, Chinese or Greek grocery shops. Chemists are another good source, as spices are often used for medicinal or cosmetic purposes. For instance, saffron, star-anise and rosewater may be available in your local chemist's shop even though your supermarket has never heard of them. Wholefood and health-food shops usually stock an extensive range of both herbs and spices. As in ethnic shops, they may be bought loose and are therefore much cheaper than those expensive little bottles from supermarkets, though the quality may be more variable.

Storing spices

Whole spices – that is spices which are sold as whole seeds such as peppercorns or coriander – may be stored indefinitely in glass jars or tins without losing their flavour. This is much the best way to buy them if you can. However, many recipes call for ground spices, so you will also need a coffee grinder. Wipe it out well after use so that the spices do not flavour your coffee. Whole spices can also be pounded in a mortar and pestle or placed between layers of kitchen paper and beaten with a rolling pin.

All this takes time and trouble, and some people prefer to buy small quantities of ground spices and renew them regularly. Throw away anything which has been hanging around in your store cupboard for longer than 6 months. Old ground spices quickly lose their flavour.

Using spices

Depending on the dish, spices often yield up their essential oils more wholeheartedly if they are first stir-fried for a few minutes in very hot oil. You will need enough oil to prevent burning. Any excess can be drained off before you proceed to the next stage.

Allspice: a dried berry which looks like a large peppercorn. It is used in pickles, cakes and for flavouring rice, where it gives a sweetish fragrance reminiscent of cloves and cinnamon.

Black pepper: this is now easy to buy as whole peppercorns so that it can be freshly ground at the point of cooking; greatly superior to the 'hotter' white ready-ground variety.

Capers: these are the small flower buds of a climbing plant which grows wild around the Mediterranean. Their tart flavour is unique, and nasturtium pods, often suggested as a substitute, are nothing like as pleasing. Use capers in sauces for fish or pasta. They have a special affinity with garlic and lemon. It is usually better to rinse them and then soak them in water before use: this gets rid of the vinegary brine in which they are normally pickled.

Cardamom: a superb pale green spice which comes in a pod containing tiny black seeds. Some people advocate only using the seeds, but the pod can also be used whole. Crush it lightly before using. Essential for Indian cooking, this is an expensive spice, but a few pods go a long way. Ground cardamom is a poor substitute as it loses its flavour so quickly.

Cayenne: a fiery pale orange-red ground pepper which should be used with the greatest caution. Half a teaspoon is often enough to make an Indian dish 'hot'.

Chillies: these can be fresh or dried, red or green, large or small. They are a variety of capsicum or pepper. Treat them with respect. The seeds are an irritant and must be removed, so wash your hands with great care immediately after de-seeding fresh chillies. Some chillies are much milder than others, but there is no reliable way of telling this from their size or colour. Chillies are widely used all over the world and are essential to Indian and Mexican food. They are usually finely chopped before being added to dishes, but the larger variety can be stuffed.

Cloves: a sweet spice, this is useful in savoury or pudding dishes. It is also excellent in apple purées with lemon, and in pickles and chutneys, but use it discreetly.

Coriander seed: this has a pleasing taste reminiscent of orange. It can be used lavishly – whole, crushed or ground. It is a versatile spice, popular in the Middle East and India, and is essential for any store cupboard. It is especially useful as a substitute seasoning for salt.

Cumin seed: the taste of this spice is somewhere between caraway and aniseed. It is cheap, and useful for fish and meat dishes. It is improved by being dry-roasted in a hot, clean pan, then ground.

Garlic: British people used to be renowned for their terror of garlic. Today we are more likely to accept garlic as one of the most important flavourings in the kitchen. There are many types – those with large cloves are much easier to peel. Raw garlic is an essential ingredient of marinades, and can also be used to rub flavour round a salad bowl. Garlic burns easily and can then taste bitter – discard it if this happens. Slow cooking makes garlic much less pungent. To crush garlic simply press the clove with the flat of a broad-bladed knife against a wooden board. It is often unnecessary to peel the clove.

Ginger: this is another flavouring which has suddenly become much more widely available. Fresh ginger is a pale brown, knobbly rhizome with a sharp, almost lemony flavour. The dried version used for gingerbread tastes quite different – hot and pungent. A small peeled cube of ginger with a clove or two of garlic can transform a casserole from something ordinary into something special. Fresh ginger can be unpleasantly fibrous, however. Deal with this by grating it, by processing it with a little water, or by cutting it into thread-like strips. When buying ginger look for a fresh, unwrinkled appearance and silky skin. Store ginger in your vegetable basket, or wrap it in newspaper and refrigerate it.

Juniper berries: these are black dried berries of the juniper tree. They are usually crushed before being added to pork or fish dishes, and are also used in marinades.

Lemons: Lemon juice is one of the most useful flavouring agents there is. Its sharp taste in sauces seems to reduce the need for a lot of salt. In meat and fish marinades, its acid action softens and therefore tenderises flesh. A lemon wedge garnish to be squeezed on meat looks pretty but also makes nutritional sense, as it helps the digestive system to absorb the iron in the meat.

Lemon zest has a pungent and distinctive lemony flavour of its own – very useful in stuffings, sauces and marinades. Scrub the lemon first in hot water to remove any waxy deposit or dyes. Carefully peel away the thin yellow skin, leaving the white pith behind. Where a recipe calls for finely grated lemon zest, a gadget called a lemon zester makes this job easier. Lemon zest is sometimes briefly blanched to intensify its colour.

Mace and nutmeg: mace is the outer casing of the nutmeg with a similar though stronger flavour. Nutmeg is much better if freshly grated from a whole nutmeg (use a fine grater kept for the purpose). Useful in cakes, puddings, fish, egg and cheese dishes.

Miso: see under *Soy sauce*

Mustard: there are dozens if not hundreds of different varieties of mustard, all made from the seed of the mustard plant. English mustard is hot and is excellent in cheese dishes or with rabbit and fish. Two French mustards are especially useful: Bordeaux and Dijon. These are aromatic as they contain vinegar and spices. Dijon mustard is the best to use for vinaigrette (French dressing).

Orange-blossom water (or orange flower water): this is the distilled essence of orange blossom petals. It has a delicate sweet flavour, almost a perfume. The strength varies considerably – 'triple distilled' is the strongest. It can be used to flavour yoghurts, dried fruit compotes, and puddings. It is excellent beaten into fromage blanc, or yoghurt. Ask for it in chemists where it is sold as a skin tonic.

Paprika: a ground spice made from red peppers, not to be confused with cayenne (though many cooks have, with disastrous results). Paprika is a mild, sweet, bright red spice, best known for its use in Middle-European cookery. It need not be used with the same caution as cayenne. Also useful as a garnish for dips and purees.

Rosewater: this is distilled from rose petals and, like orange-blossom water, is available from chemists. Popular in the Middle East, it is used in the same way as orange-blossom water.

Salt: Salt seems undoubtedly to be implicated in the widespread phenomenon of high blood pressure in all Western societies. Since high blood pressure is rarely seen in societies consuming little salt, it would seem wise to reduce our intake. A safe level is reckoned to be between 0·9 and 2·3 grams of sodium (salt) a day (*Food Facts*, David Briggs and Mark Wahlqvist, Penguin 1984). A teaspoon of salt contains about 2 grams of sodium. Many of us are consuming anything between 3 and 20 times that amount. The World Health Organisation recommends 5 grams a day as a safe level. Salt occurs naturally in many foods, but it is also added liberally by food manufacturers to all kinds of products, even to sweet biscuits.

Common salt, or table salt, is pure sodium chloride. Rock and sea salt are almost entirely sodium chloride, but they have traces of other elements which change their flavour slightly. The vogue for freshly ground salt has been a bonanza for some kitchen shops who sell it in pretty little bags or boxes, often at extraordinary prices. Some sea salt does have a pleasantly piquant flavour, it is true, but you cannot get away from the uncomfortable fact that, however it tastes and whatever it costs, it is still the same basic sodium.

Sodium also occurs in various other common ingredients: bicarbonate of soda, soy sauce, monosodium glutamate (MSG) and in some preservatives. Salt is a good preservative, which perhaps accounts for the large amount found in hard cheeses and bottled sauces. Other foods very high in salt include smoked meat and fish, crisps, bacon, ham, patés, sausages and salami, stock cubes, yeast extract and packet soups.

Some people find it is relatively easy to modify their salt intake immediately. Others find it hard to cut down suddenly, especially on salt in cooked food. However, usually over a period of time, a gradual reduction slowly but surely modifies the taste buds. A large proportion of the salt we eat – as much as 80% – comes from processed, highly refined foods, so cutting down on these will immediately reduce your salt intake.

Steamed vegetables have so much flavour that there is no need for added salt. Avoid eating too much canned food: in this book we have nearly always suggested fresh equivalents, as so often the food, particularly vegetables, is canned in brine. However, some foods can only conveniently be obtained canned. Prolonged soaking will usually remove excess salt from fermented black beans, capers, anchovies or olives. Herbs and spices can replace the need for salt or for the salty bottled sauces which some people add to their food at the table. It is usually easiest to make a start in salt-reduction by never putting salt on the table.

Salt substitutes: You can now buy low-salt products to sprinkle on food. These usually contain a mixture of sodium chloride and potassium. However, scientific opinion seems to favour caution where these products are concerned, as it is possible that unrestricted use of potassium could cause a whole new set of problems.

Saffron: this is one of the most expensive spices in the world. Fortunately a little goes a long way. It is the dried, thread-like stigma of the Saffron Crocus, and there is nothing to compare with it for the flavour and colour it can impart to, for instance, rice or fish dishes. Release the yellow colour and flavour by soaking it first in hot milk or water for 20 minutes, then add this liquid to the food to be cooked. Discard the threads. Alternatively, the threads may be quickly roasted in a medium, dry pan until they turn red. Transfer them to half a cup of milk and leave this to soak for several hours. Strain the milk and add it to pilaus or stews.

Soy sauce (Shoyu): this is a fermented product of the soya bean. It is very salty so use it discreetly. It is a uniquely useful flavouring, however, essential for Chinese and Japanese cookery. It comes in 'dark' and 'light' varieties.

Dark soy sauce is labelled 'soy superior sauce' and is less salty. Use it for braised dishes.

Light soy sauce is usually labelled 'superior soy' and is more salty. Use it for stir-frying.

'Soya sauce' is a cross between the two and is the one normally sold in supermarkets.

There are two other salty products of the soya bean which have a similar flavour to soy sauce. *Miso* is a thick paste which needs to be dissolved in water. *Tamari* is the more watery residue left behind when miso is made. It has a milder flavour than soy sauce.

Star anise: this is perhaps the prettiest spice – a star-shaped dried berry with a strong aniseed flavour. Useful for marinades and in fish dishes, it is sometimes stocked by chemists and is always available in Chinese shops.

Tabasco: this is a ready-prepared thin chilli sauce. It is very hot so a few drops are normally sufficient to flavour a dish.

Turmeric: a cheap yellow spice, normally sold ground, this should not be over-used as too much is unpleasant. It makes a poor substitute for saffron in taste, although the colour is good.

Vanilla: the strange-looking, long, thin, whole pods of vanilla are expensive, but may be used over and over again if they are carefully wiped and dried. Vanilla essence is the convenient way to obtain the uniquely sweet flavour of this spice which is so useful for puddings and icecreams. It is worth paying a little more for the real thing – look for the label 'pure vanilla essence'. Anything labelled 'vanilla flavouring' is made from a crude synthetic substitute.

Stocks

A stock cube is a good emergency stand-by, but many stock cubes are heavy concentrates of monosodium glutamate, ordinary salt and anonymous synthetic 'flavourings'. Stock cubes vary enormously in quality and flavour. Some of the best are the low-salt vegetable cubes which you can buy in health shops. Vegetable bouillon powder is the same thing in powder form.

Home-made stock is simple and cheap to prepare. In general, it is healthier and tastes better than stock made with a cube. All home-made meat stock draws out fat. The best way to deal with this is to strain the stock, refrigerate it for a few hours and then to remove the solidified fat from the top. In a hurry you can skim off the fat from the surface of hot stock. A good way to do this is to drop an ice cube into the hot stock. This will force the fat to rise to the top.

Good stock always requires bones. For brown stock you can buy marrow bones from your butcher extremely cheaply. Ham stock can be made from a pig's trotter or knuckle which is very cheap. Chicken stock is excellent made from a cooked or raw carcass. For fish stock, ask your fishmonger for a few heads and tails – he may give them to you for nothing.

Stock-making takes time and dedication which is perhaps what puts people off, as few of us have the time to stand over a stock pot for several hours. A slow-cooker, however, makes good stock and requires little attention. Carry out the initial stages in the same way as the conventional method described below. The simmering stage can be done in the slow cooker, but you should allow 8 hours for a good result, and the quantities will need to be reduced to whatever size your cooker will comfortably accept. Pressure cooking is another excellent alternative. All the processes can be carried out in the one pan, but again the quantity of stock will be smaller, as pressure cookers cannot normally be filled above two-thirds of their capacity. However, the cooking time at 15 lb pressure can be as little as 30 minutes for chicken stock, 50 minutes for beef stock, and the end product will have a very concentrated taste (dilute it if necessary). Unsalted stock freezes well and keeps for about 9 months.

BROWN STOCK

2–3 lb (1 kg approx.) beef or veal bones
4 carrots
3 onions

Pre-heat the oven to its highest temperature. Wash the bones and pat them dry. Break them up into small pieces with a cleaver (or you could ask the butcher to do this for you). Put the bones into a roasting tin just as they are for 30–45 minutes or until they look almost blackened. Now transfer them with any juices into a very large pan. Cover the bones with 4 pints (2·3 litres) of water. Roughly chop the carrots. Halve the onions, but leave their skins on as they give a good colour and flavour. Add the vegetables and bring the water to the boil. As scum rises to the top, remove it with a skimming ladle and reduce the heat so that the water is barely trembling. Put the lid on and leave the stock at this heat for 4–5 hours. Skim it from time to time if necessary. Remove the lid for the last half hour. Strain the stock, refrigerate it and remove the fat.

Variations:

Other vegetables can be added, for instance, celery or turnips. Brown stock can also be lightly flavoured by adding herbs and spices, eg bayleaves, peppercorns, coriander seeds, juniper berries, parsley and thyme.

CHICKEN STOCK

(the same method may be used for turkey)

Ingredients:
A cooked or raw chicken carcass
2 onions
2 carrots
1 bouquet garni (see page 44)
1 teaspoon black peppercorns

Break up the chicken carcass with a cleaver and put it in a wide pan. Add any odd bits of skin, meat or jelly left over from a cooked bird. Cut the onions in half but leave the skins on, and roughly chop the carrots. Put the vegetables, bouquet garni and peppercorns into the pan. Add enough water to cover the carcass completely. Bring it to the boil and immediately lower the heat. Skim off the scum, and adjust the heat until the liquid is barely simmering. Complete the cooking as for brown stock.

Variation:

QUICK CHICKEN GIBLET STOCK

This produces a small quantity of light brown stock with an excellent flavour. Put all the giblets into a medium-sized pan and add 1 chopped onion, 1 chopped carrot, 1 chopped celery stalk and a bouquet garni. Cover the giblets and vegetables with 1½ pints (900 ml) of water. Bring this to the boil and remove the scum as before. Now reduce the heat a little to a steady simmer. Keep skimming, replacing the lid each time. After 45 minutes strain the stock with a sieve lined with kitchen paper and remove any visible fat. This stock can be made in 15 minutes with a pressure cooker.

FISH STOCK

Fish stocks are the exception to the rule with stock where long, slow cooking is normally required to produce a good flavour. Fish stock can be ruined by being cooked for too long when it acquires an unpleasantly sour taste. 20–30 minutes is all that is needed to produce a wonderfully aromatic liquor which will make an excellent sauce for any fish dish.

1 ½ lb (700 g) fish heads and tails
2 small onions
1 carrot
2 sprigs of fresh dill (or a pinch of dried dill weed)
5 sprigs of fresh parsley (or ½ teaspoon dried)
1 bouquet garni
5 whole black peppercorns, lightly crushed
1 teaspoon coriander seeds
5 fl oz (150 ml) white wine

Rinse the fish in cold water. Cut the onions in half, leaving their skins on. Chop the carrot. Put the fish and vegetables in the pan with the wine, herbs and spices. Now add enough water to cover the fish – about 1 ½ pints (900 ml). Bring it to the boil, skim it if necessary, reduce the heat and simmer for about 20 minutes. Strain the stock. It can be used immediately.

Sweeteners

It is always pleasant to have something sweet as part of a meal, and eating healthily does not mean doing without sugar and sweetness altogether.

Refined sugars: whether white, demarara, light brown, or dark brown are all equally sweet, though some have stronger flavours than others. Refined sugar, whether white or brown, contains no minerals or vitamins: it has no nutritional value. Honey, golden syrup and treacle are just alternative, syrupy forms of sugar, though honey has minute traces of vitamins and minerals. It is better to cut down on all these forms of sweetness.

Sugar is a preservative, which is one of the reasons it is so popular with manufacturers: it helps prolong the shelf-life of their food. Some of the cake and biscuit recipes we give in this book have much less sugar (and fat) in them than is conventional, so they need to be eaten fairly soon after they are made.

All sweet foods, 'natural' or not, can have undesirable effects on your waistline, teeth and digestion, so it is still desirable to use them with discretion. However, some useful and pleasant alternatives to refined granulated sugar are:

Carob ('locust bean' or 'St John's Bread'): This is the pod of a tree which grows all over the Mediterranean. It is sold at health and wholefood shops in powdered form and in bars (as confectionery – but beware, some of these have a lot of added sugar) and is a good substitute for chocolate. It has a natural sweetness, no caffeine, and a great many vitamins and minerals. It can be used in baking (see our recipe for Carob Cake, page 182) and for home-made sweets (see page 177) and drinks.

Dried fruit: a huge range of dried fruit is available now, not just from wholefood stores, but from supermarkets too. There are often startling differences in price, so if you buy a lot of dried fruit it is worth doing some market research first.

Apples, apricots, plums, nectarines, grapes, pears . . . these all dry successfully and are all extremely sweet as the flavour is so concentrated. They are full of vitamins, minerals and fibre.

Almost all the dried fruit sold in Britain has been treated with sulphur dioxide, a preservative which prevents drying out and keeps the fruit supple. Sulphur dioxide may indeed be as harmless as the manufacturers claim. However, until proved innocent, it is probably wiser to wash all dried fruit under running water in a colander. It is possible to buy unsulphured fruit in some health shops. Californian raisins are usually unsulphured.

Dried fruit has innumerable uses. Mix it as it is with nuts for a snack, and include it in packed lunches too. It is an essential ingredient in muesli. Some dried fruit – for instance, prunes or apricots – make excellent sweet, moist stuffings for meat; stoned dried fruit can be stuffed with nuts (see page 208) and simmered in wine for an elegant dessert; dried fruit purées make good substitutes for jam on toast (page 189). Some of the simplest and most delicious dishes are dried fruit compotes where a mixture of fruit soaks in water overnight, or even for several days. A quicker way to produce the same effect is to simmer the fruit for about 20 minutes. Cool it, then refrigerate for about an hour.

Malt extract: Malt extract is a syrup sold in wholefood shops and chemists. It is a sugary by-product of barley, but is only about one third as sweet as white sugar. It has a strong flavour which is pleasant in bread, cakes and biscuits.

Molasses: Molasses is available in wholefood shops and some super-markets. It is a dark, almost black treacly spread, and contains the residue left after the first stage of refining sugar cane.

The taste is strong, smokey and bitter. It is mostly sugar and water, but 5% is minerals. It is useful in small quantities for baking where it gives an interesting flavour. Some people like to add a teaspoonful to plain yoghurt or muesli.

Fruit juice: Fresh fruit juice is much better for children than sugary, dyed orange squash. (However, too much can be bad for tooth enamel so it is probably wise to dilute it a little.) Watch out for brands with added sugar which taste syrupy. Natural fruit juices are useful for home-made fruit jellies (page 184) and ice-lollies.

Wholefood shops sell fruit juice concentrates – usually apple or grape. These have no added sugar or preservatives. Dilute them as with squash to make drinks, or use them in concentrated form for baking. They are cheap and have a pleasant taste.

Sugarless jams and spreads: Sugarless jams are sold in health food shops. The range usually includes, among others, raspberry and blackcurrant as well as a number of 'hedgerow' jams. They are made from concentrated fruit and added pectin. Because no sugar is added, the colour is usually pale and the texture rather wobbly. The flavour is mild: some people find it refreshing, others think it insipid. Young children are unlikely to notice the difference. These jams are good spread on pancakes and of course they can be used on bread and toast exactly like conventional jams. Once opened, they must be kept refrigerated.

Pear and apple spread is smooth and dark – it looks at a quick glance exactly like chocolate spread. It is sold in plastic tubs at health food shops and contains no added sugar. It has a sweet-sour taste and can be used as a jam or as a substitute for sugar in puddings (page 198).

Tofu (Bean curd)

This is a useful food which deserves to be more widely appreciated. It is high in protein and has no fat. Tofu is made from soya bean curd and is widely used throughout the Far East. Its taste, unseasoned, is completely bland. However, its great redeeming feature is its ability to accept other flavours.

It comes in two forms:

Firm tofu is sold in little white blocks, usually in oriental shops and now, increasingly, in some health food stores. It can be cut into smaller cubes or slices and gently fried or steamed with spices, herbs and other flavourings (see our recipe on page 130).

Silken tofu is much more widely available – look in the refrigerated displays at health and wholefood shops. It is sold in small cartons and looks like cream. Use it for salad dressings, dips and sauces.

Vinegar

Malt vinegar is excellent for making pickles, and you can't beat it for fish and chips. Real malt vinegar is brewed from malted barley and should not be confused with 'Non-Brewed Condiment', a cheap and synthetic tasting substitute derived from crude oil.

Malt vinegar is too strong for salad dressings, so it is worth accumulating a collection of flavoured vinegars for different culinary uses. They add subtlety and distinction to all sorts of dishes – for instance, a dash of tarragon vinegar can transform a chicken casserole; garlic vinegar is wonderful in salad dressings; white wine vinegar is excellent in marinades for fish or meat as it helps to soften the flesh; a tablespoon of cider vinegar adds a robust flavour to a beef casserole.

Most large supermarkets sell at least red and white wine vinegar and cider vinegar. Many now also sell ready-flavoured tarragon vinegar and garlic vinegar. However, it is extremely simple and probably more fun to make your own flavoured vinegars – that way you can experiment with flavours. You also have the advantage of being able to make smaller quantities than you can buy in shops.

Herb vinegars: You can use any lidded glass container as long as it does not have a metal top which can come into direct contact with the vinegar. Small, recycled, glass fizzy-drink bottles, preserving jars or even jams jars with plastic-lined tops are all suitable, though a bottle with a narrow top will be easier to pour from later. Wash the bottle carefully and let it dry thoroughly.

Pick or buy a generous bunch of your chosen herb. It is probably sensible to concentrate on the herbs which are unobtainable or expensive in winter – for instance basil, tarragon and dill. The leaves should be dry and clean (it is better to wipe them rather than wash them if they are dirty). There is no need to crush or chop the herbs.

Now put the herbs into the container, cramming in as much as you can. Pour white wine vinegar over the herbs, filling it to the top to prevent evaporation. Press down any herbs that spring to the top, then screw the lid on the jar or bottle. Leave on a warm sunny windowsill for 3–4 weeks: the time varies for different herbs, so keep testing by tasting and sniffing. If you wish, you can leave the vinegar as it is. However, most people prefer to strain the vinegar, then pour it back in the bottle, topping it up with more white wine vinegar. Adding a small fresh sprig of the herb looks pretty and also enables you to see what it is at a glance.

Fruit vinegars: Fruit-flavoured vinegars used to be the basis of many popular drinks in Britain. They fell out of favour, but now their use is being revived for salads and in cooking generally. They give a sweet-sour fruity flavour to salad dressings. Any fruit may be used to flavour vinegar, but the most popular and successful are raspberries, stoned cherries, and red or white currants. Red fruit gives the vinegar a delightful colour.

The basic method is the same as for making herb vinegars. Use only sound, dry, wiped fruit and discard any that look over ripe. A wide, lidded, glass jar is easier to use than a bottle. A small amount of fruit is enough to give a strong flavour. Use about 4 oz (110 g) to each 10 fl oz (275 ml) of vinegar. Put the fruit in the jar and pour the vinegar on top.

Fruit vinegars are ready to use in 2–3 weeks. Vinegar is a preservative and the fruit remains whole indefinitely. It looks attractive in the jar, but strain it if you prefer.

Other vinegars: It is worth experimenting with any of your favourite fruit, herbs and spices alone or in combination to produce interesting vinegars. For instance, all these flavourings added to 10 fl oz (275 ml) of vinegar will produce a pleasing result:

Garlic – 3 large peeled cloves, each cut in half

Spicy 'Oriental' – a small, peeled, sliced cube of fresh ginger, 6 peppercorns, 2 juniper berries, 1 teaspoon coriander seeds, 2 cardamom pods and roughly chopped zest of half a lemon

---

Greengage – stone and halve 7–8 greengages. Add 3 thin slices of peeled, fresh ginger, a clove of garlic and the roughly chopped zest of half a lemon

---

Gooseberry and thyme – wipe, top and tail 4 oz (110 g) of green or yellow gooseberries. Add the zest of half a lemon and two sprigs of thyme.

STARTERS, SNACKS AND LIGHT MEALS

The recipes in this section can all be used as first courses, or, with the quantities adjusted, as the basis of a light supper or lunch. For instance, the Avocado Dip (page 86) served with thin slices of toast will make a pleasant starter to a three-course meal. However, a more generous serving with plenty of fresh wholemeal bread and a tomato salad will also make an excellent light lunch; the Spinach and Artichoke Timbales with Carrot Sauce (page 88) make a striking and pretty first course, but served with new potatoes and a salad they could equally well be a satisfying supper dish.

FISH SOUP

Caldillo de Pescado

SERVES 4   ELISABETH LAMBERT ORTIZ

Chile has magnificent fish and shellfish and many of their dishes reflect this abundance. It is usually necessary to substitute other fish as those in Chilean waters are not available here. I have found cod an excellent substitute for the congrio that would be used in Chile. Though modestly called a soup, this is substantial enough for a main course or light lunch. Each person's fish is served in one piece surrounded by a chunky sauce of vegetables so it is best eaten with a spoon and fork!

2 lb (900 g) skinned filleted cod, cut into 4 steaks
Salt, freshly ground black pepper
2 fl oz (50 ml) lemon juice
2 medium-sized onions
2 cloves garlic, crushed
1 red pepper
1 yellow or green pepper
1 fresh red or green chilli
2 lb (900 g) small potatoes
2 tablespoons corn oil
½ teaspoon dried oregano **or 1 teaspoon fresh chopped marjoram**
10 fl oz (300 ml) dry white wine
1¾ pints (1 litre) fish stock
Fresh chopped herbs for garnish

Season the cod steaks with a little salt and pepper, then pour over the lemon juice. Meanwhile, finely chop the onions and the garlic, de-seed and chop the peppers, de-seed and finely chop the chilli (wash your hands afterwards), and peel and slice the potatoes wafer-thin. In a large heavy casserole, heat the oil and gently fry the onions, chilli, and pepper until they are soft. Add the garlic, the cod steaks, and after a few minutes the potatoes. Sprinkle with the oregano or marjoram and more pepper if you like. Pour in the wine and fish stock. Simmer, covered, for about 20 minutes or until the potatoes are tender. Serve the soup in large individual bowls, garnished with a few freshly chopped herbs and accompanied by crusty bread.

BLACK HARICOT BEAN SOUP WITH PRAWNS

Sopa de Frijoles negros con Camarónes

SERVES 4   ELISABETH LAMBERT ORTIZ

This wonderfully dark brown soup from the Mexican State of Oaxaca has a most exciting flavour, the rich flavour of the beans contrasting well with the fresh prawns. Black kidney beans are available from health food shops, but when I cannot get them, I use red kidney beans or pinto beans instead. The latter are pale brown beans with mottled pinkish markings and are sometimes sold as 'crab eye' beans. I like to follow this soup with a light main course, as the beans are rather filling.

6 oz (175 g) black haricot, red kidney or pinto beans
¼ teaspoon ground cumin
½ teaspoon ground oregano
1 bay leaf
2 fresh chillies
1 medium-sized onion
1 clove garlic
5 oz (150 g) fresh tomatoes
1 tablespoon corn oil
Salt, freshly ground black pepper
15 fl oz (400 ml) chicken stock
8 oz (225 g) peeled cooked prawns, thoroughly defrosted if frozen

In a medium-sized saucepan combine the beans, cumin, oregano and bay leaf with 1¼ pints (720 ml) of cold water. Bring this to the boil and boil vigorously for 10 minutes. Reduce the heat to low, cover, and simmer until the beans are tender (about 2½ hours). The time will vary according to the freshness of the beans so test them from time to time. Allow to cool a little, then remove and discard the bay leaf. Strain the beans, reserving the liquid. Now transfer the beans to a blender or food processor. (Alternatively, you could mash the beans with a potato masher.) Using some of the liquid, purée the beans and return them to the rinsed-out saucepan, together with the reserved liquid.

De-seed and chop the chillies. Chop the onion and garlic. Peel and chop the tomatoes. Heat the oil in a frying pan and sauté the onion, garlic and chillies until they are soft. Add the tomatoes and simmer the mixture until it is well blended (about 5 minutes). Season to taste with salt and

STARTERS, SNACKS AND LIGHT MEALS

pepper, then purée in the blender or food processor. Add to the bean purée, stirring the mixture well. Stir in the chicken stock and simmer over a moderate heat for 2 or 3 minutes. Remove from the heat and add the prawns. Allow the mixture to stand, covered, for a few minutes to heat the prawns through. Serve immediately.

COLD TOMATO SOUP
Gaspacho Andaluz

SERVES 4   CHRISTOPHE BUEY

This traditional Spanish dish can be long and complicated to cook if you keep to the Andalusian traditions. This is my 5-minute recipe which comes as near to the same delicious result as possible. It is a wonderfully light and refreshing chilled soup to serve at the start of a special meal.

Ice cubes
10 oz (275 g) tomatoes
½ cucumber
½ green pepper
½ red sweet pepper
1 medium-sized onion
1 pint (570 ml) tomato juice (tinned or fresh)
1 clove garlic
1 fl oz (25 ml) tarragon vinegar
Salt, freshly ground black pepper
1 fl oz (25 ml) olive oil
1 dessertspoon fresh herbs, such as parsley, chervil, tarragon, chives

Make sure you have a batch of ice cubes ready to chill the soup.

Wash all the vegetables well and cut them into chunks. Reserve a little of each for the garnish. Place half the tomato juice in a liquidiser or processor with the vegetables and garlic, and liquidise for 2–3 minutes. Gradually add the rest of the juice, the vinegar, salt and pepper and finish with the olive oil. Add the ice cubes to the soup and refrigerate it for 10 minutes. Remove the ice cubes and serve the soup garnished with the reserved chopped raw vegetables.

SWEET RED PEPPER SOUP

Sopa de Pimientos Morrones

SERVES 4   ELISABETH LAMBERT ORTIZ

This is a beautiful, light, refreshing soup with a deep, rich, red colour. It makes a wonderful first course. The recipe comes from Mexico where sweet red peppers and other chilli peppers originated in remote times. Sweet red peppers are now grown all over the world, are available nearly all the year round and are the ripe form of our familiar green bell peppers. Choose fresh, shiny, unwrinkled ones for the best flavour.

4 large sweet red peppers
1 medium-sized onion
1 teaspoon corn oil
1 ¼ pints (700 ml) chicken stock
10 fl oz (300 ml) tomato juice
Salt, freshly ground black pepper
Sprigs of fresh herbs for garnish (optional)

Put the peppers under a grill, a few inches from the heat, and grill them, turning them from time to time, until they are blackened and blistered all over. Lift them out with tongs and put them into a plastic bag. Close the bag, and leave them for about 20 minutes, then take out the peppers and rinse them. Most of the skin will wash away under cold water. Pull away any blackened bits but do not bother if small pieces of skin remain. Pull away the stem and remove the seeds. Chop the flesh coarsely and transfer it to a food processor or blender. Chop the onion. Heat the oil in a frying pan and sauté the onion until it is soft. Add the sautéed onion to the blender or food processor (a blender will give a smoother texture) and purée with a little of the chicken stock. Transfer the purée to a saucepan, add the rest of the stock and the tomato juice. Season it to taste with salt and pepper and simmer, covered, for 10 minutes. Serve in soup cups garnished, if you like, with a sprig of any fresh herb, such as basil, chervil, parsley or mint.

HOT BEETROOT SOUP

SERVES 6   MICHAEL QUINN

This is a thick soup with a bright reddish-purple colour. A wonderful hot soup for winter, it can also be served cold in the summer. For the best flavour, use raw beets and cook them yourself.

1 lb (450 g) raw beetroot
3 pints (1.7 litres) home-made chicken stock (page 68)
6 peppercorns
8 coriander seeds
½ teaspoon fennel seeds
A few sprigs of parsley
1 leek
2 celery stalks
2 carrots
4 shallots
1 garlic clove
Salt, freshly ground black pepper
5 oz (150 g) yoghurt
Fresh tarragon leaves for garnish (optional)

Scrub the beetroot, but do not peel it. Keep a little aside to use for garnish. Put the beetroot in a large saucepan with the chicken stock. Put the peppercorns, coriander seeds, fennel seeds and parsley into a piece of muslin and tie this onto the saucepan handle so that the muslin bag hangs in the stock. Bring the stock to the boil, lower the heat and cook gently for just over an hour. Then roughly chop the leek, celery, carrots, shallots and garlic, add these to the pan and continue cooking for 20 minutes. Remove the pan from the heat, lift out the beetroot and allow to cool. Rub off the skin, then purée the beetroot in a processor or blender together with the other vegetables and the stock (discard the muslin bag). It is essential to sieve the soup after processing it to remove the fibrous threads. Season to taste with salt and pepper.

To serve, pour the soup into bowls, grate a little of the reserved raw beetroot over the top and swirl a teaspoon of yoghurt in each bowl. Garnish with a few tarragon leaves if available and serve immediately.

CARROT SOUP
Potage Crécy

SERVES 4   CHRISTOPHE BUEY

Potage Crécy is a traditional French soup which normally uses cream and butter. In this version I have substituted healthier ingredients which make for a lighter and more delicate soup. It has a velvety smooth texture, a pale golden colour and a delicate flavour. The basic carrot purée is flavoured with chicken stock, onions and leeks. You should really use a good home-made chicken stock (see page 68). Surprisingly, this soup does not really need salt as the carrots and leeks provide enough flavour.

1 onion
1 leek
Dash of safflower oil
1 lb (450 g) carrots
2 pints (1 litre) home-made chicken stock (page 68)
Fresh chives for garnish
5 oz (150 g) natural yoghurt

Chop the onion and leek thinly. Heat the oil in a saucepan, and sweat the onion and leek; put the lid on the pan and continue to cook them gently. Meanwhile, scrape or peel the carrots (according to the season) and cut them into thin slices. Add the carrots to the onion and leek and sweat them for 5 minutes or until the vegetables have softened but not coloured. Bring the stock to the boil. Add the boiling liquid to the vegetables and simmer them for 10 minutes, or until the carrots are cooked. Liquidise in a food processor or blender. Using scissors, snip the chives into a warmed soup terrine, add most of the yoghurt and mix well. Gently pour the soup into the bowl, swirl the rest of the yoghurt on top and serve immediately.

OPPOSITE: FROM TOP TO BOTTOM
Spinach and Artichoke Timbales with Carrot Sauce (*page 88*)
Carrot Soup (*page 80*)
Marinated Fish Seviche (*page 91*)

LUSCIOUS LENTIL SOUP

SERVES 6   LESLIE KENTON

Although a simple soup, this dish is a meal in itself, when served with a
beautiful mixed salad and home-made bread. If you are in a hurry, make it
with orange split lentils, which need no soaking; it is then ready in a mere
30 minutes. I prefer to use whole lentils, particularly the tiny, very dark
brown Chinese lentils rather than the brown or green whole variety,
although whole lentils take much longer. To the lentils add whatever
vegetables you happen to have in the garden or refrigerator – from
parsnips and carrots to leeks and cabbage. Feel free to be creative. You'll
never make the same soup twice, but here are some general guidelines:

1 large onion
3 carrots
4 celery stalks
1 tablespoon olive oil
3–4 tomatoes or 14 oz (400 g) tinned tomatoes
1 lb (450 g) whole green, brown or Chinese lentils soaked for several hours or overnight
2 cloves garlic, crushed
1 tablespoon parsley
2 bay leaves
1 tablespoon ground cumin
4 pints (2·3 litres) stock or water with 1 tablespoon vegetable bouillon powder (see page 66)
Dash or two of red wine (optional)

Chop the onion, carrots and celery. Put the oil in a heavy saucepan or soup
pot, sauté the onion, then add the carrot and celery and sauté these for five
minutes. Chop the tomatoes, then add them, together with the lentils,
crushed garlic and herbs, to the vegetables. Pour in the stock. When it
begins to simmer, reduce the heat to very low and continue to simmer for
1½ to 2 hours. Add the red wine a couple of minutes before removing the
soup from the heat. Serve piping hot.

OPPOSITE: FROM TOP TO BOTTOM
Fish Kebabs (*page 212*)
Submarines (*page 221*)
Grilled Vegetables (*page 214*)

POT BARLEY AND TOMATO SOUP

SERVES 4   EVELYN FINDLATER

Most people cook with pearl barley, which is refined barley; the bran and most of the germ have been taken away. Try to buy pot barley instead, which has all the goodness and flavour of the whole grain.

Served with some chunky granary bread, a little cheese and some fresh fruit to follow, this soup makes a tasty and nourishing light meal.

2 oz (50 g) pot barley
2 tablespoons (30 ml) corn or sunflower oil
1 medium-sized onion, finely chopped
1 clove garlic, crushed
2 medium-sized carrots, finely chopped
1 medium-sized potato, chopped into ¼ inch (5 mm) cubes
2 small stalks celery, very finely chopped
1 tablespoon fresh parsley, chopped, or 1 teaspoon dried
1 tablespoon fresh mixed herbs, chopped, or 1 teaspoon dried mixed herbs
14 oz (400 g) tinned tomatoes
1 pint (450 ml) home-made chicken or beef stock (see pages 67–8) or 1 low-salt vegetable stock cube
Freshly ground black pepper
1 dessertspoon shoyu (naturally fermented soy sauce) or 1 teaspoon (5 ml) soy sauce

Soak the barley in 1 pint (570 ml) of water overnight. Drain the barley, and, if you are making stock from a cube, reserve the water and top it up with enough water to make exactly 1 pint.

Heat the oil in a saucepan and add the onion and garlic. Gently fry them for 5 minutes with the lid on. Add the prepared carrots, potato, celery and drained barley. Let this fry over a low heat for another 5 minutes. Stir in the parsley and mixed herbs. Chop the tinned tomatoes and stir these, together with their juice, into the vegetables. Simmer this mixture gently for about 10 minutes with lid on.

Heat the water used for soaking the barley and dissolve the stock cube, or alternatively heat through your home-made stock. Add the hot stock to the simmering vegetables, together with the freshly ground black pepper. Mix everything well and simmer the soup for 20–25 minutes. Finally add the shoyu or soy sauce according to taste. This soup is delicious just as it is, but you can liquidise it if you prefer a smooth texture. Serve piping hot.

SCALLOPS IN TOMATO SAUCE

Coquilles St Jacques à la Tomate

SERVES 4   CHRISTOPHE BUEY

This easily prepared appetiser of scallops is cooked in an unusual home-made tomato sauce. The sauce can be made ahead of time and reheated, before adding the scallops at the last minute. Ask your fishmonger to clean the scallops and separate the coral as that will save you time! This dish looks pretty when garnished with peeled, blanched cucumber.

8 scallops
1 lemon
Dash of safflower oil
1 shallot or small onion, finely chopped
1 lb (450 g) very ripe tomatoes, quartered, or 14 oz (400 g) tinned tomatoes, drained
Salt, freshly ground black pepper
Sprig of fresh thyme or ½ teaspoon dried thyme
Bay leaf
1 clove garlic
Sprigs of fresh herbs, such as parsley, chervil, tarragon, or a pinch each of dried
4 slices of hot toast (optional)

Shell the scallops. Slice each one in half horizontally and marinate the slices with half the juice and the grated zest of the lemon for 10–15 minutes.

Heat the oil gently and sweat the chopped shallot or onion. Add the tomatoes, a little salt and pepper, and the thyme, bay leaf and garlic. Cover and simmer this mixture for 10 minutes. Remove the lid, raise the heat to high and reduce the quantity of liquid by half. Remove the sprig of thyme, if using, and the bay leaf. Now press the sauce through a sieve into a frying-pan.

Re-heat the tomato sauce to boiling point. Discard the marinade from the scallops, and dry them on a paper towel. Add the rest of the lemon juice and the scallops to the sauce, and gently poach them for 2 minutes, being careful not to allow the sauce to boil. The scallops should now be white and tender. Serve either in the reserved shells or on toast, garnished with the fresh or dried herbs.

CRUDITÉS

PAUL LAURENSON AND ETHEL MINOGUE

Crudités – fresh or lightly cooked, chilled, prime quality vegetables, well presented, are one of the best beginnings to a meal. They can be served just as they are, or with a selection of dips, or coated lightly with vinaigrette. Any crisp, young vegetables may be used. Crudités give the cook a chance to blend the wonderful colours and textures of raw vegetables creatively for a healthy start to a meal. Use any selection of prettily cut and well chilled young vegetables. For example:

Slice into matchstick strips: red, green and yellow peppers, carrots, celery, fennel, courgettes and cucumbers.

Serve tomatoes according to type: cherry tomatoes whole, larger tomatoes quartered and beef tomatoes sliced crossways.

Blanch and serve whole: young green beans, asparagus, broccoli and cauliflower florets, globe artichokes.

Chill and serve whole: lettuce hearts, chicory, spring onions, radishes.

AVOCADO DIP FOR CRUDITÉS

SERVES 4–6

Avocados make an excellent dip for crudités, but this version is also a good substitute for butter or other fat spreads in many kinds of sandwich. Try it with lettuce, spring onions and tomatoes or piped onto slices of beef tomatoes and topped with an olive.

2–3 large ripe avocados
Juice of 1 lemon
1 tablespoon olive oil
2 drops chilli sauce (or to taste)
4 cloves garlic, crushed
¼ teaspoon paprika
A pinch of sea salt
Fresh coriander or parsley for garnish

Put all the ingredients except the garnish in a large bowl and mash with a potato masher. This gives a better texture than a blender, which tends to make it a bit like baby food. Chill, then serve, garnished with coriander or parsley.

BROAD BEAN DIP TO SERVE WITH CRUDITÉS

SERVES 4–6

In this recipe dried broad beans are cooked with a variety of interesting flavourings and then puréed to make an earthy-tasting dip for raw vegetables, or to serve with hot pitta bread or wholemeal toast. Any dried beans or lentils may be used, though the cooking times vary (see page 56).

8 oz (225 g) dried broad beans
1 small onion
6 garlic cloves
2 bay leaves
Bunch of fresh thyme
4 fl oz (110 ml) olive oil
Juice of 1 lemon
Salt, freshly ground black pepper

Soak the dried broad beans for a few hours, or overnight, until they swell, then discard the water and put the beans into a saucepan. Cover them with cold water. Tie the whole onion, 3 whole cloves of garlic, bay leaves and bunch of thyme loosely in muslin and suspend the bag in the water. Simmer until the beans are tender and have absorbed the water. Discard the muslin bag and put the beans into a food processor together with the olive oil, lemon juice, salt, pepper and remaining 3 garlic cloves, crushed. Process them until they form a smooth purée, or mash them with a potato masher. Cover and serve the purée chilled.

SPINACH AND ARTICHOKE TIMBALES WITH CARROT SAUCE

SERVES 6   MICHAEL QUINN

This is a pretty and fresh-tasting starter though it can also be served as a light meal with crusty bread. The timbales are cooked in individual ramekins, then turned out and surrounded with the sweet carrot sauce: a wonderful contrast of flavours and colours. Best of all, it is quick and simple to prepare, and can be made in advance if you wish to serve it cold. If not, the timbales can be kept hot in their dishes in the bain marie until you wish to serve them. Asparagus is a good alternative to spinach in this dish.

Timbales
A little polyunsaturated margarine
1 lb (450 g) Jerusalem artichokes
A little chicken stock or water
1 lb (450 g) spinach
4–6 fl oz (175–225 ml) skimmed milk
4 eggs
Salt, freshly ground black pepper
Parsley or chervil for garnish

Sauce
4 oz (110 g) carrots
6 fl oz (200 g) light chicken stock
5 oz (150 g) natural yoghurt
1 tablespoon tarragon or white wine vinegar
1 fl oz (25 ml) white wine
Salt, freshly ground black pepper

Pre-heat the oven to gas mark 4, 350°F (180°C). Lightly grease the 6 ramekin dishes with the margarine (or a 7 in (18 cm) soufflé dish). Peel the artichokes, then just cover them with chicken stock and simmer them, covered, for about 10 minutes or until they are tender. Drain them and reserve the liquid. Trim the stalks from the spinach, wash it, and cook it in a large pan, without adding any water, until it is tender. Drain and squeeze the excess water from the spinach. Purée it, together with the artichokes, in a processor or liquidiser, and leave to cool. Put the cooking liquid from the artichokes into a measuring jug and add enough skimmed milk to bring the liquid up to the 10 fl oz (275 ml) mark. Pour the mixture into a pan and bring it to the boil, then leave to cool. Once the purée is cool, add the eggs, artichoke liquid, salt and pepper and mix briefly. Pour the mixture into the greased ramekin dishes and cover them with foil or greaseproof paper. Place them in a bain-marie or baking dish and pour in some boiling water to come about a third of the way up the sides of the ramekins. Bake them in the oven for 30–45 minutes or until they are firm to the touch.

Meanwhile, slice the carrots thickly and cook them, covered, in the chicken stock until they are tender. Purée them with their cooking liquid in the processor or liquidiser, then add the yoghurt, vinegar, wine, salt and pepper. To serve, ease the sides of each timbale from its dish with a sharp knife and turn the timbales out onto plates. Garnish with the parsley or chervil, then pour the carrot sauce round and serve.

TROPICAL SAVOURY FRUIT SALAD

SERVES 4   CLAUDIA RODEN

Now that tropical fruits are in the supermarkets and they are no longer too expensive, it is worth making use of them for a savoury salad which can be served as a first course or taken on a picnic. Its exotic flavour never fails to enchant.

½ small melon
1 paw paw (papaya)
1 avocado
1 kiwi fruit
Juice of ½ lemon
2 tablespoons (30 ml) olive oil
Salt, freshly ground black pepper
A few sprigs of fresh mint, finely chopped

Cut the fruits open, and scoop out the seeds from the melon and the paw paw and the stone from the avocado. Remove the skins and cut the flesh into cubes or pieces. Skin the kiwi and cut it into slices. Mix together the lemon juice, olive oil, seasoning and chopped mint, then pour this over the salad and toss lightly. Serve chilled.

STEAMED SARDINES GARNISHED WITH FRESH CORIANDER

SERVES 4   LYN HALL WITH ANTON MOSIMANN

Sardines in their silver skins, garnished with graceful fronds of coriander and a spoonful of dark, glossy sauce, make one of the easiest and most successful dishes I have ever cooked. The sardines may be replaced with baby herring, and the coriander with flat-leafed parsley. Serve them with a potato and chive salad dressed with yoghurt for a quick light meal.

8 fresh or frozen sardines
Salt, freshly ground black pepper
1 cube of fresh ginger, peeled
3 tablespoons lemon juice
1 dessertspoon sugar
3 dessertspoons soy sauce
Fresh coriander leaves for garnish

If you do not have a steamer, see page 22 for various ways of improvising. Ideally you need a flat rack resting in a wide, lidded pan.

Put 2 inches (5 cm) of water in the pan, place the steaming rack in position above the water, and bring the water to the boil.

Scale the sardines by rubbing them gently with your fingers. For a neater finish, you can gut the fish as follows. Using a pair of tweezers, reach deep inside the fish through the gills to draw out the innards, leaving the heads on. Wash the fish thoroughly, sluicing the water through the fish until it runs clear, from mouth to back vent. Season the sardines lightly with salt and pepper and steam them for 4–5 minutes.

Meanwhile, using a very sharp knife, cut the ginger into fine strips as thread-like as you can manage. Place the lemon juice, sugar, soy sauce and ginger in a saucepan and bring to a simmer, then remove it from the heat.

Arrange the sardines on individual plates, spoon a little sauce over each and garnish with coriander leaves.

MARINATED FISH SEVICHE

SERVES 6   SHIRLEY RILLA AND JILL COX

This is a superb recipe from Mexico, although other Latin American countries also have their own versions. Popular in countries where the ingredients are abundant, seviche is a refreshing and exotic dish, and unusual in that the fish is 'cooked' not by heat but solely by the acidic juices of the lime or lemon marinade. You can use any firm, white fish, such as cod, halibut, or sole, but try to find limes rather than lemons for a truly authentic taste. Serve with hunks of crusty wholemeal bread to mop up the juices.

2–3 large juicy limes or lemons, enough to produce 3 fl oz (75 ml) juice
1 cube of fresh ginger, peeled
1 tablespoon chopped fresh coriander leaves, or parsley if coriander is unavailable
1 lb (450 g) firm white fish
3 large tomatoes
1 yellow pepper
1 fresh green chilli
1 large ripe avocado
Freshly ground black pepper

First prepare the marinade. Squeeze the limes or lemons and put the juice into a glass dish. Slice the peeled ginger into matchstick threads and mix it thoroughly with the juice. Add most of the chopped coriander to the juice. Neatly skin, fillet and cube the fish, using a very sharp knife, and place the cubes in the marinade, turning them to ensure they are well coated. Leave in the bottom of the refrigerator overnight, giving the fish an occasional stir with a fork. The fish is 'cooked' when it has turned from a translucent to a firm, milky-white colour.

Skin and de-seed the tomatoes, then finely chop them and reserve. De-seed and finely chop the yellow pepper, then de-seed and chop the fresh chilli, taking care to wash your hands immediately.

To serve, drain the fish, reserving the marinade, and mix the fish with the chopped tomatoes, pepper and chilli. Put the mixture on a flat serving dish. Peel the avocado, cut it into thin slices and dip them into the marinade to prevent discolouration. Use the slices to garnish the seviche. Pour the remaining marinade over the top, add freshly ground black pepper to taste, and sprinkle with the remaining chopped coriander.

MUSSELS IN WHITE WINE

Moules marinière

SERVES 4   PAUL LAURENSON AND ETHEL MINOGUE

Mussels have always been considered the poor man's shellfish in the UK but this does the mussel a disservice. Surely, there can be no more magnificent a sight than a huge bowl of hot gleaming mussels on a winter's evening. One word of caution, however: don't ever overcook mussels – they shrink and become rubbery.

4 pints (2·3 litres) fresh mussels
1 onion
1 shallot
2 cloves garlic
Sprigs of fresh thyme and parsley
8 fl oz (225 ml) dry white wine
Freshly ground black pepper

Clean the mussels thoroughly (see page 39), discarding any that are open.

Chop the onion, shallot, garlic, thyme and half the parsley, and place in a heavy pan. Add the wine and boil until nearly all the liquid has gone. Add the mussels and cover the pan. Cook over a high heat until the shells open – this takes about 5 minutes. Shake the pan from time to time so that the heat is evenly distributed. Do not overcook. The mussels will exude a lot of liquor during cooking. Strain this liquid into a small pan and boil it over a high heat for a couple of minutes so that the flavour is intensified.

Discard any mussels that are still closed, then put the mussels in a serving dish and pour the sauce over them. Add black pepper to taste, garnish with the reserved parsley and serve immediately.

EVERYDAY EATING

This long section of the book contains 32 recipes for main meals. Pasta, pulses and grains figure prominently, as do fish and poultry.

    This section falls into three parts. In the first, we have tried to provide recipes for ordinary eating where shortage of time or money are not the key elements. These are recipes perhaps for family weekends or for eating with friends. In the second section 'Cheap Food' (page 109) we have concentrated on meals which cost very little but which will also be healthy, filling and delicious. Some of these dishes will involve a slightly longer preparation time than those in the other two sections. In the third section 'Cooking in a Hurry' (page 129), we have assumed that many busy people have little time to spare for elaborate cooking or shopping, so this is a group of recipes where the whole dish can be prepared and cooked in about half an hour.

POTATOES WITH FISH AND VEGETABLES

Causa a la Chiclayana

SERVES 4   ELISABETH LAMBERT ORTIZ

This delicious and unusual dish is hearty and healthy at the same time and perfect for a dinner or luncheon party. It demonstrates the culinary genius of the Peruvians, whose ancestors first cultivated the potato.

1 medium-sized onion
3 fl oz (75 ml) lemon juice
¼ teaspoon cayenne pepper, or less according to taste
Salt, freshly ground black pepper
2 lb (900 g) potatoes
8 fl oz (225 ml) olive or corn oil
1 lb (450 g) sweet potatoes (optional)
2 under-ripe or green bananas
2 ears sweetcorn
1 lb (450 g) – or 4 small fillets – of any non-oily, firm-fleshed, white fish, eg haddock, cod or halibut
1 small sweet red pepper
8 oz (225 g) Cheshire, Wensleydale or fresh goat's cheese
Lettuce leaves
Black olives

Finely chop an onion and put it into a small bowl with the lemon juice, cayenne pepper, a little salt and freshly ground pepper. Set it aside. Boil the scrubbed but unpeeled potatoes, covered, until they are tender. Drain, and allow them to cool a little, then peel them. Mash the potatoes with the olive or corn oil and the onion, lemon juice and pepper mixture, mixing thoroughly. Make a mound of the potatoes in the centre of a large platter and keep them warm, but not hot. Boil the sweet potatoes, if using, until they are tender, cool and peel them, then cut them into 4 slices. Boil the green bananas, in their skins, for 15 minutes. Cool, peel and cut them into 8 slices. Boil the sweetcorn ears for 5 minutes, drain, cool and cut them into 8 slices horizontally. Set aside the vegetables, keeping them warm. Lightly grill the fish about 5 inches (12·5 cm) from the heat, turning once, for about 3 to 4 minutes each side. Halve the fillets crosswise and keep them warm.

Thinly slice the second onion and put the onion rings into a small bowl of salted water. Let it stand for 15 minutes, then drain. De-seed the pepper and cut it into strips, then blanch these in boiling water for one minute and drain. Cut the cheese into 6 wedges.

To assemble the dish, garnish the edge of the platter with lettuce leaves. Arrange the fish fillets and the vegetables round the mound of potatoes, on the lettuce. Scatter the onion rings and pepper strips over the potatoes. Finally, garnish the dish with wedges of cheese and the black olives and serve hot.

STUFFED TURKEY THIGH

Gigot de Dinde farci

SERVES 4   CHRISTOPHE BUEY

This is a wonderful supper dish and simple to make. Turkey thigh has a strong flavour and can sometimes be dry if it is roasted in the conventional way. Here, it stays moist because the boned meat has a delicate stuffing made from curd cheese, Parmesan cheese and courgettes. Serve it with steamed broccoli or cauliflower, baked potatoes and fresh tomatoes cooked with herbs in the same oven.

½ green or red pepper
½ onion
1 clove garlic
1 tablespoon olive oil
1 large uncooked turkey leg
4 oz (110 g) lean cooked ham
12 oz (350 g) curd cheese (eg ricotta, quark, or a low-fat curd cheese)
2 oz (50 g) freshly grated Parmesan cheese
1 egg
1 dessertspoon various freshly chopped herbs such as parsley, tarragon, chives, chervil, or 1 teaspoon dried mixed herbs
Freshly ground black pepper

Pre-heat the oven to gas mark 7, 425°F (220°C).

De-seed, then chop the pepper into neat dice; chop the onion and garlic finely and sweat them, covered, in olive oil. Remove them from the pan and leave to cool. Meanwhile, bone the meat. Cut right through to the bone along the length of the leg, and lift out the bone. Remove the tendons and nerves, and any excess fat.

Dice the ham. Mix the curd cheese, Parmesan cheese and egg together well, then add the ham, the herbs and the onion, pepper and garlic. Mix them well and season with pepper. Place half the stuffing under the skin of the turkey, turn it over and place the rest where the bones and tendons were. Roll it into a long sausage shape and secure it neatly with a piece of fine string.

Put the turkey into a shallow oven-proof dish, just large enough for the meat to sit comfortably. Turn the oven temperature down immediately to gas mark 6, 400°F (200°C) and cook the turkey on a high shelf for 10 minutes. Turn the heat down again to gas mark 4, 350°F (180°C) and cook it for a further 10 minutes, then turn the heat off and leave the meat to rest for 5 minutes with the oven door open. Transfer the turkey to a serving dish and slice the meat at the table.

PIGEON WITH APRICOTS AND COUSCOUS

SERVES 4   PAUL LAURENSON AND ETHEL MINOGUE

This recipe is inspired by Moroccan cuisine, in our opinion one of the world's most interesting and healthy. Pigeon is now being sold in many of the larger supermarkets chains as well as by butchers. This method of cooking it is a good way of tenderising what can be rather tough meat. If possible use wild or *hunza* apricots for this dish. They are smaller than the conventional sort and are dried with their stones intact. The flavour is superb, but they can be very sweet so lemon juice has been added to the sauce in this recipe. You can buy hunza apricots in most health or wholefood shops. Serve this dish with sliced, steamed carrots.

4 tablespoons olive oil
4 pigeons
3 pints (1·5 litres) chicken stock or water
1 large bouquet garni (celery, parsley, thyme, bay leaf)
8 oz (225 g) wild, or other, dried apricots, soaked until soft
Salt, freshly ground black pepper
Lemon juice
1 lb (450 g) couscous
Bunch of coriander or parsley, roughly chopped, to garnish

Heat half the oil in a flame-proof casserole and brown the pigeons all over. Cover them with the stock or water. Add the bouquet garni. Bring to the boil and simmer until the pigeons are tender. This will take at least 1½ hours and possibly as long as 3 or even 4 hours, depending on the age of the pigeon. If the birds are cooked, you should be able to pull a wing easily away from the body. The skin, however, will usually remain tight and tough.

While the pigeons are cooking, make the sauce. Stone the softened apricots, then put them into a small pan with their soaking water, plus 1 tablespoon of the cooking liquid from the pigeons. Boil the mixture hard to reduce it. The apricots should break up and soften, thickening the liquid. This will take about 10 minutes. The sauce should now be thick, almost syrupy. Add seasoning and lemon juice to taste, then set the sauce aside.

An estimated hour before the pigeons are cooked, prepare the couscous. Sprinkle water on the couscous and mix it up so that it swells lightly. Put it in a couscoussier, a steamer, or a colander set over boiling water and let it cook gently uncovered for 30 minutes (see page 22). Then sprinkle some more water over it, fluff it up and continue steaming for another 30 minutes. Add some oil and a little salt to the couscous and stir well. Re-heat the sauce gently. Place the couscous on a heated serving dish with the cooked pigeons on top. Pour over the sauce. Garnish the pigeons generously with the chopped coriander or parsley.

RABBIT IN PLUM SAUCE

SERVES 4   PAUL LAURENSON AND ETHEL MINOGUE

Wild rabbit as food has had a very bad press in recent times, but it is actually healthier and lower in fat than most meat, and has much more flavour than the paler flesh of domestic rabbit. As a variation, cooking apples can be used instead of plums, to provide a tart contrast to the meat. The dish is delicious served on a bed of noodles or long-grain brown rice.

3 lb (1.4 kg) rabbit, preferably wild
1 dessertspoon flour
Salt, freshly ground black pepper
1 tablespoon olive oil
1 lb (450 g) purple plums
1 onion
2 cloves garlic
1 teaspoon each of fresh chopped thyme and rosemary, or ½ teaspoon of each, dried
½ teaspoon fresh chopped sage, or pinch of dried
2 whole cloves
4 fl oz (110 ml) sherry or port

Pre-heat the oven to gas mark 3, 325°F (170°C). Get the butcher to joint the rabbit. Wash it in cold water and dry it. Dip the joints in flour seasoned with salt and pepper and sauté the joints in a frying-pan for a few minutes in the olive oil. Stone the plums, slice the onion wafer-thin, and crush the garlic. As soon as the rabbit joints are golden, take them from the pan and drain them on kitchen paper. Put the sliced onion and garlic in the bottom of a casserole. Scatter over the herbs and cloves, then put the rabbit joints on top. Pour the sherry or port into the frying pan and boil for a minute, scraping the pan with a spatula to blend with the juices. Pour the juices into the casserole. Arrange the plums on top and cover the casserole with foil and a lid. Cook in the oven for 1½ hours. If necessary, spoon off any excess liquid and boil this over a high heat to reduce the amount and concentrate the flavour. Then return the liquor to the casserole and serve immediately.

OPPOSITE: FROM TOP TO BOTTOM
Rice with Shellfish (page 108)
Chicken Breast with Ginger and Garlic (page 105)

CASSOULET

SERVES 10   MICHAEL QUINN

Cassoulet is a great French provincial dish, where different meats are cooked very slowly with haricot beans to produce a richly flavoured stew, served straight from the cooking pot. Traditionally an earthenware pot is used, but a heavy-based casserole is also suitable. The cassoulet gives great scope for variation, as almost any kind of meat can be used. For my healthy variation I have used beef and best end of neck with a spicy sausage. It may not be authentic but it will be much better for you! As it is a filling meal, serve it on its own with some hot crusty bread and a green salad, and be prepared to take a siesta afterwards! Any leftovers may be re-heated and eaten the next day.

6 oz (175 g) each of haricot beans, dried peas and lentils
1 pint (570 ml) home-made beef stock (page 67)
4 tablespoons tomato purée
2 celery stalks, chopped
2 leeks, cleaned and sliced
1 onion, sliced
2 shallots, sliced
6 cloves garlic
Bay leaf
1 lb (450 g) beef topside
12 oz (700 g) neck fillet of lamb
4 oz (110 g) strongly flavoured French garlic sausage or smoked bacon, chopped
Sprigs of fresh thyme and tarragon
5 fl oz (150 ml) red wine
2 courgettes
1 tablespoon olive oil
6 oz (175 g) green beans
4 tomatoes
Salt, freshly ground black pepper
1 oz (25 g) Parmesan cheese
1 teaspoon freshly chopped sage leaves, or ½ teaspoon dried sage

Continued overleaf

OPPOSITE: FROM TOP TO BOTTOM
Stuffed Turkey Thigh (*page 95*),
Cassoulet (*page 101*)
Pigeon with Apricots and Couscous (*page 96*)

Soak the pulses overnight and drain them. Put them in a large flameproof casserole, cover them with the beef stock and bring them to the boil. Add the tomato purée, chopped celery, leeks, onions, shallots, garlic and bay leaf and put the casserole in the oven. Cook it for about an hour, adding more liquid part-way through the cooking, if necessary.

Pre-heat the oven to gas mark 2, 300°F (150°C). Trim the beef and lamb of all visible fat, and cut them into chunks. Put the meat into a large pan of cold water and bring it to the boil. Skim off the scum as it appears on the surface, then drain off the water. This process gets rid of most of the fat in the meat. Add the meat to the pulses in the casserole, together with the chopped garlic sausage, the thyme, tarragon and wine. Put the casserole back in the oven and cook it for 3½ hours or until the meat is tender. Towards the end of the cooking time, gently fry the courgettes in the oil, and boil the green beans until they are just cooked, but still crisp. Peel and chop the tomatoes.

Once the cassoulet is cooked, add the courgettes, green beans and tomatoes. Check for seasoning, adding salt and pepper if necessary. Cover the surface with the Parmesan cheese and sage leaves, and brown it under the grill.

MOROCCAN FISH CASSEROLE

Tagine Samak

SERVES 4   CLAUDIA RODEN

The best part of this Moroccan dish is the spicy marinade which becomes a sauce. It is called *chermoula*. In Morocco, every family has its own special recipe. Different herbs may be used, for example parsley instead of coriander, varying proportions of spices added, onion substituted for garlic, and so on. Use the following list of ingredients as a guide and suit it to your own particular taste. You are told in Morocco that any fish will do, so choose what you like – but nothing too delicate.

The principle is to cook the fish in the juice or the steam of the vegetables over which it is laid, and that can be done over the heat in a heavy pan with a tight-fitting lid. All sorts of vegetables can be used – potatoes, onions, celery, tomatoes, peppers, all thinly sliced, or cooked broad beans and artichoke hearts. Turnips, which are the vegetable in this version, make a particularly delectable dish especially in this unusual combination with dates.

Serve with bread and a salad.

1 lb 8 oz (700 g) fish, such as cod, haddock, halibut, monkfish or skate
1 lb 8 oz (700 g) young turnips, thinly sliced
6 fresh or moist dried dates, pitted and halved
For the marinade:
2–3 cloves garlic, crushed
1 teaspoon ground cumin
½ teaspoon ground coriander
1 teaspoon cinnamon
¼ teaspoon ground ginger
1 teaspoon paprika
A pinch of cayenne
Salt, freshly ground black pepper
Juice of 1 or more lemons
2–3 tablespoons olive oil
A large bunch of coriander or parsley, finely chopped

Clean the fish. Mix the marinade ingredients in a bowl and leave the fish in it for an hour in the refrigerator, turning the fish over once.

Drain the fish, reserving the marinade. In a wide casserole or heavy pan put the turnips with the dates interspersed here and there. Pour over the marinade and lay the fish on top. Let it cook, covered, on a very low heat until the fish just begins to flake and the turnips are tender. (In Morocco they like to overcook it!) Serve hot or cold directly from the casserole, garnished with chopped parsley or coriander.

DUCK WITH CHESTNUTS AND GINGER WINE

SERVES 6   MICHAEL QUINN

This is a marvellous way of using traditional English ingredients to create a festive dish. The duck is pot-roasted on a bed of vegetables and a little stock, and served with a sauce combining chestnuts and ginger wine. If you can find it, use wild duck, such as mallard, which has a rich flavour and not much fat. If you have to use the blander, larger, domestic duck, it will produce a lot of fat which must be spooned off after cooking. To feed a larger number of people more cheaply you could substitute a 10–13 lb (4·5–6 kg) turkey.

2 onions
2 celery stalks
2 leeks
2 carrots
3 wild ducks or 2 domestic ducks
Salt, freshly ground black pepper
12 oz (350 g) fresh chestnuts, or 8 oz (225 g) tin peeled chestnuts, or 8 oz (225 g) of dried chestnuts reconstituted in water, then drained
Small cube of fresh ginger, roughly chopped
7 fl oz (200 ml) ginger wine, preferably dry
8 fl oz (220 ml) chicken stock

Pre-heat the oven to gas mark 6, 400°F (200°C). Roughly chop the onions, celery stalks, leeks and carrots. Put them in a roasting tin and place the ducks on top. Season the ducks with salt and pepper, prick them all over with a fork, then cover the tin with foil. Roast the ducks for about an hour, turning the temperature down to gas mark 3, 325°F (170°C) after 20 minutes. After another 10 minutes remove the foil to crisp the skin. Meanwhile, prepare the fresh chestnuts, if using: pierce their shells with a sharp knife, cover them with water and boil them for about 3 minutes. Drain them and remove their shells and skins. Place the shelled chestnuts in a small amount of the chicken stock and simmer them gently until they are cooked. Reserve 6 chestnuts – whether freshly cooked, tinned or reconstituted dried ones – for garnish, and purée the remainder in a processor or liquidiser.

Remove the ducks from the oven and place them on a serving dish. Pour off the excess fat from the pan juices. Add the fresh ginger and the ginger wine to the pan and bring them to the boil, stirring well. After a minute, add the chicken stock and chestnut purée and cook for a further 5 minutes. Strain the sauce, discarding the vegetables and press the juices from the fresh ginger. Taste for seasoning and add more salt and pepper, if necessary.

To serve, pour some of the sauce round the ducks on the serving dish and put the rest of the sauce in a sauceboat. Garnish the ducks with the remaining chestnuts, and carve at the table.

CHICKEN BREAST WITH GINGER & GARLIC

SERVES 4 LYN HALL WITH ANTON MOSIMANN

Clean and fresh-tasting, with a most decisive and irresistible flavour, this dish only needs a little foresight: when to begin the marinade. If the breasts are left with the flavourings for an hour or so, the dish is very good, but if left overnight, the mingling of the flavours develops with an even more rewarding intensity.

4 oz (110 g) spring onions
Small cube of fresh ginger
1 dessertspoon crushed garlic
1 lemon
4 chicken breasts
15 fl oz (400 ml) chicken stock
4 oz (110 g) fromage blanc (see page 34)
Salt, freshly ground pepper

Trim the roots and any old skin from the spring onions, and set aside 3 oz (75 g). Place the remainder in a food processor with the ginger and garlic, and process to a rough paste, adding a little water if necessary. If you don't have a food processor, wrap the ginger, garlic and onion in greaseproof paper and beat it on a table-top with a heavy pan. Peel the zest from the lemon and add it whole to the paste. Skin the chicken breasts and carefully cut the flesh away from the bone with a sharp knife. Spread the paste over the chicken breasts, cover and marinate in the refrigerator for about 12 hours, or up to 24 hours. If you are in a hurry, leave them in a cool place for an hour or so. Pick out the pared lemon zest, and drop it into boiling water for 3 minutes. Cut it into fine strips. Scrape the paste from the chicken and pat the meat dry. Set the chicken aside, and place the paste in a saucepan, together with the stock. Bring it to the boil, then cover and simmer for 20 minutes. Strain, pressing hard with a spoon to extract all the liquid. Pre-heat the grill to high. Slice the reserved spring onions very finely on the diagonal. Return the stock to a small pan and boil for 10–15 minutes until reduced to about 2 fl oz (50 ml). Remove it from the heat, and whisk in the fromage blanc, a little at a time. Add lemon juice to taste. Season if necessary. Add the remaining spring onions and the lemon strips. Grill the chicken breasts for 4–5 minutes each side or until they are cooked through, but still moist and slightly spongy. Warm the sauce gently, adding a little additional stock if necessary. Cut the chicken into ½ in (1 cm) slices, cross-wise on the diagonal. Fan the slices out on each dinner plate, spoon the sauce over, and serve.

INDIAN-STYLE CHICKEN AND POTATO CASSEROLE

SERVES 4   MADHUR JAFFREY

There is a potato dish that is only sold in the bazaars of old Delhi. It is stew-like, thick and very spicy. I decided to find out what such a dish might taste like with the addition of chicken pieces. Here is what resulted! You could serve this chicken with rice, with a crusty bread or with just a green salad.

If you make this dish a day ahead, you will find that its flavour will improve. Keep it refrigerated and then heat it slowly but thoroughly.

1 lb 7 oz (650 g) potatoes
2 lb 4 oz (1 kg) chicken joints
Large cube of fresh ginger
2 cloves garlic
4 tablespoons corn oil
4 whole cardamom pods
½ teaspoon whole fennel seeds
½ teaspoon whole nigella (kalonji) seeds (optional)
½ teaspoon whole cumin seeds
7–8 whole fenugreek (methi) seeds (optional)
1 tablespoon ground coriander seeds
2 teaspoons ground cumin seeds
½ teaspoon ground turmeric
¼–½ teaspoon cayenne pepper
2 dessertspoons tomato paste
1 teaspoon salt or to taste
3 tablespoons finely chopped fresh coriander

Peel the potatoes and cut them into bite-sized cubes. Put them in a bowl of water.

Skin the chicken joints and cut them into smaller pieces. Breasts should be cut into 4–6 pieces and each whole leg into 2–4 pieces. Peel the ginger and grate it on the finest part of your grater. Peel the garlic and chop it finely.

Heat the oil in a wide, casserole-type pot over a medium heat. When it is hot, put in the cardamom pods, then the fennel, nigella, cumin and fenugreek seeds. Stir them once, then add the ginger and garlic. Cook them, stirring, for 2–3 minutes. Add the ground coriander, ground cumin, turmeric and cayenne. Stir them once, then add the tomato paste. Give the mixture a good stir. Drain the potatoes and add them to the pot, followed by the chicken, 1 pint (570 ml) water and salt. Stir and bring the stew to a simmer. Cover the pot, lower the heat and simmer for about 25 minutes or until the chicken and potatoes are tender.

You can, if you like, at this stage, mash one or two of the potato pieces with the back of a spoon to make the sauce thicker.

Sprinkle the finely chopped coriander over the chicken and serve.

Note: The whole cardamom pods should not be eaten.

RICE WITH SHELLFISH

Arroz con Mariscos

SERVES 4   ELISABETH LAMBERT ORTIZ

This is a flexible recipe as you can use whatever is best at the fishmongers.
I find monkfish accommodating as it mimics lobster and is now widely
available. The secret of success is to cook the seafood briefly as it toughens
so quickly with overcooking. The dish is substantial, with a wonderfully
subtle flavour.

1 pint (570 ml) fresh mussels
1 large onion
2 cloves garlic
1 red, green or yellow pepper
1 fresh chilli
1 tablespoon corn oil
1 lb (450 g) long-grain rice
2 pints (1·1 litre) fish stock
Salt (optional)
1 bunch fresh coriander, finely chopped
8 oz (225 g) monkfish
6 scallops, defrosted if frozen
1 lb (450 g) cooked, unshelled prawns, or 8 oz (225 g) peeled prawns

Clean the mussels thoroughly (see page 39), discarding any that are open,
and set them aside. Finely chop the onion and the garlic, de-seed the
pepper and cut it into fine strips. De-seed and chop the chilli (wash your
hands afterwards). Heat the oil in a frying pan and sauté the onion, garlic
and pepper until the vegetables are soft. Using a slotted spoon transfer the
mixture to a cast-iron casserole. Add the rice to the oil remaining in the
frying pan and sauté, stirring with a wooden spoon, until the rice has
absorbed all the oil. Do not let the rice brown. Add it to the casserole and
pour in the stock. Bring it to the boil, stir once, cover and cook over very
low heat for 20 minutes or until the rice is tender and all the liquid has
been absorbed. Taste for seasoning and, if necessary, add a little salt. Stir
in the fresh coriander and the monkfish cut into 1 inch (2·5 cm) pieces,
then cover and simmer for 4–5 minutes. Add the mussels, the scallops cut
into slices and the prawns. Cover and simmer gently for 1–2 minutes.
Discard any mussels that don't open. Leave the remaining mussels in
their shells and serve the dish piping hot straight from the casserole.

CHEAP FOOD

One advantage of 'healthier' eating is that so many of the 'right' foods are also cheap: pulses, pasta, rice and bread are a fraction of the cost of red meat. Highly refined food tends to be expensive as well as unhealthy, and avoiding it will undoubtedly help cut the size of your food bill. The recipes in this section concentrate on cheap ingredients transformed by herbs, spices and subtle sauces. We also include several recipes for the humble 'oily' fish (herring, sprats, mackerel), which are thought to have especially beneficial effects on the arteries.

BAKED STUFFED POTATOES

EVELYN FINDLATER

Many people underestimate the humble potato. When baked, it has a superb flavour which can be enhanced by an enormous variety of stuffings. Here I have suggested a few, but you will be able to think of many more. Choose large, firm potatoes for baking; the red-skinned variety is best. Avoid any potatoes that are crinkled, sprouting or green. Baked stuffed potatoes make a wholesome light meal served with a tomato or green salad and French bread.

How to bake potatoes
4 potatoes, each weighing 6–8 oz (175–225 g)
1 dessertspoon corn or sunflower oil

Pre-heat the oven to gas mark 6, 400°F (200°C). Scrub the potatoes well. Dry them and prick them all over with a fork. Cut a thin slit all round the potato as if you were going to cut it in half lengthways. This makes it easier to deal with later. Rub a very little oil over each potato to stop the skin from getting too hard when it is baking. Bake the potatoes in the oven for an hour or until a skewer will go right through the centre easily. Cut in half where you marked the slit and scoop out the pulp. Mash pulp, and add any of the following fillings:

Spiced chick pea filling
6 oz (175 g) cooked chick peas or haricot beans (see page 56)
2 tablespoons yoghurt
1 tablespoon lemon juice
1 large clove garlic, crushed
1 dessertspoon fresh mint, chopped
Freshly ground black pepper
2 tablespoons sesame seeds ground with a pinch of sea salt for the topping

When the potatoes are done, remove them from the oven and lower the temperature to gas mark 5, 375°F (190°C). Mash the chick peas or beans with a potato masher or use a food processor, but be careful not to over-process. Mash all ingredients together including the potato pulp, but not the ground sesame seeds. Spoon the filling into the potato skins. Sprinkle the ground sesame seeds on top of the potato mixture and bake them for 20 minutes, then serve immediately.

Yoghurt and cheddar filling
2 oz (50 g) ground sunflower seeds, toasted
3 tablespoons natural yoghurt
1 medium-sized onion, very finely chopped
3 tablespoons parsley, finely chopped
3 oz (75 g) mature Cheddar, Gouda or Edam cheese, grated
Freshly ground black pepper
Dash of paprika

While the potatoes are baking, toast the sunflower seeds on a baking tray on the middle shelf of the oven until they are lightly roasted; this should take about 15 minutes. Watch them so that they do not burn. Process or grind the seeds to a medium-fine texture. When the potatoes are cooked, remove them from the oven, but leave the heat on. Halve the potatoes, then scoop out the cooked potato pulp and put it in a mixing bowl together with the yoghurt, onion, sunflower seeds, parsley, 2 oz (50 g) of the cheese and the black pepper. Mash everything well together. Spoon the mixture back into the potato skins and sprinkle the rest of the cheese on top, together with the paprika. Return the potatoes to the oven and bake for another 20 minutes. If necessary, brown the cheese under the grill for a few minutes before serving.

Meat or fish filling
1 medium-sized onion, finely chopped
1 tablespoon corn or sunflower oil
2 oz (50 g) button mushrooms, thinly sliced
6 oz (175 g) minced cooked bacon, ham, chicken, smoked mackerel or tuna fish
2 tablespoons fresh parsley, finely chopped, or 1 teaspoon dried parsley
1 teaspoon fresh chopped sage, or pinch dried sage
Freshly ground black pepper

When the potatoes are done, remove them from the oven and lower the oven temperature to gas mark 5, 375°F (190°C). Sauté the onion in the oil for 4 minutes. Add the mushrooms and sauté them for 3 minutes more. Scoop out the potato pulp, mash it, then add all the other ingredients and mix thoroughly. Spoon the stuffing back into the potato skins. Bake them for 15 minutes, then serve immediately.

Continued overleaf

Cottage cheese and chive filling
8 oz (225 g) cottage cheese
1 heaped tablespoon chopped chives or spring onions
2 in (5 cm) chunk of cucumber, very finely chopped
Freshly ground black pepper
Paprika for garnish

Using a fork, mix the cottage cheese, most of the chives or spring onions (reserving a few for garnish), cucumber pieces and black pepper. When the potatoes are cooked and still hot, slit them in half, and mash the potato pulp in the skins. Make a little well in the middle and pile the cottage cheese filling on top of each half. Sprinkle with paprika and the reserved chives to garnish, and serve immediately.

PASTA BUTTERFLIES WITH TOMATO SAUCE

Farfale al sugo

SERVES 2   ANTONIO CARLUCCIO

For this delicious dish you can use home-made pasta butterflies or bought fresh or dried pasta.

2 tablespoons olive oil
2 cloves garlic, finely chopped
2 × 14 oz (400 g) tinned tomatoes
6 fresh basil leaves, torn into pieces, or a pinch of dried basil
Salt, freshly ground black pepper
1 tablespoon tomato purée
8 oz (225 g) dried pasta butterflies, or ½ quantity of fresh pasta butterflies (page 54)
Freshly grated Parmesan cheese

Heat the olive oil in a frying-pan, then add the chopped garlic and fry it gently, but don't let it brown. Chop the tomatoes and add them, together with their juice, to the frying-pan. Add the basil, salt and pepper and cook the sauce for 20 minutes until the liquid has reduced a little, then add the tomato purée.

Bring 3½ pints (2 litres) of lightly salted water to the boil and put the pasta in very gently. Stir a couple of times to prevent the butterflies sticking together. Boil the pasta for about 4 minutes if it is fresh, 8 minutes if it is dried, or until it is cooked but is still *al dente*. Drain the pasta and return it to the pan. Toss it with a few spoonfuls of the tomato sauce until evenly coated.

Transfer the pasta to a heated serving plate, pour over the rest of the tomato sauce, sprinkle with the Parmesan cheese and enjoy a real taste of Italy!

OTHER PASTA SAUCES

ANTONIO CARLUCCIO

Here are five more delicious sauces for pasta, all of them simple, wholesome and tasty.

HERB AND WALNUT SAUCE

SERVES 4

This sauce, with its freshness and simplicity, is a perfect accompaniment to pasta. You *must* use fresh herbs for it; dried are no substitute. You must also chop these and the walnuts *by hand* so that the sauce has a fairly coarse texture.

1 oz (25 g) shelled walnuts
Small bunch each of fresh parsley and chives
1 tablespoon each of *2 only* of the following fresh herbs: tarragon, dill, basil, mint
1 clove garlic
4 tablespoons olive oil
Salt, freshly ground black pepper
Freshly grated Parmesan cheese.

Using a sharp knife, finely chop the walnuts and herbs. Crush the garlic with the salt. Mix the walnuts, herbs, garlic, olive oil and salt and pepper well. Add half of this to the cooked pasta and mix well. Turn out onto a serving dish, pour the remaining sauce on top and serve with the grated Parmesan cheese.

TOMATO AND CAPER SAUCE

SERVES 4

1 onion
2 red or yellow peppers, or one of each
2 tablespoons olive oil
2 × 14 oz (400 g) tinned tomatoes
2 tablespoons capers, drained and rinsed
Salt, freshly ground black pepper
Freshly grated Parmesan cheese

Chop the onion finely, and core, de-seed and chop the peppers. Sweat them gently in the pan with the olive oil for about 5 minutes. Chop the tomatoes and add them to the pan, together with their juice and the capers. Simmer the mixture gently for 20 minutes or until it has thickened. Add salt and pepper to taste and mix some of the sauce into the cooked pasta before pouring the remaining sauce on top. Serve the dish accompanied by grated Parmesan cheese.

LEEK AND HAM SAUCE

SERVES 4

8 oz (225 g) leeks
1 tablespoon olive oil
8 oz (225 g) ricotta
4 fl oz (110 ml) skimmed milk
4 oz (110 g) lean cooked ham
1 clove garlic, crushed
Freshly grated Parmesan cheese

Wash the leeks thoroughly, and discard the tough outer leaves and tops. Chop the leeks finely and fry them gently in the olive oil, together with the crushed garlic, until the leeks are soft but not brown. Mix the ricotta with the milk to make a smooth cream and warm it through gently, but do not boil it. Dice the ham. When the leeks are soft, add the ham and continue to cook for a few minutes. Pour this mixture over the cooked pasta, mix it well, then add the milk and ricotta mixture and toss again. Sprinkle the dish with grated Parmesan cheese and serve. There is no need to add salt, as both the ham and cheese already contain enough to season the sauce.

EGG AND TOMATO SAUCE

SERVES 4

Stracciatella is a Roman term used to denote the addition of beaten eggs to a broth at the end of cooking, so the eggs are cooked in the hot liquid. This sauce is based on onions, with eggs added at the last moment to give a creamy texture. Spanish, or red onions, are best for this recipe as they give a gentler flavour than other onions.

2 Spanish or red onions
2 tablespoons olive oil
2 × 14 oz (400 g) tinned tomatoes
2 basil leaves, or a pinch of dried basil
3 eggs
Salt, freshly ground black pepper
Freshly grated Parmesan cheese

Finely slice the onions. Heat the olive oil in a frying-pan and sweat the onions gently until they are transparent, but not brown. This will take 15–20 minutes. Roughly chop the tomatoes, then add them, together with their juice and the basil, to the pan and cook for another 10 minutes or until the sauce has thickened a little. Beat the eggs and, just before serving, slowly pour them into the sauce, stirring continuously. After a minute the sauce will turn creamy. Immediately mix some of it into the cooked pasta, then serve the pasta on a dish or on plates with the remaining sauce on top, sprinkled with Parmesan cheese.

COURGETTES AND GARLIC SAUCE

SERVES 4

12 oz (350 g) courgettes
2 cloves garlic
2 tablespoons olive oil
Salt, freshly ground black pepper
Freshly grated Parmesan cheese

Finely slice the courgettes and crush the garlic. Heat the oil in a frying-pan, and slowly fry the courgettes until they are soft. Add the garlic after a couple of minutes, and stir the courgettes occasionally to prevent them browning. Add salt and pepper, and mix the courgettes and pan juices into the cooked pasta. Serve it immediately with the Parmesan cheese handed round separately.

CANNELLONI WITH RICOTTA AND SPINACH

Cannelloni alla Ricotta

SERVES 4   ANTONIO CARLUCCIO

There are many variations of this classic Italian dish, using meat and fish filling inside tube-shaped pasta. This recipe, however, is especially for vegetarians, though I must say that non-vegetarians love it too. Based on the ricotta cheese so popular in Italian cooking (see page 34), the dish makes a pleasant light meal, served with a fresh green salad.

1 tablespoon olive oil
8 pieces of lasagne 6 × 7 inch (15 × 18 cm), fresh or dried
1 lb (450 g) spinach
12 oz (350 g) ricotta cheese
Freshly grated nutmeg
Salt, freshly ground black pepper
1 quantity of Tomato Sauce (see page 112)
Freshly grated Parmesan cheese

Pre-heat the oven to gas mark 9, 475°F (240°C). Put a generous quantity of lightly salted water plus the olive oil on to boil. Immerse the pieces of lasagne one by one and boil until they are cooked but still *al dente*. Drain them and lay them out in a single layer on a cloth. Wash the spinach, then put it in a saucepan and cook it, without any additional water, until it has wilted. Let it cool, then chop it finely, but do not use a food processor as it makes the spinach too wet. Mix the spinach, the Ricotta cheese, grated nutmeg, and salt and pepper. Put 2 tablespoons of this mixture in the centre of each piece of pasta and roll it, overlapping one side, to form a tube. Spread about 3 tablespoons of the tomato sauce in a shallow ovenproof dish. Place the cannelloni side by side in the dish and pour over the rest of the sauce. Sprinkle the Parmesan cheese on top and bake for 15–20 minutes or until well browned. Serve immediately.

OPPOSITE: FROM TOP TO BOTTOM
Tagliatelle with Leek and Ham Sauce (*page 114*)
Pasta Spirals with Herb and Walnut Sauce (*page 113*)
Pasta Butterflies with Tomato Sauce (*page 112*)

GREEN RISOTTO
Risotto verde

SERVES 2 AS A MAIN COURSE, 4 AS A STARTER   ANTONIO CARLUCCIO

The soft cooked broccoli makes this risotto as creamy as 'buttered' risotto, with the added advantages of being extremely digestible, healthy and an authentic Italian dish. Italian risotto should be prepared with Arborio rice, a large-grain rice which is very absorbent but remains *al dente*. You can buy it in Italian shops and in large supermarkets. A useful substitute is short-grain 'pudding' rice, which has a similar texture, but not the delicate flavour of Arborio. The preparation of this dish takes about 20 minutes. You could use the same idea to prepare risottos based on asparagus or courgettes.

1 lb (450 g) broccoli or calabrese
3 pints (1·7 litres) chicken stock
1 tablespoon olive oil
1 small onion, chopped
2 cloves garlic, chopped
10 oz (275 g) Arborio rice
Freshly grated Parmesan cheese
Salt, freshly ground black pepper (optional)

Chop the broccoli, including the tender part of the stalks, and cook it in the chicken stock for about 3 minutes. Drain it, returning the stock to a low heat. Put the olive oil, onion and garlic into a large cast-iron casserole and sweat them gently over a moderate heat for 4 minutes or until they are cooked. Add the rice and stir a couple of times until it is coated with the oil. Add the broccoli, and continue to stir to mix the ingredients thoroughly. Now add the hot stock, ladle by ladle, as required, and keep stirring for about 20 minutes or until the rice is *al dente*, shiny and creamy. Check the seasoning, adding salt and freshly ground black pepper to taste. Spoon the risotto onto pre-heated plates, sprinkle with the Parmesan cheese and serve immediately.

OPPOSITE: FROM TOP TO BOTTOM
Baked Stuffed Potatoes with Ham and Mushroom,
Cottage Cheese and Chive, and Yoghurt
and Cheddar Fillings (*pages 110–112*)
Chick Pea Rissoles (*page 122*)
Yoghurt and Cucumber Salad (*page 159*)
Baked Sardines (*page 127*)

BAKED SAVOURY RICE WITH TOASTED CASHEW NUTS

SERVES 4   EVELYN FINDLATER

Tasty, slightly chewy, whole-grain rice is far healthier than the white and fluffy sort, and is equally versatile. This recipe can be varied enormously by adding cubed, left-over chicken sautéed with the vegetables, or substituting cooked chick peas or kidney beans for the cashew nuts. Add a little curry powder for a change of flavour. Any of the variations are delicious served with bean sprout or coleslaw salad.

8 oz (225 g) Italian short- or long-grain brown rice
½ teaspoon salt, preferably sea salt
1 bay leaf
3 oz (75 g) unsalted cashew nuts
2 tablespoons sunflower or olive oil, plus extra for greasing
1 large onion, finely chopped
1 clove garlic, crushed
2 medium-sized carrots, cut into matchstick strips
2 celery stalks, finely chopped
1 tablespoon fresh chopped basil, or 1 rounded teaspoon dried basil
1 dessertspoon fresh chopped tarragon, or ½ teaspoon dried tarragon
6 ripe, skinned and chopped tomatoes, or 14 oz (400 g) tinned tomatoes, drained and chopped
1 tablespoon tomato purée
1 tablespoon Shoyu (naturally fermented soy sauce) or 1 teaspoon soy sauce
3 oz (75 g) Cheddar cheese, grated

Put the rice in a sieve and wash it under cold running water for 30 seconds.

Prepare and cook the rice by your preferred method (see page 59 for a foolproof way of cooking brown rice), adding the salt and bay leaf to the cooking water. While the rice is cooking, toast the cashew nuts on a baking sheet in the oven, gas mark 3, 325°F (170°C) for 15 minutes or until golden. Grilling is a quicker but riskier method, as the nuts may burn.

Meanwhile, heat the oil in a large frying pan with a lid. Raise the oven temperature to gas mark 5, 375°F (190°C).

Sweat the onion, garlic and carrots for 7 minutes with lid on. Add the celery and herbs and continue to cook them for 3 more minutes. Stir in the chopped tomatoes, tomato purée and Shoyu or soy sauce. Cook for another minute only and set it aside. Fork the sautéed vegetables into the cooked rice. Stir in the toasted nuts and put this mixture into a greased ovenproof dish. Top this with the grated cheese and bake in the centre of the oven for 25–30 minutes, then serve.

LENTIL PATTIES

SERVES 4–6   CAROLE HANDSLIP

You can use ordinary orange split lentils for this recipe; they cook quickly so there is no need to soak them first. These little patties are lovely served with a tomato sauce and buckwheat spaghetti, but they are equally good with a potato accompaniment and a crisp green salad to complete the meal. They can also be eaten cold and are useful to take on picnics.

2 tablespoons sunflower oil
1 onion, finely chopped
3 cloves garlic, crushed
2 carrots, finely chopped
2 celery stalks, chopped
8 oz (225 g) orange lentils
1 tablespoon soy sauce
Freshly ground black pepper
2 tablespoons chopped parsley
2 tablespoons tomato purée
5 oz (150 g) wholemeal breadcrumbs

Heat half the oil in a pan, add the onion and garlic and sauté them until they have softened. Add the carrots, celery, lentils, 1 pint (570 ml) water, soy sauce and pepper, and bring the mixture to the boil, stirring all the time. Cover and simmer, stirring occasionally, for 55–60 minutes or until all the water has been absorbed and the lentils reduced to a stiff purée. Mix in the parsley, tomato purée and 2 oz (50 g) breadcrumbs and leave to cool. Dampen your hands and shape the mixture into small patties, then shake the remaining breadcrumbs over them.

Pour a little of the remaining oil into a heavy frying-pan and place it over moderate heat. When hot, add the patties and fry them until they are crisp and golden on both sides. These patties also freeze well.

CHICK PEA RISSOLES
Falafel

SERVES 4   PAUL LAURENSON AND ETHEL MINOGUE

Falafel or Ta'amia, made with dried broad beans, are one of the great national dishes of Egypt. In Israel, chick peas are used, as they are in this recipe. The falafel are an excellent appetiser served with yoghurt or vegetable purées. Alternatively they make a good snack at any time of day. Falafel are delicious served with salads, but they are also excellent tucked inside pitta bread with a crunchy coleslaw or crisp shredded lettuce salad.

8 oz (225 g) dried chick peas
2 Spanish onions, finely chopped
3 tablespoons finely chopped parsley
2 teaspoons ground coriander
2 teaspoons ground fennel
2 teaspoons ground cumin
½ teaspoon baking powder
4 cloves garlic
Salt, freshly ground black pepper
A little flour (optional)
A little sunflower oil for frying
Paprika for garnish

Soak the chick peas in water for several hours, or overnight, until they double in size. Change the water as often as you remember during the soaking as this reduces the likelihood of their causing flatulence. Put the chick peas into a food processor and process until you have a smooth paste. Add the onions and parsley to the chick peas and process again for a few seconds. Add all the ground spices, baking powder, crushed garlic, and salt and pepper. Knead the mixture for a moment or two to mix the ingredients well, then let it rest in the refrigerator for 30 minutes.

Take small pieces of the mixture and form them into little flat cakes about 2 inches (5 cm) across. If they are sticky, roll them in a little flour.

Heat the oil and quickly fry the falafel – about 2 minutes each side. Sometimes they begin to break apart as they are cooking; if this happens, just pat them together again. Handle them gently when you turn them over. Drain on kitchen paper and sprinkle a little paprika over the top. Serve hot or cold.

LENTILS AND RICE

Megadarra

SERVES 4   CLAUDIA RODEN

The extreme simplicity of the ingredients for this common and homely dish belies its wonderful taste. Since ancient times in Arab folklore, lentil, bean and chick pea dishes have been branded as dishes of the poor or the mean, but in reality they have always been extremely popular. *Megadarra* is inexpensive and makes an excellent light supper dish.

There is no absolute proportion of rice to lentils but equal quantities are a good combination. Serve this dish with a Yoghurt and Cucumber Salad (page 159), or a simple tomato salad.

6 oz (175 g) green or brown lentils
6 oz (175 g) basmati rice
2 very large onions
3 tablespoons olive oil
Salt, freshly ground black pepper
1–1 ¼ pints (570–700 ml) chicken stock, or water

Wash the lentils and the rice separately. It is usual but not really necessary (especially if you are in a hurry) to soak them for a few hours.

Drain and cook the lentils in about 1 pint (570 ml) of the chicken stock or water for 10–15 minutes or until they are just tender but not quite done. Remove from the heat and set aside. Meanwhile, cut the onions in half, then into thin slices, and fry them in the oil until they are brown and almost caramelised. Stir half into the lentils. Add the drained rice and salt and pepper to taste. Stir and cook, covered tightly, over a very low heat for 20–25 minutes or until the rice and lentils are cooked, adding a little more stock or water if the liquid is absorbed too quickly. (You can also cook the lentils and the rice separately and mix them when they are done.)

Serve cold or warm, topped with the remaining onions and with the olive oil from the pan poured all over the dish.

CABBAGE LEAVES STUFFED WITH MEAT AND RICE

SERVES 4–6   CLAUDIA RODEN

In the Middle East they say that a woman shows her love by the amount of work she does in preparing a dish. Stuffed vegetables come into the category of dishes that show a great deal of caring, but it is pleasant work, even fun, and the end result is delicious. This is a very economical and healthy dish as it uses so little meat. It is an example of the perfect harmony between meat, grain and vegetables that exists in so much Middle Eastern food. Serve the stuffed cabbage as a main dish with a green salad.

1 medium-sized white cabbage
Bunch of parsley
1 medium-sized onion, chopped
1–2 tablespoons sunflower oil
6 oz (175 g) lean minced beef
1 tomato, chopped
Salt, freshly ground black pepper
1 teaspoon cinnamon
½ teaspoon allspice
3 oz (75 g) short grain or pudding rice
2 cloves garlic, thinly sliced
Juice of 1 lemon or 1 tablespoon tamarind paste (available in Asian and Greek shops)
½–1 teaspoon sugar

Using a sharp pointed knife, carefully cut the core out of the cabbage: this helps speed up the cooking of the inner leaves. Boil the cabbage whole in a large saucepan of water for 10–15 minutes or until leaves are soft enough to detach without breaking. After removing the cooked outer leaves, you may need to return the inner leaves to boiling water for a few minutes more, if they are still stiff. When all the leaves are detached, simmer them yet again if they are not soft enough to roll. Chop the parsley finely and reserve some for garnishing.

For the filling, fry the onion in oil, then add the meat, and stir well. When it has changed colour, add the chopped tomato, salt and pepper, cinnamon, allspice, rice and parsley and pour in 3 fl oz (75 ml) water. Stir, then cover tightly and cook the filling over a very low heat for about 10 minutes. The rice should have absorbed the liquid completely and be slightly undercooked.

Line a heavy-bottomed saucepan (preferably non-stick) with small or torn cabbage leaves, to prevent the rolls sticking to the pan. Put a tablespoon of filling at one end of each cabbage leaf and roll it up like a cigar. (You may need to cut out some of the very thick stalks.) Fold the sides of the leaves in so that the filling does not fall out.

Arrange the rolled leaves in layers, packing them tightly together and tucking a slice of garlic here and there between them.

Mix 5 fl oz (150 ml) water with the lemon juice and a little sugar, or dilute the tamarind paste in the same quantity of boiling water and sugar, then pour this over the rolls. Cover and simmer gently for 30–45 minutes, then remove the lid and simmer for another 15–20 minutes or until the stuffed cabbage leaves are very tender and the liquid has been absorbed. Check them from time to time and add a little water if necessary. Serve the stuffed cabbage rolls hot, garnished with the remaining parsley.

MACKEREL IN FOIL WITH HERBS

Sgombro al Cartoccio

SERVES 4   ANTONIO CARLUCCIO

Mackerel is a beautiful fish, inexpensive and superbly nutritious. In this recipe, fresh herbs provide more than enough flavouring, and no butter or other fat is necessary. Baked in foil in the oven, the fish retains its own juices while the herbs lose none of their aroma. Serve this dish hot with Fennel Gratin (see page 146) or cold with a potato salad.

4 medium-sized fresh mackerel, gutted
Juice of one lemon
Salt, freshly ground black pepper
4 small bunches of 4 different fresh mixed herbs, eg tarragon, chives, parsley and sage
A little olive oil

Pre-heat the oven to gas mark 9, 475°F (240°C). Wash the mackerel and sprinkle the insides with lemon juice. Add a little salt and a generous sprinkling of pepper. Put a bunch of mixed herbs inside the cavity of each fish and brush the skin with olive oil to avoid sticking. Wrap each fish individually in foil, quite tightly, and bake for 10–12 minutes. Take them out of the foil, leaving the herbs inside them, and place them on a hot platter with their own juices.

OAT-STUFFED MACKEREL

SERVES 4   LESLIE KENTON

Some of the best fish dishes are made, not with sole, salmon or other expensive fish, but with the more modest monkfish, angler, gurnet or mackerel – one of my favourites. Here orange and rosemary provide a sharp contrast to the rich, oily taste of mackerel. This dish looks like a gourmet's delight – something special to serve for guests – but is simple to prepare.

4 mackerel, gutted
2 large oranges
4 tablespoons porridge oats
1 medium-sized onion, finely chopped
1 tablespoon fresh parsley, finely chopped
1 tablespoon raisins
1 apple, grated
1 teaspoon vegetable bouillon powder (see page 66), or a pinch of salt
4 sprigs of rosemary, or 1 teaspoon dried rosemary
10 fl oz (300 ml) cider

Pre-heat the oven to gas mark 5, 375°F (190°C). Wash the mackerel. Grate the zest of the oranges and reserve. Chop the flesh of the oranges into small pieces, discarding the pips and any tough pith. Mix the orange zest and flesh with the oats, the finely chopped onion, parsley, raisins and grated apple and season with vegetable bouillon powder or salt. (If you prefer a smooth-textured stuffing, you could process the mixture briefly.) Divide the mixture into 4, then loosely stuff the fish. Place a sprig of fresh rosemary or a pinch of dried rosemary in each fish, then lay them in a shallow oven-proof dish. Pour the cider over the fish, then cover tightly with foil. Bake them for about 40 minutes. Transfer the fish to a heated serving dish, then reduce the juices by boiling them, uncovered, to concentrate the flavour. Pour a little liquid over each fish and serve immediately. Alternatively, drain the fish and serve cold, accompanied by a fresh green salad garnished with orange slices.

BAKED SARDINES
Sardine gratinate

SERVES 4   ANTONIO CARLUCCIO

The anchovy, herring, mackerel and sardine belong to the same family. Italians call sardines 'blue fish' (*pesce azzurro*) because of the colour of the skin. Vast quantities of sardines are caught in the Mediterranean; in Italy you can buy them fresh but in Britain they are almost always sold frozen. Nonetheless they have an excellent flavour, and you will no doubt be able to invent your own variations on my recipe. A bottle of light Italian white wine, such as Frascati, would be an ideal accompaniment to this meal.

24 small sardines
A small bunch each of: fresh dill, fresh parsley, fresh chives, fresh sage, fresh rosemary
1 oz (25 g) walnuts or almonds
1 clove garlic, finely chopped
2 tablespoons olive oil
Juice of one lemon
1 oz (25 g) fresh breadcrumbs
Salt, freshly ground black pepper

Pre-heat the oven to its highest temperature. Using kitchen scissors, remove the heads and tails from the fish, and trim off the lower fins. Slit and gut each fish, then, using your thumb, loosen the central bone from the flesh, leaving the two halves still attached along the back by the skin. Wash the fish and dry them on kitchen paper, then lay the sardines out flat. Finely chop the herbs, roughly chop the walnuts or almonds, and mix them well, together with the garlic.

Grease a large baking tray with a little olive oil. Put 12 of the flat sardines on the tray, skin side down, each next to the other. Sprinkle them with lemon juice and spread each one with a heaped tablespoon of the herb and nut mixture. Cover each of these fish with another sardine, with the skin side up, to make a sandwich. Sprinkle the breadcrumbs over the top, add salt and pepper, then sprinkle over a little oil. Bake for 8 minutes. Serve the sardines hot or cold, accompanied by a tomato and onion salad.

MARINATED SPRATS

SERVES 6   PAUL LAURENSON AND ETHEL MINOGUE

This is a Moroccan recipe in which the sweet-sour mixture of the marinade complements the oiliness of the sprats. Whiting and other small fish, such as sardines, pilchards and whitebait can be substituted for the sprats.

1 lb (450 g) sprats
1 bunch of coriander
3 large cloves garlic
3 tablespoons olive oil
Juice of 1 lemon
1 tablespoon ground cumin
½ teaspoon chilli powder
1 tablespoon paprika
Lemon wedges for garnish

If the fishmonger has not already done so, clean and gut the sprats. Use a tweezer to gut them through the gills (see page 38); if you slit them they will fall apart as they cook. Using a blender or food processor, blend most of the coriander, the garlic, olive oil, lemon juice, cumin, chilli and paprika. Cover the sprats with this mixture and leave to marinate for at least 2 hours.

Pre-heat the grill to its highest temperature. Using a slotted spoon, remove the sprats from the marinade and grill until brown. Serve hot or cold, garnished with the rest of the coriander and some lemon wedges.

COOKING IN A HURRY

One reason so many of us fall for the lures of those bright packs of 'oven-ready' food is that they save time and trouble. Unfortunately much of this food is also full of salt, fat and sugar, as well as artificial flavourings and colourings. Those other standbys of the hard-pressed cook, chops and steaks, also contain too much saturated fat for wise eating every day. So our challenge was to produce 'healthy' recipes which busy people could prepare speedily. Many of the dishes in this section use fish. Apart from its benefits to our health, fish has the tremendous advantages of cooking quickly and of offering a wide variety of flavours and textures. We have also included a recipe which uses tofu (page 130) and one featuring stir-fried lean pork (page 138).

TOFU WITH PEAS

SERVES 4   MADHUR JAFFREY

The very popular North Indian dish *mattar paneer* is made with peas and paneer, a fresh cow's milk cheese. Here I have substituted tofu (see page 71), a freshly curdled soya milk cheese. After all, both paneer and tofu are bland soft cheeses which get most of their flavour from the accompanying ingredients or food. Both are white, nutritious, quick to cook and easy to digest, but are very slightly different in taste and texture. The sauce itself is light and mild, but you can add more spices if you prefer and use less water. Try to find fairly firm tofu as it should not disintegrate during cooking.

You can serve this delectable dish in several ways: hot, with hunks of dark, crusty bread, followed by a fresh green salad, cheese and fresh fruit; hot, with plain rice and Onion and Green Coriander Relish (see page 156); or cold, ladled onto a crisp lettuce leaf and accompanied by wholewheat crispbreads.

4 oz (110 g) onion
1 cube of fresh ginger
1 clove garlic
1 lb (450 g) tomatoes
8 oz (225 g) firm tofu (beancurd), cubed
2 × 10 oz (275 g) packets of frozen peas
3 tablespoons corn oil
1 tablespoon ground coriander
1 teaspoon ground cumin
¼ teaspoon ground turmeric
Salt, freshly ground black pepper
⅛–¼ teaspoon cayenne pepper

Peel the onions and chop them very finely. Peel the ginger and grate it on the finest part of the grater. Put the garlic through a press; you do not need to peel it first. Chop the tomatoes finely; cut the tofu into small bite-sized cubes. Run the peas under warm water just enough to separate them.

Heat the oil in a wide, casserole-type pot over a medium-high heat. When it is hot, add in the onion, ginger and garlic, then stir-fry them for about 4 minutes or until the onion pieces are brown at the edges.

Add the coriander, cumin and turmeric, stir once, then add the tomatoes. Continue to cook, stirring, for 4–5 minutes, crushing the tomatoes with the back of a slotted or wooden spoon.

Add 10 fl oz (300 ml) water and bring the liquid to a simmer. Cover it, lower the heat and cook for 3–4 minutes. Add the peas, salt and black pepper to taste and cayenne pepper. Bring to a simmer again, add the tofu cubes and bring them to a simmer. Cover the pan again and cook gently for 3–4 minutes or until the peas are just cooked. Serve immediately.

MONKFISH WITH GARLIC
Gigot de Mer

SERVES 4   PAUL LAURENSON AND ETHEL MINOGUE

Monkfish is always sold without its head as it is considered so ugly. This is a pity as it has rather an interesting head with huge jaws. It consumes large quantities of fish and seabirds too, hence its other name, angler fish. It has firm white flesh and is a great favourite with the French as it can be served with many sauces. This recipe is called *Gigot de mer* or 'leg of the sea', as the large monkfish tail resembles a leg of lamb, called a *gigot* in French. Noodles or boiled potatoes would make a good accompaniment.

2 monkfish tails
10 cloves garlic
1 lb (450 g) tomatoes
2 tablespoons olive oil
4 fl oz (110 ml) white wine
1 tablespoon fresh mixed herbs, finely chopped, or 1 teaspoon of dried mixed herbs
½ teaspoon fennel seeds
Salt, freshly ground black pepper
Extra chopped fresh herbs to garnish

Pre-heat the oven to gas mark 8, 450°F (230°C). Remove the skin and membrane from the fish, if the fishmonger has not done this for you, then wash the fish and pat it dry. Peel 10 cloves of garlic, then cut 4 into slivers and insert them into the flesh of the fish as if it were a leg of lamb. Heat the oil in a cast-iron, ovenproof pan, add the remaining garlic cloves, and sauté the fish on all sides. Skin, de-seed and chop the tomatoes. Add the white wine and the tomatoes to the pan, and continue cooking for a minute or so. Add the herbs, fennel seeds, salt and pepper. Cover and cook in the oven for 10–15 minutes.

Garnish with the remaining mixed herbs and serve immediately straight from the dish.

PORK TENDERLOIN PROVENÇAL STYLE

Filet mignon de Porc à la Provençal

SERVES 4   CHRISTOPHE BUEY

Pork tenderloin has very little fat, an excellent flavour and cooks quickly. This dish can be made in two stages: the vegetables can be prepared the day before and gently re-heated. The meat takes only a few minutes to cook. Serve the dish with brown rice and a green salad.

½ aubergine
1 courgette
Salt, freshly ground black pepper
1 lb (450 g) tomatoes
1 onion
1 clove garlic
1 shallot
1 teaspoon safflower or olive oil
½ red pepper
A sprig fresh thyme, or a pinch of dried thyme
1 bay leaf
1 lb (450 g) pork tenderloin
4 fl oz (110 ml) red wine
A few basil leaves, or a pinch of dried basil

Cut the aubergine and courgette into large matchstick strips, sprinkle them with salt and leave them in a colander. Peel the tomatoes, cut in half, de-seed, then cut again into large chunks. Finely chop the onion, garlic and the shallot. Heat a dash of oil in a saucepan, add the onion and garlic, cover and sweat them over a low heat. Chop the red pepper finely, add it to the saucepan and cover. Rinse the aubergine and courgette under the cold tap, dry them well on kitchen paper, add them to the saucepan and sweat gently. Add the tomatoes to the rest of the vegetables, together with the basil, thyme and bay leaf, and cook for 10–15 minutes. Meanwhile, cut the tenderloin in ¼ inch (0·5 cm) thick slices. Cover them with a film of greaseproof paper and flatten them with the base of a saucepan. Heat a dash of oil in a frying-pan and sauté the slices for 1 minute on each side, then remove from the heat and keep warm. Add the shallot to the frying-pan and sweat it gently, then add the wine, turn the heat to high and reduce the sauce by half. Add the shallot and wine to the vegetables and simmer for 1 minute. Season to taste, then transfer the vegetables to a heated dish, arrange the meat on top and serve.

RED MULLET ORIENTALE

SERVES 4   PAUL LAURENSON AND ETHEL MINOGUE

The liver of red mullet is considered a great delicacy and is left in the fish when it is cleaned. In France this fish is known as 'woodcock of the sea' because the liver of woodcock is also considered a delicacy. In summer red mullet are caught around our shores and they are now readily available in many supermarkets and fishmongers.

In this recipe the fish is cooked very briefly in a mild sauce made from wine and spices. Serve on a bed of plain rice with a seasonal salad.

4 red mullet weighing about 8 oz (225 g) each
10 fl oz (275 ml) dry white wine
1 tablespoon whole coriander seeds
1 teaspoon whole cloves
1 teaspoon whole black peppercorns
2 cloves garlic, lightly crushed
Pinch of saffron
Bunch of fresh parsley and fennel leaves, or 1 teaspoon fennel seeds
2 bay leaves
Salt
1 lemon and fresh parsley or fennel for garnish

Scale and gut the fish but leave in the liver. The liver of a fresh red mullet is the largest single organ in the guts. It is terracotta-coloured and is nearest the head. (If the fish has been frozen, the liver usually disintegrates and is unusable.) Lightly crush the spices and put them with the fish and the wine in a large pan. Add the garlic, saffron, fresh herbs and salt to taste. Bring to the boil, reduce the heat immediately and simmer the fish, uncovered, for 5 minutes. Set the pan aside and leave the fish to cool in the liquid for about 30 minutes to let the flavours develop.

Gently re-heat the fish, then transfer to a serving dish and keep warm. Boil the cooking liquid to reduce it by about half. Strain the sauce, then spoon a little over the fish. Garnish with the remaining parsley or fennel and thin slices of lemon. Serve immediately, with the rest of the sauce handed separately.

SQUID WITH TOMATOES AND CAPERS

SERVES 4   PAUL LAURENSON AND ETHEL MINOGUE

Squid is becoming more popular, now that people have tasted it on Mediterranean holidays and know how delicious it can be. The quality of the squid we can buy is excellent, fresh or frozen, and cooked carefully it should be sweet and tender. In this recipe, the capers add an extra piquancy to the sauce.

3 tablespoons olive oil
1 onion
3 cloves garlic
1 shallot
2 lb (900 g) squid
2 × 14 oz (400 g) tinned tomatoes, chopped
2 tablespoons capers, rinsed
Bouquet garni
4 fl oz (110 ml) dry white wine
Salt, freshly ground black pepper
Black olives
Parsley or coriander

Heat the oil in a large pan. Slice the onion finely. Chop the garlic and shallot finely. Add the onion to the pan and cook it slowly to soften but not brown it. Prepare the squid (see pages 40–1) and keep the ink sack, if it is intact. Cut the body into rings ⅓–½ inch (0·8–1 cm) thick and the tentacles into 2 inch (5 cm) lengths. Add the shallot and garlic to the onion and cook them, stirring, for a minute or until they are soft. Increase the heat a little. Add the squid and cook it, stirring, until it has turned opaque. Remove the squid and set it aside. Add the tomatoes, capers, bouquet garni and wine, increase the heat again and cook for about 10 minutes to reduce the sauce. Lower the heat and return the squid to the pan. This should be perfectly tender after very little further cooking. If not, continue cooking it slowly until it is done. Add the reserved ink to the sauce, then add seasoning if necessary. Serve the squid on a bed of rice and garnish it with black olives and freshly chopped parsley or coriander.

OPPOSITE: FROM TOP TO BOTTOM
Squid with Tomatoes and Capers (*page 134*)
Filleted Grilled Fish with
Spring Onions and Ginger (*page 140*)

PLAICE IN HERBS AND BREADCRUMBS

SERVES 4

This fish dish is quick and simple. The plaice is coated in a herb and breadcrumb mixture then quickly fried in minimal oil, making a change from the inevitable batter – healthier and lighter too! A simple green salad and some plain baked potatoes would be perfect accompaniments.

3 oz (75 g) plain flour
Salt, freshly ground black pepper
1 large egg
A little skimmed milk
4 oz (110 g) stale wholemeal bread
Handful of fresh mixed herbs, such as parsley, coriander, marjoram
1 tablespoon ground coriander
4 large cloves garlic, crushed
8 plaice fillets
A little sunflower oil
A little parsley and some lemon wedges for garnish

Prepare the coating for the fish, using 3 shallow dishes. In the first, mix the flour with salt and pepper. In the second, lightly beat the egg and milk. The third will contain the breadcrumb mixture. Using a blender, gradually drop in chunks of the wholemeal bread, the herbs, the ground coriander and the crushed garlic. Blend until you have a fine green breadcrumb mixture. Transfer this to the third dish.

Pat the fish dry with kitchen paper. Dip each fillet first in the flour, then the egg and milk mixture, and finally the breadcrumbs. Smear some oil onto a heavy non-stick frying-pan. Quickly fry the first batch of fish, carefully flipping them over to fry the second side. Don't overcook them – about 3 minutes each side is ample. Transfer the fish to a heated serving dish and keep warm while cooking the next batch: smear the pan with more oil as necessary. Serve immediately, garnished with lemon wedges and a little finely chopped parsley.

OPPOSITE: FROM TOP TO BOTTOM
Drunken Prunes (*page 201*)
Fruit Salad on a Red Wine Jelly (*page 202*)
Orange Soufflé (*page 196*)

STIR-FRIED CHINESE CABBAGE AND PORK

SERVES 4   LYN HALL WITH ANTON MOSIMANN

Although a frying-pan may be used in the preparation of this dish, stir-frying in a wok is easier, quicker and much more fun (see page 20).

Pork fillet may be replaced by chump, loin or boned-out pork cutlets; the vegetables should be as fresh as possible.

Once you have prepared your meat and vegetables, they may be kept in the refrigerator covered with cling-film, and then cooked briefly at the last moment. The Chinese-style sauce enhances the vivid colour, natural flavour and crisp texture of the vegetables.

10 oz (275 g) well trimmed pork fillet
½ small onion
½ clove garlic
¼ small cauliflower
1 large carrot
A small bunch of spring onions
¼ Chinese cabbage
½ oz (10 g) fresh ginger root
3 tablespoons safflower oil
3 tablespoons dry sherry
1 dessertspoon brown sugar
3 tablespoons chicken stock
1 dessertspoon soy sauce
Salt, freshly ground black pepper

Cut the pork fillet into thin strips with the grain of the meat. Chop the onion and crush the garlic. Cut the cauliflower into small florets, the carrot into long thin strips (wider than the pork), the spring onions into 1 inch (2·5 cm) slices on the diagonal, and the Chinese cabbage similarly. Peel and grate the ginger: you should end up with ½ teaspoon.

Heat the wok, a large deep frying-pan, or even a wide pot. The secret of stir-frying is intense heat and split second timing, spacing out your ingredients in the order you need to add them to the pan. Sprinkle a drop of water into the pan; if it sizzles instantly and evaporates, the pan is hot enough to add half the oil. Heat it for a second or so, then swirl the oil round the pan to coat it evenly. If this is not done, the meat will stick to the side of the wok, then scorch and crumble.

Pat the strips of meat dry with kitchen paper. Just before the oil begins to smoke, scatter in the strips of pork and immediately begin to toss, turn and flip with a wooden spoon or fork, so that the meat is covered with oil and the natural juices are seared in. Remove the meat from the pan and set it aside.

Heat the pan again, add the rest of the oil and stir-fry the onion, garlic, cauliflower and carrots for 3 minutes. With brisk circular movements of your spoon make the vegetables tumble and slither across the hot oil.

Add the remaining ingredients to the pan. Cover and simmer gently for 2 minutes, then return the pork to the pan. Heat the pan until crackling noises tell you there is little or no liquid left. After a few fast turns serve immediately in a heated dish.

FILLETED GRILLED FISH WITH SPRING ONIONS AND GINGER

SERVES 4–6   MADHUR JAFFREY

I have always loved to eat fish that is steamed whole in the Cantonese style. The seasonings are often very simple – just spring onions and ginger – but the flavour is superb. Sometimes I do steam my fish in this very traditional Chinese way, but when I am rushed, I use grilling as an easy alternative. The results taste as good as steamed fish.

Filleted fish can be used. I like halibut, haddock or cod fillets that are 1–1¼ inches (2·5–3 cm) thick. As a result I sometimes have to ask my fishmonger to give me the thickest sections from several different large fillets. The sesame oil in this recipe is the dark, aromatic, oriental oil sold in Chinese, Japanese and health food stores. If you cannot find it, replace it with extra corn oil. Serve this dish with plain rice, and a stir-fried green vegetable or a green salad to complete the meal, either of which could be made while the fish is under the grill.

4 spring onions
½ inch (1 cm) cube of fresh ginger
2 lb (900 g) filleted halibut, haddock or cod, 1–1¼ inches (2·5–3 cm) thick
2 dessertspoons oriental sesame oil
2 dessertspoons corn oil
3 tablespoons soy sauce
½ teaspoon sugar

Pre-heat the grill. Cut the spring onions into fine diagonal slices all the way up, including the green part. Peel the ginger and cut it into very thin slices, then stack up the slices and cut them into fine slivers.

Use a baking or grilling tray that is ¾–1 inch (2–2·5 cm) deep and is large enough to hold the fish easily in a single layer. Line the tray with aluminium foil if you wish. Rub the fish on both sides first with the sesame oil and then with the corn oil, and put the fillets in the centre of the tray. Lift the fish up and scatter half the spring onions and half the ginger just where the fish was. Replace the fish over the onion and ginger, then sprinkle the remaining spring onions and ginger over the top.

Put the soy sauce in a small bowl and add the sugar, mixing well. Spoon this soy mixture over the fish. Pour 5 tablespoons of water around, but not over, the fish. Place the fish under the grill and cook it for 10–12 minutes or until the fish is lightly browned on top and still very moist inside. Baste once or twice during the grilling with the juices in the tray. Check with the tip of a knife to see if the fish is cooked through. Transfer the fish to a warm serving plate. Pour all the juices from the grilling tray over the fish and serve immediately.

GRILLED STUFFED TROUT

Truites farcies grillées

SERVES 4   CHRISTOPHE BUEY

Trout are now easy to buy and fairly cheap. River trout have a better flavour, but farmed trout are a reasonable substitute. Ask your fishmonger to bone and gut them for you. In this recipe they are stuffed with a wonderful filling made from spinach, prunes, almonds and mushrooms. Serve them with a yoghurt sauce, plain potatoes and a salad for a satisfying supper dish.

1 onion
2 oz (50 g) button mushrooms
Dash of safflower oil
1 lb (450 g) spinach
2 oz (50 g) pitted prunes
4 trout weighing about 10 oz (275 g) each
2 oz (50 g) flaked almonds, lightly toasted
For the sauce:
5 oz (150 g) yoghurt, preferably Greek cow's milk yoghurt
1 teaspoon each of freshly chopped chives, parsley, chervil, and tarragon
Dash of olive oil
Freshly ground black pepper

Finely chop the onion and roughly chop the mushrooms. Heat the safflower oil in a saucepan and sweat the onion and mushrooms with the lid on. Wash the spinach, removing any tough stalks, and chop it roughly. Add the spinach to the onion and mushroom mixture and toss briskly over a medium heat for 5 minutes. Chop the prunes and add them to the mixture, then transfer it to a plate and allow to cool.

Pre-heat the grill to medium heat. Check the trout to make sure they have been well boned and gutted; use tweezers to remove any remaining bones. Rinse the fish under the tap, and dry them with kitchen paper. Add the almonds to the spinach mixture and stir. Divide into 4 portions and stuff the belly of each trout. Be careful not to overstuff the fish; put the mixture towards the head rather than the tail if necessary. Secure the opening with cocktail sticks or skewers. Now rub each trout with a little oil and grill for 5 minutes. Then turn them over, rub the newly exposed side with a little oil and grill them for another 5 minutes. Remove from grill, cover them with foil and keep warm.

In the meantime prepare the sauce by beating the yoghurt with the fresh herbs, olive oil and pepper. Serve the trout accompanied by the sauce.

VEGETABLES, SALADS AND DRESSINGS

Vegetables and salads are surely destined to play a much larger part in our diet than ever before. This section gives you a range of ideas for serving original and attractive vegetable dishes. All the cooked vegetable dishes form a complete meal if served with some cheese and crusty wholemeal bread: otherwise, both they and the salads can be served to accompany a main course.

IMAM BAYELDI

CLAUDIA RODEN

Aubergines are perhaps the most popular vegetable in the Middle East. This dish is a speciality of Turkey which boasts no less than 100 ways of cooking them. *Imam bayeldi* means 'the Imam fainted' because, according to legend, the Imam (priest) fainted with joy on tasting this dish as it was so delicious.

Aubergines, when fried, taste wonderful but they soak up an enormous amount of oil; when they are boiled they never really taste good. In this recipe, the aubergines are lightly braised in tomato juice with a little olive oil and garlic.

The dish is served garnished with softened onions, currants, golden pine-nuts and parsley – a wonderful combination of flavours and textures. Serve it alone as a starter or as part of a buffet meal. It is also lovely to present out of doors on a summer's day.

2 large aubergines
Salt
Tomato juice mixture for cooking:
10 fl oz (300 ml) tomato juice
2 tablespoons olive oil
2 cloves garlic, crushed
Salt, freshly ground black pepper
½–1 teaspoon sugar
Juice of 1 lemon
1 tablespoon fresh, chopped mint, or 1 teaspoon dried mint
For topping and garnishing
1 tablespoon pine-nuts
1 Spanish onion
1 tablespoon olive oil
2 tomatoes
1 tablespoon currants
Large bunch of fresh parsley, finely chopped

Cut the aubergines into thick slices. Sprinkle with salt, leave to drain in a colander for 30 minutes and then rinse. Combine all the ingredients for the tomato juice mixture in a covered pan and bring to a simmer. Stew the aubergines in the liquid for about 30 minutes or until they are tender.

Remove the lid towards the end of cooking to reduce the sauce to almost nothing. Remove from the heat and leave the aubergines to cool in the liquid.

Meanwhile, toast the pine-nuts for the topping in a dry frying-pan until they are golden. Slice the onion thinly and fry it in the olive oil. Peel and chop the tomatoes, then add them to the onions, together with the currants, the toasted pine-nuts, and most of the parsley. Mix them well and simmer for a few minutes then leave to cool. Arrange the aubergine slices on a serving dish. Spread the onion mixture carefully over the aubergines and garnish with the remaining parsley.

SPINACH WITH ALMONDS

SERVES 4   CLAUDIA RODEN

This dish is tasty, looks beautiful, and the nuts make a marvellous contrast to the spinach. Served as a side dish it goes particularly well with stuffed tomatoes.

2 lb (900 g) fresh spinach or 1 lb (450 g) frozen spinach, defrosted
1 large onion, coarsely chopped
1 tablespoon oil
Salt, freshly ground black pepper
2 large tomatoes, peeled and sliced
2 tablespoons split almonds
Juice of ½ lemon (optional)

If using fresh spinach, clean it and remove any hard stalks. Fry the onion in oil in a large pan until it is soft, then add the spinach. Season with salt and pepper to taste and cook gently and briefly; fresh spinach should just wilt into a soft mass. Add the tomatoes and cook until they are only slightly softened. Toast the almonds and stir them in just before serving. Serve hot or cold. If served cold, the spinach is best with a good squeeze of lemon.

FENNEL GRATIN

SERVES 4

1 lb 8 oz (700 g) fennel bulbs
Slice of lemon
Salt, freshly ground black pepper (optional)
Chicken stock
1 tablespoon olive oil
1 oz (25 g) Parmesan cheese, freshly grated

Trim the fennel and remove any discoloured skin with a potato peeler. Cut the fennel vertically into slices about ¾ inch (2 cm) thick. Put them in a saucepan, add the lemon slice, a little salt and just enough light chicken stock or water to cover them. Simmer the fennel for about 20 minutes or until it is tender, then drain it, discarding the lemon slice. Arrange the slices in a gratin dish. Sprinkle over the Parmesan and black pepper and place the dish under a grill for a few minutes to brown the cheese. Serve immediately.

POTATO GRATIN

SERVES 4   MICHAEL QUINN

1 lb 8 oz (700 g) waxy potatoes
A little oil
3 cloves garlic
Salt, freshly ground black pepper
5 oz (150 g) fromage blanc (see page 34)
3 fl oz (75 ml) skimmed milk
Grated nutmeg

Pre-heat the oven to gas mark 5, 375°F (190°C). Cut the potatoes into slices ⅛ inch (3 mm) thick. Brush an ovenproof dish with oil and slice the garlic cloves thinly. Layer the potatoes with the garlic, and season with salt and pepper. Mix the fromage blanc with the milk and nutmeg to taste and pour over the potatoes. Bake for about an hour or until the potatoes are browned. Serve immediately.

SPINACH GRATIN

Gratin d'Épinard

SERVES 4   CHRISTOPHE BUEY

This easily prepared dish only requires a little skill in chopping the raw spinach. Roll the leaves in your hand and chop the spinach with a large knife. Do not be afraid of its bulk: as soon as it is mixed with the batter it loses its volume! Serve this dish as a light meal with a salad and warm wholemeal bread.

A little oil
1 lb (450 g) fresh spinach
4 oz (110 g) ricotta cheese
2 oz (50 g) Parmesan cheese, freshly grated
2 fl oz (50 ml) milk
1 egg
2 oz (50 g) hazelnuts, chopped
Salt, freshly ground black pepper
Nutmeg
Juice of ½ lemon

Pre-heat the oven to gas mark 4, 350°F (180°C). Lightly oil an 8 inch (20 cm) shallow ovenproof dish. Wash the spinach thoroughly and re-move the stalks. Dry it well and chop it thinly, compressing it tightly in your hands. Mix the ricotta and Parmesan cheese and the milk in a large bowl, and beat in the egg. Add the chopped spinach, half the chopped hazelnuts, the salt, pepper, nutmeg and lemon juice and mix them thoroughly. Press the mixture down into the ovenproof dish and sprinkle the rest of the hazelnuts on top. Cover the dish with foil and bake for 20–30 minutes. Remove the foil for about 5 minutes before the end of cooking. Serve immediately.

AUBERGINE PIE

SERVES 8–10   CAROLINE WALDEGRAVE

This is a very pretty layered vegetable pie flavoured with basil. It is better made several hours ahead of time and served cold, but it can also be served warm as a supper dish. If you are serving it as a main course, a crisp green salad and basmati rice make suitable accompaniments.

This quantity fits tightly into a 6½ inch (16 cm) diameter, 3½ inch (8·5 cm) deep loose-bottomed cake tin.

4 large aubergines
Salt, freshly ground black pepper
2 onions
2 cloves garlic
2 lbs (900 g) medium-sized tomatoes
2 tablespoons sunflower oil, plus extra for greasing
1 bunch fresh basil or 1 teaspoon dried basil
1 lb (450 g) yoghurt

Wash and slice the aubergines. Sprinkle them with salt and leave them to stand in a colander for 30 minutes, then rinse the slices well and pat dry. Meanwhile chop the onions finely, crush the garlic, and peel, quarter, de-seed and roughly chop the tomatoes. Cook the onions and garlic in the oil for 3 minutes. Add the tomatoes and pepper and cook for a further 25 minutes. Chop the basil finely.

Pre-heat the oven to gas mark 4, 350°F (180°C). Set the aubergines over a pan of hot water and steam them until tender. This may take up to 20 minutes. Drain them well on kitchen paper. Lightly oil the cake tin and line the base with greaseproof paper. Arrange a close fitting layer of aubergines along the bottom and up the sides of the cake tin. Add the basil to the tomatoes and layer the remaining aubergines with the tomatoes, then the yoghurt, finishing with a layer of aubergines.

Cover the top layer with a piece of wet greaseproof paper. Place the tin on a baking sheet (with a lip, as the pie will leak slightly) and bake in the centre of the oven for 30 minutes. Leave it to cool in the tin, then carefully remove the greaseproof paper and turn it out. Soak up the liquid, which runs out, with kitchen paper. If you are going to serve it cold, it is better to refrigerate the pie for a few hours. This makes it easier to cut. Use a sharp knife and cut it in wedges like a cake.

Note: Any extra tomato sauce or yoghurt can be mixed together and handed separately.

VEGETABLES, SALADS AND DRESSINGS

AUBERGINE WITH PARMESAN

Parmigiana di Melanzane

SERVES 4   ANTONIO CARLUCCIO

This is a typical Italian main course made with fresh vegetables. Slices of brown bread are sufficient accompaniment, with perhaps a small green salad.

2 lb 4 oz (1 kg) aubergines
A little olive oil
2 × 6 oz (175 g) mozzarella cheese
1 quantity of prepared Tomato Sauce (see page 112)
Parmesan cheese, freshly grated

Pre-heat the oven to gas mark 7, 475°F (240°C). Cut the aubergines into long slices ¼ inch (0·5 cm) thick. Brush both sides of the slices with olive oil, and grill on both sides until brown. Cut the mozzarella into thin slices. Spread 3 tablespoons of the tomato sauce in an ovenproof dish. Place some grilled aubergine slices side by side on the sauce, top with a few slices of cheese and sprinkle with 3–4 tablespoons of sauce. Repeat the layers until everything is used, taking care to finish with a few slices of cheese. Sprinkle the dish with the Parmesan cheese and bake for 20–25 minutes. Cut it into 4 portions with a sharp knife and serve on warmed plates.

POTATOES WITH CHEESE, WALNUT AND HOT CHILLI PEPPER SAUCE

Ocopa Arequipeña

SERVES 4   ELISABETH LAMBERT ORTIZ

The potato was first cultivated in what is now Peru, and many recipes were invented using ingredients introduced by the Spanish conquest: walnuts, for example, which are less sweet than New World pecans. This dish makes a splendid main course and though Peruvians traditionally like their food 'hot', the quantity of chilli peppers used is a matter of taste. I like to use a fresh crumbly goat's cheese in the sauce, but you could use any light cheese. ✴

4 large dried red chilli peppers, or to taste
1 medium-sized onion
1 clove garlic
3 tablespoons corn or olive oil
3 oz (75 g) shelled walnuts
3 oz (75 g) white crumbly cheese, such as Cheshire, Wensleydale or fresh goat's cheese
6 fl oz (175 ml) milk
Salt (optional)
Lettuce leaves, preferably cos
4 large potatoes
2 eggs
12 black olives
1 sweet red pepper, de-seeded and cut into strips

Pull off the stems and shake the seeds out of the dried chilli peppers and put the peppers to soak in plenty of warm water for 30 minutes. (Always wash your hands after handling chilli peppers.) Drain them and set aside.

Cut the onion into 3 thick slices and crush the garlic, if using. Heat the oil in a small, heavy saucepan and cook the onion and garlic over very low heat, uncovered, until the onion is golden. Let it cool slightly. Meanwhile grind the walnuts finely. Add them to a food processor or blender, together with the onions and oil from the pan, the chilli peppers, and the cheese, crumbled. Add the milk, and salt if necessary, and blend to a smooth sauce, about the consistency of thick cream. Set aside.

Prepare a large platter by arranging lettuce leaves to cover it, with small leaves decoratively round the edge.

Boil the potatoes whole in their skins. Allow them to cool a little, then peel them and cut them into halves, lengthwise. Hard boil the eggs, cool and peel them. Arrange the potatoes, cut side down, on top of the lettuce. Mask the potatoes with the sauce. Halve the eggs lengthwise and arrange them, cut side up, among the potatoes. Garnish with the black olives and strips of sweet red pepper.

PEANUT SAUCE
Salsa de Mani

SERVES 4   ELISABETH LAMBERT ORTIZ

Peanuts have been grown in South America and Mexico since pre-historic times and were widely used in the kitchen as a thickening agent in casseroles, in soup, and in a ground form very like our modern peanut butter, by the time Christopher Columbus reached the New World. Peanut sauce, in different versions, has spread all over the world and is popular in Indonesia (where tamarind is always added), far from Brazil. This sauce comes from Ecuador, once part of the Incan Empire. Today it is eaten with the local potato cakes (*llapingachos*). It has a special affinity with steamed cabbage, but is equally good with chopped raw cabbage.

1 medium-sized onion
1 clove garlic
5 oz (150 g) tomatoes
1 dessertspoon corn oil
2 oz (50 g) unsalted, roasted peanuts,   **or 2 tablespoons smooth peanut butter**
1 tablespoon tamarind juice or the juice of ½ lemon
10 fl oz (400 ml) chicken stock
Salt, freshly ground black pepper

Finely chop the onion. Chop the garlic. Peel, de-seed and chop the tomatoes. In a frying-pan heat the oil and add the onion, garlic and tomatoes. Cook over a moderate heat until the onion is soft and the mixture well blended. If you are using whole nuts, grind them finely until they turn to peanut butter, and stir it into the tomato mixture. If you are using peanut butter, stir it in. Add the tamarind or lemon juice, and enough chicken stock to make a pouring consistency. Season to taste with salt and pepper, then simmer it, stirring, for a few minutes longer. Serve hot or cold.

CREOLE SPROUTS

SERVES 6   LESLIE KENTON

A new variation on the Southern American creole tradition, this dish is quick to prepare, and an inexpensive alternative to curry when served on a bed of brown rice, buckwheat or couscous. Okra is available from West Indian and other specialist stores; substitute cubed kohlrabi for the okra if you have trouble finding it.

2 onions
3 celery stalks
1 lb (450 g) okra
2 tablespoons sunflower oil
8 fresh tomatoes, or 14 oz (400 g) tinned tomatoes
3 bay leaves, crumbled
2 cloves garlic, crushed
2 teaspoons vegetable bouillon powder (see page 66)
1 pint 15 fl oz (1 litre) fresh bean sprouts
4 tablespoons fresh parsley, chopped
A little paprika

Finely chop the onions, celery and okra. Heat the oil in a wok or frying-pan and gently fry the chopped vegetables until they are golden. Add the tomatoes, bay leaves, crushed garlic and bouillon powder and simmer for 10 minutes. Add the sprouts, then add the chopped parsley and a little paprika to taste.

OPPOSITE: FROM TOP TO BOTTOM
Japanese-style Cucumber and Carrot Salad (*page 160*)
Sprouty Fruit Salad (*page 162*)
Tofu Dressing (*page 156*)
Peanut Sauce (*page 151*)
Onion and Green Coriander Relish (*page 156*)

BULGAR AND NUT SALAD

Bazargan

SERVES 4   CLAUDIA RODEN

Many different cracked wheat (bulgar) salads are made in the Middle Eastern countries where wheat is the staple. Each village has its own version incorporating tomatoes, spring onions, green peppers, parsley and mint in summer, and in winter making use of tomato concentrate and the nuts that grow locally. This winter salad lasts for days without spoiling.

8 oz (225 g) bulgar (cracked wheat)
1 large-sized onion, finely chopped
3 tablespoons olive oil
4 oz (110 g) tomato purée
A bunch of fresh mint, or 1 tablespoon dried mint
1 teaspoon ground cumin
1 teaspoon ground coriander
½ teaspoon ground allspice
4 oz (110 g) walnuts and/or hazelnuts, very coarsely chopped
Juice of 1 lemon

Soak the cracked wheat in plenty of fresh cold water for 15 minutes. Drain it well and squeeze out as much of the water as you can. Fry the chopped onion in a tablespoon of oil until very soft but not yet coloured. Mix all the ingredients in a large serving bowl and leave it for about an hour for the bulgar to absorb the flavours and become plump and tender.

OPPOSITE: FROM TOP TO BOTTOM
Imam Bayeldi (*page 144*)
Bulgar and Nut Salad (*page 155*)
Potato Gratin (*page 146*)

ONION AND GREEN CORIANDER RELISH

SERVES 4   MADHUR JAFFREY

For those who like raw onions, this simple relish may be served with almost any meal. It goes particularly well with Indian-style Chicken and Potato Casserole on page 106.

4 oz (110 g) onion
2 tablespoons fresh coriander, finely chopped
¼ teaspoon salt, or to taste
5 teaspoons (25 ml) white vinegar
⅛ teaspoon cayenne pepper

Peel the onion and chop it.

Put the onion and chopped coriander in a bowl. Add all the other ingredients and mix well. Test for the balance of salt and sour, and add more salt or vinegar as necessary.

TOFU DRESSING

LESLIE KENTON

Tofu – soyabean curd – is the pride of the Orient, and it is eaten daily as a source of high-quality, low-fat protein. Tofu makes excellent creamy salad dressings.

9 oz (250 g) silken tofu (see page 71)
Juice of 1 lemon
½ teaspoon vegetable bouillon powder (see page 66)
1 clove garlic, crushed
3 tablespoons olive oil, or juice of 1 orange
A handful of fresh mint, or ½ teaspoon dill seeds

Put the ingredients in a blender or food processor and blend well. This dressing will keep in the refrigerator for up to a week.

COLD PASTA SALAD
Pasta fredda

SERVES 4   ANTONIO CARLUCCIO

This dish is healthy, extremely easy to prepare and is equally good the next day. As most of the ingredients are inexpensive it is well worth using the very best olive oil for its superb flavour. Look for the dark green 'virgin' cold-pressed oil. The dressing is also excellent made with a herb- or fruit-flavoured vinegar (see page 72).

For variations on this cold pasta salad, include tuna, olives, red peppers, courgettes or garlic.

4 oz (110 g) pasta wheels
4 oz (110 g) pasta shells
1 celery heart
1 thin slice of Mortadella sausage
6 oz (175 g) cheese, preferably mozzarella
A few leaves of fresh basil, or ½ teaspoon of dried basil
1 small bunch of fresh mint
1 tablespoon chopped parsley
4 spring onions
3 tablespoons olive oil
1 tablespoon tomato juice
1 tablespoon wine vinegar
Salt, freshly ground black pepper

Boil the pasta in plenty of lightly salted water. Drain it and leave it to cool. Cut the celery, Mortadella and mozzarella in fine strips. Tear the basil leaves and chop the mint and parsley. Finely chop the spring onions including the green leaves. Put the prepared herbs into a salad bowl and mix well with the olive oil, tomato juice, vinegar and salt and pepper to taste. Add all the other ingredients, toss lightly until thoroughly coated with the dressing and serve.

COLESLAW

SERVES 4–6   EVELYN FINDLATER

The home-made version of this classic salad is much tastier than the shop-bought variety, which tends to be drenched in cheap vinegary 'salad dressing'. The slicing blade of a food processor takes all the hard work out of the preparation of coleslaw. Alternatively, use a small, very sharp knife to shred the cabbage. Have the dressing ready, because once the cabbage is chopped, the valuable vitamin C will leach away unless immediately sealed in with the acid of the dressing.

1 lb (450 g) white or red cabbage
1 bulb of fennel (optional)
2 crisp eating apples
Juice of ½ lemon
2 oz (50 g) raisins or sultanas
2 medium-sized carrots
2 tablespoons walnuts, chopped

Shred the cabbage and fennel (if using) finely. Core the apples, chop them finely and sprinkle them with lemon juice to prevent browning. Wash the dried fruit, grate the carrots. Mix all the ingredients thoroughly.

Lemon and Oil Dressing:
3 tablespoons sunflower oil
1 tablespoon fresh lemon juice or cider vinegar
½ teaspoon mustard powder
1 teaspoon apple juice concentrate (see page 70)
1 clove garlic, crushed
Dash of herb salt (optional)

Shake all the dressing ingredients in a screw-top jar. Pour the dressing over the prepared salad and toss well.

YOGHURT AND CUCUMBER SALAD

Cacik

SERVES 6   CLAUDIA RODEN

This Middle Eastern favourite is already very popular in this country. The salad can often be watery, though, because the cucumber releases its juices into the yoghurt, and the yoghurt itself is quite thin.

If you have time, pour the yoghurt into a colander lined with dampened muslin or kitchen paper. Let it drain into the sink for about an hour before you turn it into the serving bowl. This will result in thicker yoghurt. Ewe's milk yoghurt, which can now be found in supermarkets, is already thick enough for this salad.

1 lb (450 g) yoghurt, or 1 lb 8 oz (700 g) if you are going to drain it as described above
Salt, freshly ground black pepper
1–2 cloves garlic, crushed
A small bunch of fresh mint or dill, finely chopped
1 large cucumber, chopped or grated

Use the yoghurt as it is or thicken it by draining as described above. Season it lightly with salt and pepper; beat in the crushed garlic and some of the herbs. Stir in the cucumber when you are ready to serve and garnish with the rest of the herbs.

JAPANESE-STYLE CUCUMBER AND CARROT SALAD

SERVES 4–6   MADHUR JAFFREY

The Japanese serve exquisite little first courses: a salad of watercress, a combination of crab and cucumber or, as I had in a Japanese restaurant recently, a combination of cucumber and carrot. The salads are invariably heaped in the centre of small individual bowls or plates and then eaten with chopsticks, but a fork would do just as well.

1 large cucumber
1 small carrot
1 tablespoon unhulled sesame seeds
2 tablespoons soy sauce
2 dessertspoons distilled white vinegar

Peel the cucumber and cut it diagonally into wafer-thin, long, oval shapes. Put them in a bowl. Peel the carrot and cut this too diagonally into wafer-thin, long, oval shapes. Put them into the bowl with the cucumber.

Put the sesame seeds in a small cast-iron frying-pan and place it over a low heat. Cook, shaking the pan, until the sesame seeds begin to brown evenly; it takes just a few minutes. When they start popping, they are ready. You can also spread the sesame seeds out in a tray and roast them under the grill. They should turn just a shade darker.

Pour the soy sauce and vinegar over the salad, and mix thoroughly. Sprinkle in the sesame seeds and mix again. Serve immediately.

CHARISMATIC CARROT SALAD

SERVES 6   LESLIE KENTON

This is a recipe my daughter Susannah created one day when we had nothing raw in the house but a few carrots and some herbs. The salad tastes exquisite and has a brilliant colour which goes beautifully with the modest earth shades of most pulses and grains. It is cheap and easy to prepare and the ingredients are available all year round.

The Salad:
8–10 crisp fresh carrots
4 spring onions
Carton of mustard and cress or a handful of alfalfa sprouts
The Dressing:
Juice of 1 lemon and 1 orange
1 teaspoon whole-grain mustard
1 dessertspoon honey
½ teaspoon vegetable bouillon powder (see page 66)
3 tablespoons olive oil
1 tablespoon fresh chopped parsley
Freshly ground black pepper

Scrub the carrots well, and top and tail them. Don't peel them, or many of the vitamins will be lost. Slice the carrots crosswise very thinly, using a food processor with the slicing blade or the slicing part of a stainless steel grater. Finely chop the spring onions and add them to the carrots, together with the mustard and cress or alfalfa sprouts. Combine the dressing ingredients, pour them over the salad, toss and serve.

SPROUTY FRUIT SALAD

SERVES 6   LESLIE KENTON

We often serve this salad with curry or spicy hot dishes because it balances them beautifully, with its crunchy freshness and sweet aroma.

8 leaves of crisp lettuce, such as **Webbs Wonder or Iceberg**
1 large pineapple
2 oranges
4 oz (110 g) mung bean sprouts
3 celery stalks, thinly sliced
4 oz (110 g) fresh lychees, peeled, or 1 small tin of lychees, drained
2 oz (50 g) splintered almonds
1 teaspoon tamari soy sauce (or ordinary soy sauce)
3 oz (75 g) natural yoghurt
1 dessertspoon honey
Juice of ½ lemon
½ teaspoon powdered ginger
½ teaspoon cinnamon

Wash and dry the lettuce. Cube the pineapple, then peel the orange and cut out the segments, removing the pithy 'walls'. Toss the pineapple cubes, orange segments, sprouts, celery slices, lychees and almonds together, and arrange them on the lettuce leaves in a large bowl. Cover and chill it thoroughly in the refrigerator. Mix the tamari, yoghurt, honey, lemon and spices and pour it over the salad just before serving.

COOKING FOR CHILDREN

It is clearly very important indeed to give children the healthiest possible start to life, and this must include steering them away from the processed, sugary, salty and fatty foods for which, unfortunately, they so quickly acquire a taste. It is chilling to learn that the beginnings of arterial disease are now found in children as young as five.

No-one would pretend that changing children's tastes is easy. The recipes in this section have been devised by people who are parents themselves, and know the problem at first hand. All the food has been tried and tested, not just by their own children but by many others as well. Much of it is designed to have a superficial resemblance to unhealthy 'junk' food to minimise consumer-resistance, so there is an excellent recipe for baked beans, for real hamburgers, a home-made pizza, and a healthy version of fish-cakes. Since most children can only be weaned away gradually from cakes and biscuits, some 'healthy' versions of these have also been included.

Presentation and colour is just as important with children's food as it is with adults'. A child who spurns a cottage cheese salad may eat it if it is presented inside a scooped-out tomato, garnished with a slice of red apple. A young child may accept grilled chicken served in bite-sized portions on a cocktail stick where he would refuse a whole chicken joint. Home-prepared spaghetti left in long strands may be too difficult for children to manage: chopped up small, it may be much more acceptable.

There are no soup recipes in this section (see pages 75–84 for several ideas) but most children enjoy soup and this is often a good initial way of bringing pulses and other unfamiliar tastes into children's diets. Other recipe ideas for dishes which often appeal to children include Baked Stuffed Potatoes (page 110), Baked Savoury Rice with Toasted Cashew Nuts (page 120) and most of the Outdoor Eating section (pages 209–224).

BOSTON BAKED BEANS

SERVES 6   LESLIE KENTON

It always saddens me to find how many people have never tasted real home-made baked beans. Boston Baked Beans bear no resemblance to the ghastly little things drenched in sugar and salt which come out of tins. Boston Baked Beans are a typically American delicacy which costs very little to prepare, especially if you are lucky enough to have a solid fuel cooker, because the longer you cook them at a low temperature the better they taste. The beans are traditionally made with streaky pork or salty bacon but I prefer the vegetarian variety – not only because it is low in fat but because I find the addition of a little vegetarian bouillon powder to replace the flavour of the pork is an improvement on the traditional recipe and far less salty. If you prefer, a well flavoured stock cube can be used instead. You will also need the best black molasses you can get, preferably one made from unsulphured sugar. This is a particularly good winter dish and pleasant served with black rye bread and Apple and Cinnamon Spread (see page 190).

1 lb (450 g) dried haricot beans or pinto beans
2 tablespoons molasses
1 teaspoon dried mustard
2 tablespoons vegetable bouillon powder (see page 66), or 1 pint (570 ml) chicken or beef stock (see pages 67–8)
4 tablespoons tomato purée
2 tablespoons raw cane sugar, the darker the better
2 bay leaves
Sprig of fresh thyme, or a pinch of dried thyme
2 sage leaves, finely chopped, or a pinch of dried sage

Wash the beans and soak them for 4–6 hours or overnight. Cover them with 2 inches (5 cm) of unsalted water, bring them to the boil and let them boil hard for 10 minutes. Then reduce the heat and simmer them, covered, for 1½ hours. Drain the beans, retaining the cooking water. Pre-heat the oven to its lowest possible setting. Put the beans into a deep ovenproof dish with a lid and add the molasses, mustard, vegetable bouillon powder, tomato purée, sugar, herbs and the cooking water and mix well. (If you are using chicken stock omit the bean cooking water.) Cover the dish and cook for 4–6 hours, adding more liquid if necessary. (This dish is ideal to make if you are going out and are uncertain about when you will return since if it stays on an extra hour or two it makes no difference to the final result.)

PIZZA SCONES

The aroma of these little pizza scones as they come fresh from the oven will bring your children running in to tea. Pizza scones are much quicker to make than the traditional pizza, and can also be made into 4 larger pizzas if you prefer, served with a salad at lunch-time. Fresh tomatoes can be used in season, but do skin them first: you may also need to add a little tomato purée to strengthen the flavour.

8 oz (225 g) wholemeal flour, plus extra for flouring
1 teaspoon cream of tartar
½ teaspoon bicarbonate of soda
2 oz (50 g) polyunsaturated margarine
4 fl oz (110 ml) milk
Topping:
1 tablespoon sunflower oil
1 onion, chopped
14 oz (400 g) tinned tomatoes
½ teaspoon dried marjoram
Salt, freshly ground black pepper
4 oz (110 g) mozzarella cheese, sliced

Pre-heat the oven to gas mark 7, 425°F (220°C). Place the flour in a bowl and sift in the cream of tartar and soda. Rub in the margarine until the mixture resembles fine breadcrumbs, then add the milk and mix everything to a soft dough.

Turn the mixture onto a floured surface and knead the dough lightly, then roll it out till it is ½ inch (1 cm) thick. Cut out 2½ inch (6 cm) rounds with a plain cutter and place them on a floured baking sheet. Bake them for 10–12 minutes or until they are golden brown. Transfer them to a wire rack to cool.

To make the topping, heat the oil in a pan, add the onion and fry it until it has softened. Drain and chop the tomatoes. Add the marjoram, tomatoes and seasoning and cook the sauce for about 3 minutes to reduce it to a jam-like consistency.

Cut the scones in half and place them, cut side up, on the baking sheet. Place a spoonful of tomato mixture on each one and spread this to the edges. Place a piece of cheese on each one, then bake them in the oven at gas mark 5, 375°F (190°C) for 10–12 minutes or until they are golden brown and bubbling. Serve immediately.

REAL PIZZA

MAKES 1 LARGE PIZZA: ENOUGH FOR 10 SERVINGS   EVELYN FINDLATER

Here I have adapted the usual pizza dough base by using wholemeal flour and sesame seeds. Sesame seeds are a good source of protein, vitamins, fibre and minerals.

This recipe produces a thin crisp pizza base and a moist savoury topping.

For the dough:
12 oz (350 g) wholemeal flour
1 heaped tablespoon sesame seeds
1 heaped teaspoon dried yeast
½ teaspoon blackstrap molasses, or ½ teaspoon brown sugar
6 fl oz (150 ml) warm water
1 teaspoon malt extract
1 dessertspoon corn oil, plus extra for greasing
Bran for rolling out the pizza
For the pizza topping:
2 tablespoons corn or sunflower oil
1 medium-sized onion, chopped
2 celery stalks, finely chopped
1 large clove garlic, crushed
1 small green pepper
2 oz (50 g) small button mushrooms
2 tablespoons chopped fresh basil, or 1 teaspoon dried basil
1 small bay leaf
14 oz (400 g) tinned tomatoes
1 tablespoon tomato purée
¼ teaspoon freshly ground black pepper
6 oz (175 g) Cheddar cheese, grated
1 oz (25 g) pumpkin or sunflower seeds (optional)

Grease a round pizza tin 11 inches (28 cm) in diameter.

To make the dough:

Put the flour and sesame seeds into a bowl. Mix them well, lifting the flour to get air into it. Measure 3 fl oz (75 ml) of the warm water in a jug. Sprinkle on the dried yeast and the molasses or sugar. Stir it well, cover it with a clean cloth and leave it to froth in a warm, not hot, place for 5–7 minutes.

Put the rest of the warm water in another jug. Stir in the malt extract and the dessertspoon of oil. Make a well in the flour and pour the frothy yeast liquid and the malt liquid into it. Using your hands mould the mixture into a soft dough. You should not need to add any more liquid but if the dough seems very dry, add a little more warm water. Keep working the ingredients together in the bowl. Rub a little flour on your hands to loosen any dough clinging to them. Knead the dough on a flat work surface for 7 minutes, then put it into a large greased polythene bag. Press out the air and tie the opening. Leave the dough to rise in a warm, but not hot, place for 40 minutes or until it has doubled in size.

Knead the dough again for 1–2 minutes. Sprinkle bran on the work surface. Roll out the dough into a circle the size of your pizza tray. Place it on the greased tin and stretch it, if necessary, to the edge of the tin. Slide the tin into a greased plastic bag and leave the dough to rise again.

Meanwhile, pre-heat the oven to gas mark 6, 400°F (200°C).

To make the topping:

Heat the oil in a medium-sized heavy-bottomed saucepan. Sweat the onion, celery and garlic for 5 minutes with the lid on. Finely chop the pepper and the mushrooms, and add them to the pan. Continue to cook the vegetables for 3 more minutes. Stir in 1 tablespoon of the chopped, fresh basil or most of the dried basil, if using, and the bay leaf. Drain off about a third of a cup of the juice from the tomatoes and save for use in another recipe. Chop the tomatoes and add these, together with the tomato purée and black pepper, to the sautéed vegetables. Put the lid on the pan and simmer the sauce for 15 minutes.

By this time your pizza base should have risen and be ready to fill. Remove it from the plastic bag and spoon the hot sauce over the top to within 1 inch (2·5 cm) of the edge. Sprinkle on the grated cheese, then the pumpkin or sunflower seeds and finally the remaining basil. Bake in the centre of the oven for 30 minutes. Let the pizza stand for 10 minutes before cutting it.

MEAT BALLS AND TOMATO SAUCE

SERVES 4   CAROLINE WALDEGRAVE

Always buy lean beef and mince it yourself, as any bought mince is inevitably going to be fatty. If you use a processor rather than a mincer, the final texture of the meat balls is much smoother. The ground rice in this recipe 'stretches' the meat and makes it a very economical dish.

For a more 'adult' flavour, follow the recipe but use chopped coriander instead of parsley and add some minced spring onions, crushed garlic and soy sauce; add herbs such as thyme, basil and dried fennel seeds to the basic tomato sauce. Serve these meat balls with noodles or wholewheat spaghetti.

8 oz (225 g) lean beef, such as brisket or shin
4 tablespoons ground rice
1 tablespoon chopped fresh parsley, or 1 teaspoon dried parsley
1 small onion
Freshly ground black pepper
Dash of Worcestershire sauce (optional)
Sunflower oil
1 quantity of Tomato Sauce (see opposite)

Mince the beef finely or, preferably, process it well in a food processor. Add the ground rice and chopped parsley. Chop the onion and beat it into the beef mixture. (If you have a processor simply cut the onion into quarters and process briefly.) Season with freshly ground black pepper and add a dash of Worcestershire sauce if your children like it.

Shape the mixture into balls the size of a pingpong ball and fry slowly in a non-stick frying-pan, with the minimum amount of oil, for 10 minutes. Re-heat the tomato sauce and add the meat balls.

TOMATO SAUCE

SERVES 4   CAROLINE WALDEGRAVE

1 small onion
1 carrot
1 celery stalk
14 oz (400 g) tinned tomatoes
1 clove garlic, crushed
1 bay leaf
Salt, freshly ground black pepper
1 teaspoon lemon juice
Dash of Worcestershire sauce
Pinch of sugar
1 teaspoon freshly chopped basil, or a pinch of dried basil

Chop the onion, carrot and celery. Put all the ingredients in a heavy-bottomed saucepan and simmer for 30 minutes. Remove the bay leaf, sieve the sauce, or purée it in a liquidiser or processor. Return the sauce to the pan and reduce it by rapid boiling to the required consistency. Check the seasoning and serve.

CORN FRITTERS

MAKES 12–15 FRITTERS   EVELYN FINDLATER

When my children were younger and invited friends for tea these fritters were top of the list of favourite foods.

Use frozen sweetcorn, as the canned variety has added sugar. There is no need to add salt to the fritters, as the cheese already has quite a lot.

8 oz (225 g) frozen sweetcorn
4 oz (110 g) wholemeal flour
1 teaspoon baking powder
1 large egg
8 fl oz (225 ml) milk
1 tablespoon onion, very finely chopped
3 oz (75 g) Cheddar cheese, coarsely grated
Corn or sunflower oil for frying

Cook the sweetcorn for 4 minutes in boiling water. Drain it and leave to cool while you make the batter. Sieve the flour and baking powder into a mixing bowl. Make a well in the middle and break the egg into it. Add half the milk and, using a fork, blend the ingredients together until they are smooth. Gradually add the rest of the milk and stir again until it is well mixed. Add the onion, cheese and cold sweetcorn. Stir these in well and leave the batter for 15 minutes to thicken. Stir it again before making the fritters.

Using a heavy non-stick pan, gently heat a little of the oil, spreading it to cover the whole surface. Use 1 tablespoon of batter for each fritter, flattening them as they cook, using the back of the spoon. Add more oil as necessary. Cook the fritters on one side for 2 minutes until crisp and golden, then turn them with a palette knife or fish slice and cook the other side for another 2 minutes. Serve immediately on warmed plates.

OPPOSITE: FROM TOP TO BOTTOM
Spiced Fruit Sweets (*page 179*)
Curry Burgers (*page 173*)
Corn Fritters (*page 170*)

CURRY BURGERS

MAKES 4 BURGERS   CAROLE HANDSLIP

These curry burgers are always a success with children – I like to serve them with Granary Baps (see page 28). My children adore them with pickled dill cucumber and thinly sliced onion rings, together with a home-made tomato sauce. A small amount of meat goes a long way because it is mixed with bulgar wheat.

1 ½ oz (40 g) bulgar wheat (see page 60)
A little sunflower oil
1 onion, chopped
1 celery stalk, chopped
1 carrot, chopped
1 clove garlic, crushed
2 teaspoons curry powder
3 oz (75 g) minced lean pork
1 teaspoon soy sauce
Salt, freshly ground black pepper

Soak the bulgar in cold water for 15–20 minutes. Drain it thoroughly, then, using your hands, squeeze out all the extra water. Place the bulgar in a large mixing bowl. Heat a little oil in a non-stick pan and fry the onion until it has softened but not coloured. Add the celery and carrot and cook for a further 5 minutes, then add the garlic and curry powder and cook for 1 minute, stirring, so that it cooks evenly.

Add the cooked vegetables to the drained bulgar in the mixing bowl. Let it cool.

Mix in the pork, soy sauce, and seasoning until all the ingredients are well blended. Heat the non-stick pan and lightly grease it with a little oil. Shape the mixture into 4 burgers. The mixture will seem rather wet at this stage.

Fry the burgers gently for 4 minutes on each side or until they are firm and golden brown. Serve in a granary bap with a little tomato sauce on each one. (See page 169 for a good home-made tomato sauce recipe.)

OPPOSITE: FROM TOP TO BOTTOM
Boston Baked Beans (*page 164*)
Carob Cake (*page 182*)
Pizza Scones (*page 165*)
Orange Jelly (*page 184*)

FISH-CAKES

MAKES 8 FISH-CAKES   CAROLINE WALDEGRAVE

These are simple and economical to make and I often make them using left-over cooked fish and potatoes. If you are using left-over potatoes you will need 6 oz (175 g) of cooked potato purée. Fish-cakes really need an accompanying sauce, such as yoghurt, Tomato Sauce (page 169) or a white sauce made from the fishy milk, thickened with a little cornflour or arrowroot.

10 oz (275 g) filleted white fish, such as cod or haddock
10 fl oz (300 ml) skimmed milk
1 small onion
1 bay leaf
6 peppercorns
1 parsley stalk
12 oz (350 g) potatoes
Freshly ground black pepper
Sunflower oil
1 beaten egg

Put the fish, skin side up, in a large flat saucepan. Pour in the milk. Peel and chop the onion and add it to the saucepan, together with the bay leaf, peppercorns and parsley stalk.

Cook slowly until the fish is tender, about 7 minutes. Strain. Skin and flake the fish. Meanwhile, peel the potatoes and cook them in boiling water until they are just tender. Drain well and push them through a sieve. Mix with the fish and add most of the beaten egg to make a soft but not sloppy mixture. Taste and season.

Pre-heat the grill to its highest temperature. Brush the grill pan lightly with oil. Shape the fish and potato mixture, as best you can, into 8 flat cakes. Brush the tops with some of the remaining beaten egg and grill the fish-cakes until they are lightly browned. Turn them over, brush them again with beaten egg, and grill them for a further 3 minutes or until they are golden brown.

REAL HAMBURGERS

MAKES 4 SMALL BURGERS

Home-made hamburgers are quick and simple to make and much healthier than the bought variety. Serve them plain or in baps with lettuce or home-made relishes. These burgers are equally suitable for barbecuing when they can be brushed first with Barbecue Sauce (page 210).

8 oz (225 g) lean beef
3 thick slices stale wholemeal bread
1 small onion
Salt, freshly ground black pepper
Oil for greasing

Cut away any visible fat from the meat. Cut the crusts off the bread, soak it in water, then squeeze it out. Process or blend the meat with the bread, onion and seasonings until it has a paste-like consistency. Alternatively, pass the meat and onion twice through the finest blades of a mincer. Pre-heat the grill to its hottest setting and oil it lightly. Form the meat into evenly sized balls, then flatten them into neatly shaped burgers. Grill the burgers for 2–3 minutes on each side and serve immediately.

FRUIT CRUMBLE

SERVES 4   EVELYN FINDLATER

This is the easiest hot pudding of all. You will need an 8 inch (20 cm) pudding dish at least 3 inches (7·5 cm) deep, a mixing bowl and cool hands! The sesame seeds make an unusual crunchy topping, and you can vary the filling according to whatever fruit is cheap and in season. Apple juice concentrate replaces sugar in the fruit fillings.

Crumble topping:
3 tablespoons sesame seeds or chopped sunflower seeds
3 oz (75 g) cold polyunsaturated margarine
6 oz (175 g) wholemeal flour
1–2 rounded tablespoons muscovado sugar
1 teaspoon ground cinnamon

Apple filling:
Oil for greasing
3 cooking apples, thinly peeled, cored and thinly sliced
¼ teaspoon powdered cloves or 4 whole cloves
6 tablespoons apple juice concentrate (see page 70)

Toast the seeds by heating a heavy-bottomed saucepan and stirring the seeds continuously over a moderate heat until they are golden brown, but not burnt. When the seeds start popping, they are ready. Let them cool. In a mixing bowl rub the margarine into the flour until the mixture resembles breadcrumbs. Stir in the toasted seeds, the sugar and the cinnamon.

Pre-heat the oven to gas mark 5, 375°F (190°C). Grease the pudding dish well. Put in the sliced apples. Mix the clove powder, if using, with the apple juice concentrate and pour this over the fruit. If your children don't object to whole cloves, tuck these among the apple slices, then pour over the concentrate. Sprinkle the crumble mixture over the fruit, pressing the mixture down gently. Bake the crumble for 40 minutes.

Some alternative fillings:

Blackberry and apple filling:
Oil for greasing
2 large cooking apples, thinly peeled, cored and thinly sliced
8 oz (225 g) fresh blackberries
½ teaspoon freshly grated nutmeg
5 tablespoons apple juice concentrate (see page 70)

Grease the pudding dish well. Put in the sliced apples and blackberries. Mix the grated nutmeg with the apple juice concentrate and pour over the fruit. Sprinkle the crumble mixture over the fruit, pressing the mixture down gently. Bake as in the previous recipe.

Apricot filling:
4 oz (110 g) dried apricot pieces
4 tablespoons apple juice concentrate (see page 70)
2 large cooking apples, thinly peeled, cored and thinly sliced
½ teaspoon freshly grated nutmeg
¼ teaspoon powdered cloves

You need to start preparing this filling a day in advance. Wash the apricots well and soak them in 15 fl oz (400 ml) water and the apple juice concentrate overnight. Add the apple slices and spices. Spread the mixture in the baking dish. Sprinkle on the crumble topping. Bake as in the previous recipe.

CAROB FUDGE

LESLIE KENTON

Carob (see page 69) looks and tastes a great deal like chocolate, but in fact it is better for you and many people find it more delicious.

4 oz (110 g) sesame seeds
2 oz (50 g) dried grated coconut
2 oz (50 g) carob powder
1 dessertspoon honey
Few drops vanilla essence
Juice of ½ orange

Grind the seeds in a food processor. Add the other ingredients and process again. Form the mixture into little balls. Chill well and serve in petit-four cases.

CARROT CAKE

Gâteau de Carottes

MAKES A 7 INCH (18 CM) CAKE   CHRISTOPHE BUEY

This recipe combines a French type of sponge cake known as Genoise and a Swiss carrot cake. The natural sweetness of the carrots means that little added sugar is necessary. This recipe produces a surprisingly moist, dense cake.

4 oz (110 g) carrots
1 oz (25 g) hazelnuts
1 oz (25 g) sultanas or raisins
1 dessertspoon rum
3 eggs
2 oz (50 g) muscovado sugar
3 oz (75 g) wholemeal flour
½ teaspoon baking powder
½ teaspoon ground allspice

Pre-heat the oven to gas mark 4, 350°F (180°C). Line a 7 inch (18 cm) cake tin with greaseproof paper. Grate the carrots, roughly chop the hazelnuts and soak the sultanas in the rum.

Put the eggs and sugar in a bain-marie, or in a bowl over a saucepan of freshly boiled water, and remove it from the heat. Whisk the eggs and sugar to the 'ribbon' stage (ie when the whisk is lifted, the batter falling from it forms a ribbon). Sift the flour with the baking powder and the allspice, and fold it gently into the batter. Quickly add the carrots, hazelnuts, sultanas and rum.

Pour the mixture into the cake tin and bake for 20–30 minutes until the cake springs up when touched. Turn the cake out of the tin and place it on a wire rack to cool. Do not remove the greaseproof paper until the cake has cooled. Leave the cake in a container for 24 hours, then sprinkle very lightly with icing sugar pressed through a sieve, and serve.

SPICED FRUIT SWEETS

MAKES 36 SWEETS   LESLIE KENTON

If you have a food processor, you can make a range of sweets from dried fruit and nuts. The processor pulverises the food, and the resulting stiff paste can then be rolled into little balls.

Spiced fruit sweets are a real children's favourite. They not only like to eat them but also love to help make them. Adults will also enjoy spiced fruit sweets served as an after-dinner treat. They keep well for up to a week in the refrigerator – that is if you can hang on to them for that long. In our house they tend to disappear the day they are made! There are many variations of this basic recipe: raisins and sultana balls rolled in carob powder, for example, or apricot and Brazil nut balls.

4 tablespoons each of sesame, sunflower and pumpkin seeds
12 oz (350 g) mixed dried fruits, eg pitted dates, apricots, peaches, figs
4 oz (110 g) raisins
Juice of 1 orange
Freshly grated nutmeg
Pinch of freshly ground cloves
1 teaspoon ground cinnamon
2 oz (50 g) grated dried coconut

Finely grind the 3 seeds in a food processor or grinder. Add the dried fruits and raisins and process them finely, adding as much orange juice as necessary to make the food processor run smoothly without the mixture becoming runny. When the fruit is finely chopped, sprinkle in the 3 spices and process again briefly. Form the mixture into small balls, and roll them in coconut until they are completely covered. Arrange the sweets on a plate, chill for an hour or more, then serve.

TEA CAKES OR HOT CROSS BUNS

MAKES 12–15 BUNS   EVELYN FINDLATER

These hot cross buns are traditional at Easter-time but of course they can be made at any time of the year. They have a much better taste than shop-bought buns and are far healthier, as they are made with wholemeal flour.

1 oz (25 g) fresh yeast, or 1 dessertspoon dried yeast
½ teaspoon Barbados sugar
10 fl oz (300 ml) warm (not hot) milk
2 large egg yolks
Roughly grated rind of 1 small orange
Roughly grated rind of 1 lemon
1 lb (450 g) 100% wholemeal flour, plus extra for flouring
½ teaspoon each of mixed spice, cinnamon and nutmeg
2 oz (50 g) polyunsaturated margarine
1 dessertspoon malt extract
5 oz (150 g) dried fruit, eg sultanas and raisins
1 teaspoon honey for glaze
Oil for greasing

Cream the fresh or dried yeast with the sugar and a little of the warm milk until it is smooth. Add the rest of the milk and leave for 10 minutes in a warm place, until the yeast is frothy.

Put the egg yolks in a mixing bowl, stir in the grated orange and lemon rind and the frothy yeast mixture. Gradually stir in 8 oz (225 g) of the flour, mixed with the spices. Melt the margarine and the malt together, but don't let them get too hot. Trickle the melted margarine and malt into the flour mixture, stirring continuously.

Gradually add the dried fruit and the remaining flour, handful by handful. You will have to mould the dough with your hands as you near the end of adding the fruit and flour, and it will be a bit sticky at this stage. Turn it out onto a lightly floured surface. Flour your hands and knead the dough for about 7 minutes, re-flouring your hands as necessary. (Do not add flour to the dough.) When the dough becomes soft and pliable, put it into a greased plastic bag and let the dough rise in a warm place for 40 minutes or until it has doubled in size. Grease 2 baking trays. Turn out the dough, flour your hands only and knead for 2 minutes.

Divide the dough into 12 equal pieces: it helps to weigh them. Each should be just under 3 oz (75 g). Put the pieces back into the bag, then take out 1 piece at a time and roll it neatly into a ball. Place 6 balls on each baking tray. Slide the trays into greased plastic bags and let the buns rise in a warm place for 30 minutes or until they have doubled in size. Pre-heat the oven to gas mark 6, 400°F (200°C).

When the buns are well risen, use the back of a knife to press a cross-shaped indent gently into the tops. Place 1 tray just above the centre of the oven and the other just below and bake for 10 minutes. Then swap the trays around and bake for another 10 minutes.

To give that attractive shiny top which hot cross buns have, just mix 1 teaspoon of hot water with 1 teaspoon of honey and brush the top of the buns as soon as they come out of the oven. Place them on a wire rack and serve them as soon as they have cooled.

STICKY CLOUDS

MAKES 16   CAROLE HANDSLIP

These little balls of malted popcorn make a good alternative to the sweets and crisps that are always so much in demand. As a variation, add toasted sesame seeds or raisins when you mix the popcorn into the malt extract.

1 tablespoon sunflower oil
1 oz (25 g) popcorn kernels
2 rounded tablespoons malt extract

Heat the oil in a large heavy pan with a lid. Add the popcorn, cover and cook, shaking the pan occasionally, until the kernels have popped. Do not lift the lid until most of the popping has stopped or the kernels will jump out of the pan. Transfer the popcorn to a bowl. Place the malt extract in the pan and bring it to the boil. Boil this for 30 seconds, then quickly stir it into the popcorn until it is as evenly coated as you can manage. Leave it to cool for a few seconds, then, using two spoons, form the mixture into 16 balls and leave them to set. Serve them as they are or in paper cases.

CAROB CAKE

MAKES A 7 INCH (18 CM) CAKE   CAROLE HANDSLIP

This is a dark, traditional-looking 'chocolate' cake, which contains very little sugar because it is made with naturally sweet carob (see page 69) rather than cocoa powder.

The cake can be made in a food processor if you have one – though the resultant lack of air during mixing will produce a rather flatter cake.

4 fl oz (120 ml) sunflower or corn oil, plus extra for greasing
2 oz (50 g) dark brown sugar
2 eggs
1 rounded tablespoon malt extract
6 oz (175 g) wholemeal flour
1 oz (25 g) carob powder
2 teaspoons baking powder
Topping:
3 oz (75 g) carob confectionery bar, chopped
4 oz (110 g) curd cheese (see page 33)
Shelled walnut halves

Pre-heat the oven to gas mark 4, 350°F (180°C). Grease two 7 inch (18 cm) sandwich tins and line with greaseproof paper. Place the sugar, eggs, oil, 4 fl oz (110 ml) water and malt extract in a bowl and mix them thoroughly. Add the flour, sift in the carob powder and baking powder and mix them thoroughly for a minute or so, until completely smooth. Divide the mixture between the prepared tins, and bake for 20–25 minutes or until the cakes are firm in the centre. Loosen round the edges and turn them out onto a wire rack to cool. To make the topping, melt the chopped carob bar in a basin over a pan of hot water, being careful not to allow any water to get into the carob. Beat the cheese in a bowl until it is smooth, then add the melted carob and mix until smooth. Use half the mixture to sandwich the cakes together. Spread the remainder over the top of the cake, mark an attractive pattern on the top using a palette knife and decorate with walnut halves.

HAZELNUT FINGERS

MAKES 20 FINGERS   CAROLE HANDSLIP

The nuts in these 'fingers' can be varied according to what you have available, but always toast the nuts first as their flavour is greatly enhanced when crisp and brown. The sesame seeds can be replaced with sunflower or pumpkin seeds for a change. These 'fingers' are delicious crumbled and sprinkled over stewed fruit for a quick dessert or served at breakfast time instead of cereal. Once your children are accustomed to less sugar, omit the honey and increase the malt extract to 4 fl oz (110 ml).

4 fl oz (110 ml) sunflower oil
3 rounded tablespoons malt extract
1 rounded tablespoon clear honey
9 oz (250 g) rolled oats
2 oz (50 g) hazelnuts, chopped
2 tablespoons sesame seeds

Pre-heat the oven to gas mark 4, 350°F (180°C). Place the oil, malt extract and honey in a pan and heat it gently until it has melted. Stir in the oats, hazelnuts and sesame seeds and mix thoroughly.

Turn the mixture out into a 12 × 8 inch (30 × 20 cm) Swiss roll tin, and press the mixture to the edges with a palette knife until the surface is smooth. Bake for 25 minutes or until golden brown. Cool in the tin for 2 minutes, then cut into fingers. Allow these to cool completely before removing them from the tin.

ORANGE JELLY

SERVES 4   CAROLINE WALDEGRAVE

The basis of this recipe is a very simple idea: fresh, carton or frozen orange juice set with gelatine. To make it more festive you can add a variety of prepared fresh fruit, such as segments of orange, peeled sliced kiwi fruit, pipped grapes, sliced bananas or sliced strawberries. In this recipe, the jelly is set in several layers, because fruit mixed with unset jelly and poured into a serving bowl immediately rises to the top.

1 pint 5 fl oz (700 ml) orange juice
¾ oz (20 g) powdered gelatine
2 oranges
1 banana
2 oz (50 g) grapes

Put 3 tablespoons of the orange juice in a small saucepan. Sprinkle in the gelatine and leave it to swell for 5 minutes, then dissolve the gelatine over a very gentle heat, without letting it boil. When the mixture is clear and liquid, combine it with the remaining orange juice.

Peel the oranges with a knife as you would an apple, making sure that all the pith is removed, and divide the orange into segments, reserving any juice. Peel and slice the banana. Halve and pip the grapes. (If the skins are tough and spotted, the grapes should be peeled; dip them in boiling water for a few seconds to make this easier.)

Rinse a ring mould out with cold water. Pour a layer of orange jelly in the bottom of the mould to a depth of about ½ inch (1 cm). Refrigerate until it has set. Arrange the orange segments on top of this layer. Pour in a little jelly to hold the oranges in place, and refrigerate until it has set. Pour in a little more jelly so that the oranges are just covered and refrigerate again. When set, arrange the bananas in the ring mould and pour in a very little jelly. Refrigerate again. Pour in a little more jelly to cover the bananas and once again refrigerate until set. Now arrange the grapes, cut side up, in the ring mould. Pour in a little orange jelly and refrigerate again. Pour in the remaining jelly and refrigerate until set.

To serve, loosen the jelly round the edges with a knife. Place a serving plate over the jelly, turn the mould and plate over together, give a sharp shake and remove the mould. If the jelly will not budge, dip the outside of the mould briefly in hot water to loosen it. If there is any prepared fruit left over, toss it in the orange juice from the segmented orange and pile it into the centre of the ring mould.

BREAKFAST

The traditional British breakfast seems to be in decline. In the last few years there has been a steady drop in the sales of eggs, bacon, butter and white bread. New ideas about healthy eating are no doubt partly responsible for this loss of sales, but another reason must be that, where breakfast is concerned, so many people feel that they have neither the time nor the inclination for cooking in the mornings.

Whatever revelations nutritionists make about the fat content of sausages or the high percentages of sugar and salt in cornflakes, they all still agree that a decent breakfast makes a good start to the day. It gives you energy and also staves off cravings for crisps, sweets or biscuits at mid-morning.

So what is a 'good' breakfast? It certainly doesn't have to be cooked. But a few rounds of wholemeal toast spread with a dried fruit conserve (page 189) or a fruit spread (see page 190) will be far healthier than cornflakes drenched in added sugar. A bowl of plain yoghurt (page 36) with some fresh fruit is just as simple for those who prefer a light breakfast. Home-made Muesli (page 190) is an excellent source of fibre, vitamins and minerals. It is not expensive (especially if you buy the ingredients in bulk) and it will not have the sickly, sugary taste typical of so many commercial brands. When you do have a little more time, perhaps at weekends, it might be worth considering the Alternative Breakfast (page 186) – a satisfying cooked breakfast without the usual bacon and eggs.

THE ALTERNATIVE BREAKFAST: DEVILLED KIDNEYS, GRILLED TOMATOES AND POACHED MUSHROOMS

SERVES 4   SHIRLEY RILLA AND JILL COX

The traditional idea of a decent hearty breakfast is something cooked, usually with meat in it. Kidneys are typical breakfast fare and, if devilled, can be cooked fat-free with a good early morning kick. While the kidneys are cooking, grill the tomato halves and poach the mushrooms so that everything is ready together. Wholemeal toast completes the meal.

4 lamb's kidneys
A little milk (optional)
2 teaspoons lemon juice
2 teaspoons Dijon mustard
1 teaspoon Worcestershire sauce
1 teaspoon paprika
Freshly ground black pepper
4 large tomatoes
2 teaspoons grated Parmesan cheese
8 oz (225 g) button mushrooms
5 fl oz (150 ml) skimmed milk
1 teaspoon chopped fresh parsley, or ½ teaspoon dried parsley

Cut the kidneys in half, skin them and remove the core. Soak them overnight in milk. (This is to remove the strong flavour, but if you don't mind it, cook them without soaking.) Drain the halves and pat them dry with kitchen paper. Mix the lemon juice, mustard, Worcestershire sauce and paprika. Make several cuts in the rounded sides of the kidneys and smear with the 'devil' mixture. Grind over some black pepper, then grill under a medium heat for about five minutes each side, until they are cooked.

If you have enough room under your grill, cook the tomatoes at the same time as the kidneys. Otherwise, keep the kidneys hot while you do this. Halve the tomatoes and sprinkle them first with Parmesan cheese and then with freshly ground black pepper. Place them on the grill grid, flat sides up, and cook till the topping is crispy.

Meanwhile, poach the mushrooms. Cut the ends off the stalks and wipe the caps with a damp cloth or piece of kitchen paper. Don't peel them, as all the nutrients are in or just under the skin. Place them in a small uncovered pan together with the milk, parsley and black pepper. Cook gently over medium heat till the milk has disappeared.

Arrange the kidneys, tomatoes and mushrooms on a large heated platter, and serve immediately.

BREAKFAST NOG

SERVES 4   LYN HALL

I like to drink this creamy nog in lieu of a breakfast if I am in a hurry, or to serve it in tall glasses with a brunch. Summer or winter, it is soothing, filling and rejuvenating. Like any good breakfast dish, it may be taken any time of the day or night. The proportions do not really matter, so adjust them to your taste.

1 pint (570 ml) skimmed milk
6 fl oz (175 ml) fresh orange juice
3 tablespoons natural yoghurt
1–2 very ripe bananas
1 egg
Grated nutmeg

Place all the ingredients except the nutmeg in the blender, and blend them until they are frothy. Pour the liquid into tall goblets or glasses, and dust the nog lightly with a little nutmeg.

WHOLEWHEAT PANCAKES WITH LOW-FAT CHEESE AND DRIED FRUIT CONSERVE

MAKES 12–15 PANCAKES   SHIRLEY RILLA AND JILL COX

Pancakes make a good, quick breakfast as you can prepare a whole batch in one go and store them, individually wrapped in cling-film, in the refrigerator. They can be easily re-heated on a plate covered with foil over a pan of hot water, or in the microwave oven.

Pancakes are tremendously versatile; they can be rolled, filled and folded, spread with a filling and stacked like a cake, or eaten just on their own with honey or lemon juice. Try pancakes filled with thick tomato sauce, dotted with Parmesan cheese, then grilled, or stuffed with a chopped mushroom and garlic mixture, folded into an envelope shape and served with a sharp yoghurt and cucumber sauce. They are particularly good with a low-fat cheese, such as quark, and Dried Fruit Conserve, spiced up with orange flower water or grated orange peel.

4 oz (110 g) wholemeal flour
10 fl oz (300 ml) skimmed milk
1 small egg
Oil for cooking
6 oz (175 g) quark (see page 34)
Dried Fruit Conserve (see opposite)

Make a thin batter with the flour, skimmed milk and egg, whisking well. Use kitchen paper to wipe a small, heavy, non-stick, frying-pan with oil and heat it until it is smoking. Pour a generous 2 tablespoons of the batter into the pan and swirl it around to cover the bottom as thinly as possible. Cook the batter for 60 seconds, then flip it over with a spatula and cook the other side for a few seconds only. If you are going to eat them straight away, tip them onto a heated plate. Otherwise stack the pancakes with cling-film in between each one. (The first pancake is often a failure – don't let this deter you.) Grease the pan again between pancakes, but only lightly – the pancakes should not fry.

To serve, put a dollop of quark on each pancake, roll it up and put it into a heatproof dish. Pour over a little conserve and quickly heat under a hot grill for a minute or two, then serve.

DRIED FRUIT CONSERVE

MAKES ABOUT 1 LB (450 G) CONSERVE   SHIRLEY RILLA AND JILL COX

Most fresh fruit, or dried fruit such as apricots and prunes, makes very good conserves or sauces. Basically, all you need to do is to choose your fruit and cook it with as little water as possible until it is soft and then blend it into a thick purée. You can perk up your conserves by adding lemon juice to prune purée, ginger to rhubarb, chopped almonds to apple, cardamom to strawberries – in fact, any spices or flavourings you fancy.

These fruit conserves have many different uses: as a filling, as a substitute for jam on toast or pancakes, poured over low-fat cream cheese as a pudding, or whipped up with yoghurt for a fast breakfast.

Because dried apricots are so easily available all year round and taste so good, this recipe is based on them.

8 oz (225 g) dried apricots
Apple juice
Flavourings – use only one of the following: **1 teaspoon orange flower water**   **1 teaspoon finely grated orange peel**   **2 oz (50 g) flaked almonds**

Soak the apricots overnight in water. Discard the water, put the apricots into a saucepan and just cover them with apple juice, using the minimum amount to ensure a thick purée. Simmer them, uncovered, for about 30 minutes or until they are thoroughly cooked and soft. Cool them and then thoroughly blend or sieve them until they have a thick, smooth consistency. Add one of the flavourings.

You should keep the purée in the refrigerator, where it will last for approximately 10 days.

APPLE AND CINNAMON SPREAD

MAKES 12 FL OZ (350 ML)   CAROLE HANDSLIP

This is a tasty spread made without sugar to serve instead of jam on toast. It also makes a quick dessert mixed with a little apple or orange juice and topped with a spoonful of yoghurt.

2 large dessert apples, peeled and chopped
4 oz (110 g) chopped dates
½ teaspoon cinnamon

Place the apples in a pan with the dates, 6 fl oz (175 ml) water and cinnamon. Cover and cook them for 10–15 minutes or until the apples are soft. If you prefer a stiffer mixture, you could take the lid off for the last 5 minutes of cooking to reduce some of the liquid. Mash them with a potato masher or fork and cool with the lid on. This spread will keep, refrigerated, for several days stored in a glass container.

MUESLI

SHIRLEY RILLA AND JILL COX

Patients of the Bircher–Benner Clinic, founded in Zurich in 1897, had never heard of muesli. The words 'fruit diet' appeared on the menu, and it was served so often it become known as 'The Dish'. Dr Bircher was reviving an old Swiss custom from the fruit-growing areas where porridge with apples, pears, berries or dried fruits was often the evening meal.

Far from growing tired of the dish, patients loved it so much that they made it in their own homes, and it became known as Bircher muesli. In the early 1920s recipes for the dish were published and it was served in Swiss restaurants.

Arriving in England, where the word muesli is used for the dry mixture of flakes, cereals, fruit and nuts, it was enthusiastically received by the health-conscious who at that time were considered slightly cranky. We know better now. It wasn't long before the nation was hooked on this cereal, buying the ingredients and combining them to taste. In fact, comparing the merits of family recipes is often the source of heated arguments. Whatever the merits of individual versions, it goes without saying that the home-made variety is infinitely superior to the packaged sort which is so often laced with sugar and powdered milk.

Here is a particularly good combination, but you can adjust it as you like, adding extra ingredients or leaving some out. It is really up to you. It is easiest if you use one measure – like a mug – for all the ingredients and make up a large air-tight container at the beginning of the week.

¼ **mug dried dates**
¼ **mug dried apricots**
1 ½ **mugs jumbo oats**
1 ½ **mugs barley flakes**
1 **mug rye flakes**
¼ **mug hazelnuts**
¼ **mug dried banana flakes**
¼ **mug dried toasted coconut chips**
¼ **mug large raisins**
1 **teaspoon powdered cinnamon**

Chop the dates and apricots, then mix all ingredients well and pack into a large jar. Use as required, served with skimmed milk. As alternatives, try it with juice – it is especially good with apple juice – or plain yoghurt. You can also add grated apples, chopped bananas or any other fresh fruit in season. Some people prefer to soak muesli overnight for a softer texture. Unsoaked, it is very crunchy.

One delectable variation is to serve the muesli mixture toasted. Spread it out on foil and grill it for about 3 minutes. The flakes become crisp and lightly browned, the raisins plump up, the dried fruit caramelises, the nuts toast and become nuttier: delicious! Serve with skimmed milk, fruit juice or yoghurt in the same way as above.

KEDGEREE

SERVES 4   SHIRLEY RILLA AND JILL COX

This is a healthy version of an old favourite. It does without eggs, except as a garnish, and doesn't need cream, butter or added salt. We have used brown rice instead of white and the light-flavoured sauce is a real revelation – made only from the liquid from the cooked fish, yoghurt and oil. For added visual appeal, the dish is garnished with shelled prawns.

Instead of the dyed yellow smoked haddock, you can buy the genuine article: a paler, more delicately flavoured fish. Just ask your fishmonger. Serve kedgeree with the Sunday newspapers for a leisurely weekend breakfast, or as a light lunch-time meal with a large bowl of green salad.

8 oz (225 g) whole-grain brown rice
2 large onions
1 dessertspoon sunflower oil
1 egg
8 oz (225 g) smoked haddock fillet
1 pint (570 ml) cooked prawns in their shells
Chopped parsley for garnish
Sauce
2 tablespoons drained liquid from cooked fish
1 teaspoon hot curry paste
2 tablespoons sunflower oil
2 tablespoons natural yoghurt
Juice of ½ lemon

Cook the rice according to your preferred method (see page 59 for a foolproof method of cooking brown rice). While the rice is cooking, peel and chop the onions. Heat the oil in a shallow pan, then stir-fry the onions. When the onions are soft but not browned, remove from the heat and set them aside. Hard-boil the egg, plunge it into cold water to prevent a black ring forming round the yolk, then remove the shell. Poach the fish by putting it in a pan with 4 tablespoons of water. Bring the water to the boil, cover the pan and turn the heat off. Leave the fish to stand for 10 minutes, then drain off all the fishy liquid into a jug or bowl. Skin the fish, making sure there are no small bones left, and flake it roughly. Once the rice is cooked, drain off any excess water and add the cooked onion and flaked fish, and keep it warm. Peel all but 8 of the prawns.

Make the sauce by blending 2 tablespoons of the fish liquid with the curry paste (more or less, depending upon how hot you like it) and sunflower oil. It is easier to use an electric hand-blender or liquidiser to achieve a thick emulsion – it simply won't work with a fork. Lastly add the yoghurt and the lemon juice. Add the peeled prawns to the rice, then pour the sauce over and lightly toss with a fork. Stir gently over a low heat until the rice is coated with the sauce and hot enough to serve. Turn the kedgeree out onto a dish and garnish it with the reserved whole prawns, quartered or sliced hard-boiled egg and chopped parsley. This kedgeree is equally good hot or cold.

GRANOLA

SERVES 4–6   SHIRLEY RILLA AND JILL COX

This crunchy, mouth-watering breakfast has its origins in America, although this version is rather different. The easiest way to describe it is as a broken-up fruity flapjack, either served with skimmed milk or yoghurt, or just on its own as a nutritious snack.

2 oz (50 g) rolled oats
2 oz (50 g) wheat flakes
2 oz (50 g) sultanas
2 oz (50 g) raw cane sugar
1 oz (25 g) dried apple flakes
1 oz (25 g) wheatgerm
1 oz (25 g) chopped walnuts
1 oz (25 g) bran
½ oz (10 g) sesame seeds
5 fl oz (150 ml) fresh apple juice
2 tablespoons sunflower oil for greasing

Pre-heat the oven to gas mark 2, 300°F (150°C). Mix all the dry ingredients together with the apple juice and turn the mixture out onto a very well greased baking tray, about 12 × 8 inches (30.5 cm × 20.5 cm). Spread the mixture firmly, using the back of a spoon, and bake for 20 minutes. Take the tray out of the oven and, using a fish slice, turn the granola over in large pieces. Bake it for a further 20 minutes.

Take the tray from the oven and leave it to get completely cold; the mixture should become crispy as it cools. Keep it in an air-tight container and it will stay crispy for several days.

As an alternative, add 1 oz (25 g) coconut flakes and substitute grapefruit juice for apple juice to give a more tropical flavour.

PUDDINGS AND DESSERTS

When you want to avoid pastry and sweet, fatty puddings, what can you give your family and guests instead? For most people, the simplest and best everyday answer is fresh seasonal fruit, either just as it is or as a fruit salad. If you want to go to a little more trouble, this section gives you a range of ideas, all of them capitalising on the natural sweetness of fresh or dried fruit.

ORANGE SOUFFLÉS

SERVES 4   CHRISTOPHE BUEY

This is an unusual way of serving oranges: cooked in a soufflé in the orange shells. If you do not have time to prepare the shells, then cook the soufflé in ramekins. In either case, remember: a soufflé does not wait, one waits for a soufflé!

4 large oranges
1 oz (25 g) wholemeal flour
6 fl oz (150 ml) skimmed milk
1 egg
2 oz (50 g) caster sugar
1 egg white
Oil for greasing (optional)

Pre-heat the oven to gas mark 4, 350°F (180°C). Cut the oranges in half and, using a grapefruit knife, cut the flesh away from the sides of the orange, and lift each half out. Slide the knife inside the thin skin surrounding each segment and cut the flesh out. Drain the orange segments, reserving the juice, then place each segment on kitchen paper to dry. Clean out any remaining pith from the orange halves. Place the flour in a small saucepan and whisk in the milk. Bring it to the boil, whisking all the time to prevent lumps, and leave it to cook for 1 minute. Remove the pan from the heat and add the yolk, sugar and 1 tablespoon of the reserved orange juice.

Whisk the egg whites and fold them into the batter, then add the orange segments.

Pour the mixture into each orange cup. Place the orange cups in a shallow rimmed baking dish, pour in enough water to cover the base of the tray and cook for 15 minutes. Serve immediately.

RICOTTA SOUFFLÉS
Soffiate di Ricotta

SERVES 4   ANTONIO CARLUCCIO

A hot dessert is a treat, but so many of them require cream or eggs or both. This dessert has been created to please both the palate and the pocket and is also very healthy. The soufflés are served in individual ramekins.

A little butter for greasing
A little white sugar
3 lemons
12 oz (350 g) ricotta cheese
3 tablespoons brown sugar
3 egg whites

Pre-heat the oven to gas mark 6, 400°F (200°C). Grease 4 ovenproof ramekins lightly with butter. Put a little white sugar in the bottom of the ramekins and tip them round so that the sugar coats the insides. This helps the soufflés to rise well. Grate the rind from the lemons, and squeeze the juice from 1½ lemons. Mix the ricotta with the brown sugar, the lemon juice and grated rind until you obtain a creamy mixture. Beat the egg whites until they are stiff and fold them carefully into the ricotta mixture, then fill the ramekins with the mixture, leaving a space for expansion at the top. Cook them in the oven for 15 minutes and serve immediately.

STEAMED FRUIT PUDDING WITH PLUM AND PORT SAUCE

SERVES 6   MICHAEL QUINN

This is an intriguing autumn version of summer pudding. Instead of refrigerating a bread mould filled with summer fruit, the mould is steamed with plums, apples and pears. Damsons give a good colour and powerful flavour, but they should be cooked gently with a little sugar for a few minutes first. Serve the pudding cold with Greek yoghurt and the magnificent hot, purple sauce made from plums and port.

Butter for greasing
Small sliced white loaf
2 oz (50 g) sultanas
2 tablespoons port or rum
8 oz (225 g) purple plums
8 oz (225 g) cooking apples
8 oz (225 g) ripe pears
1 oz (25 g) split almonds
3 tablespoons Pear and Apple Spread (see page 71)
Large pinch of powdered cloves
Large pinch of cinnamon
Greek yoghurt to serve

First butter a 2 pint (1·1 litre) pudding basin. Remove the crusts from the bread and line the basin with the slices. Soak the sultanas in the port or rum. Halve and stone the plums; peel, core and slice the apples and pears. Mix the prepared fresh fruit with the sultanas and port, almonds, Pear and Apple Spread and spices. Carefully spoon it into the bread-lined basin, cover the fruit with a layer of bread, and tie a piece of foil tightly round the top of the basin, making sure that the foil does not touch the bread. Steam the pudding (see page 22) for 1–1½ hours, then refrigerate it until completely cold. Turn the pudding out onto a plate, and pour over some hot Plum and Port Sauce (see below). Serve it accompanied by Greek yoghurt and the remaining sauce.

PLUM AND PORT SAUCE

SERVES 6   MICHAEL QUINN

8 oz (225 g) purple plums
2 tablespoons Pear and Apple Spread (see page 71)
4 fl oz (110 ml) port

Place the plums, Pear and Apple Spread and port in a saucepan. Add water to cover and simmer for 10 minutes or until the plums are cooked. Remove the pan from the heat, stone the plums and purée them, together with the cooking liquor, in a processor or liquidiser. Re-heat the sauce before you serve it.

PEAR MOUSSE

Mousse aux Poires

SERVES 4   CHRISTOPHE BUEY

This simple, delicate, uncooked mousse combines the strong flavour of Williams' pears with the lightness of whisked egg white.

1 lb 4 oz (550 g) ripe pears, preferably Williams'
Juice of ½ lemon
1 oz (25 g) muscovado sugar (optional)
4 oz (110 g) curd cheese
1 egg white

Peel and core the pears, set half a pear aside for decoration, and purée the rest in a food processor or mash with a fork. Add the lemon juice and half the sugar. Mix the pears with the curd cheese. Whisk the egg white and fold in the remaining sugar. Fold the sweetened egg white into the pear and cheese mixture, and pour it into a dish. Refrigerate the mousse for 10–15 minutes, decorate with thin slices of pear, arranged in a fan shape, and serve.

FRUIT COMPOTE

Mazamorra morada

SERVES 4   ELISABETH LAMBERT ORTIZ

This is a luscious and refreshing dessert, perfect for late summer when fresh blackberries and peaches are in season, but good at any time of the year using frozen fruit. The original Peruvian version is coloured a beautiful purple by *maiz morado* (purple corn).

4 oz (110 g) dried apricots
4 oz (110 g) dried peaches
½ small pineapple
1 fresh pear
1 fresh peach
1 apple
4 oz (110 g) blackberries
3 oz (75 g) sugar, preferably demerara
2 whole cloves
2 inch (5 cm) piece stick cinnamon
1 tablespoon lemon juice
1 oz (25 g) arrowroot or cornflour

Soak the dried apricots and peaches in enough water to cover them for 1–2 hours, until they have plumped up. Peel, core and chop the pineapple. Peel, core and chop the pear. Peel, stone and chop the peach. Peel, core and chop the apple. Combine the prepared fresh fruit in a large saucepan with the blackberries. Halve the dried apricots and quarter the dried peaches, then add these to the pan.

Add 1 pint 5 fl oz (700 ml) water, the sugar, cloves and cinnamon and simmer, covered, until the fruit is tender, about 10 minutes. Remove the cloves and cinnamon if you like. Add the lemon juice to the arrowroot with a little water, if necessary, to make a thin paste. Stir it into the fruit mixture and cook, stirring from time to time using a wooden spoon, for 5 minutes or until the liquid has thickened slightly. Do not overcook. Let the compote cool, then chill it in the refrigerator and serve.

DRUNKEN PRUNES

SERVES 4   LYN HALL WITH ANTON MOSIMANN

I have always loved the deep, rich sheen of prunes and their appealing sweetness, and regret the inevitable jocular comments from Britons around the table whenever I serve them. The prunes in this recipe are soaked in Sauterne to give them an attractive glossy appearance; a dash of mango purée adds a fresh new flavour. The sweet taste means that this dish will appeal to anyone with a sweet tooth! If you want a sharper flavour you could substitute a lemon for the orange. Serve the prunes very well chilled in individual glass dishes.

13 fl oz (375 ml) Sauterne wine
12 large prunes
1 small orange
½ small mango
3 tablespoons fromage blanc
4 sprigs mint

Boil the Sauterne until only 7 fl oz (200 ml) remain. Add the prunes and boil them for 1 minute, then allow them to soak for about an hour. Segment the orange, carefully removing the skin covering each segment. Add the segments to the prune mixture, and boil again for a minute or so. Allow to cool, then put it in the freezer for about 30 minutes, or until the mixture is well chilled.

Liquidise the mango flesh, then sieve to to remove the fibres. Drain the prunes and orange segments, reserving the liquid. Stone the prunes neatly, and place them, together with the segments, in pretty bowls. Pour over the reserved liquid. Spoon over the fromage blanc, then the mango purée, and finally decorate with a sprig of mint. Serve immediately.

FRUIT SALAD ON A RED WINE JELLY

SERVES 4   LYN HALL WITH ANTON MOSIMANN

This is one of the most graceful desserts I know with its delightful combination of flavours, textures and colours. It *looks* like a beautiful arrangement of fruit on a plate with a red wine sauce: when you place it on the table with a flourish your guests will invariably draw back to avoid being splashed. But they will then find a spiced jelly is holding everything together. Lightest of all desserts, it is neither expensive nor difficult to make.

The jelly:
½ orange
½ lemon
1 teaspoon powdered gelatine or 1 leaf gelatine
4½ fl oz (125 ml) sweet red wine
2 inch (5 cm) stick cinnamon
1 dessertspoon orange flower water
½ teaspoon vanilla essence
For the fruit salad:
2 oranges
2 grapefruit
6 strawberries
4 cherries (or small berries in season)
8 large mint leaves

Chill 4 dinner plates in the freezer. Grate the rind and squeeze the juice from the orange and lemon. Soak the grated rind of the orange and lemon in their juice for 15 minutes. Soak the gelatine in the wine for 5 minutes or until the gelatine is soft, then heat the wine gently to dissolve the gelatine. Add the cinnamon stick and leave to infuse for a few minutes. Strain the orange juice and lemon juice into the wine, discarding the grated rind, then add the orange flower water and vanilla. Strain the liquid through a coffee filter paper into a clean jug. Cool until it has slightly thickened. Pour the jelly onto the chilled plates.

To make the fruit salad, segment the oranges and the grapefruit. Halve the strawberries and the cherries, and remove the cherry stones. When the jelly is almost set, lay the fruit segments on the plates in a pretty circular design, with a cherry or berry in the centre of each. Just before serving, roll up the mint leaves, and slice them into fine shreds with a sharp knife. Scatter them over the centre of each plate, and serve immediately.

MIXED FRUIT CLAFOUTI

SERVES 4   CLAUDIA RODEN

A homely dessert of fruit baked on a pancake-type bed is made in the French countryside with whatever fruit grows locally: black cherries in the Limousin, for example, or apples in Normandy. In this version, I have used a Middle Eastern-type cream of skimmed milk, thickened with ground rice and chopped almonds, instead of the usual flour, eggs and milk mixture. The fragrant orange blossom water and rose water are available in Greek and oriental stores and some chemists (see page 64), but you can use cinnamon, bitter almond essence or vanilla as an alternative.

Clafouti is meant especially for fruits which have passed their prime or those which have not quite reached it, but, of course, perfect fruit would not be wasted on it. Apples and pears, peaches, bananas, apricots, dates, plums, greengages, cherries and all kinds of berries are suitable.

1 pint (570 ml) skimmed milk
2 heaped tablespoons ground rice
1 tablespoon sugar
3 oz (75 g) almonds, finely chopped
2 tablespoons orange blossom or rose water or a mixture of the two
1 lb 8 oz (700 g) mixed fresh fruit

Pre-heat the oven to gas mark 6, 400°F (200°C). Bring the skimmed milk to the boil. Mix the ground rice with 2 or 3 tablespoons of cold water and beat well, making sure there are no lumps. Pour into the milk and simmer, stirring constantly, for 5 minutes or until it thickens, then add the sugar and almonds and simmer for another 5 minutes over a very low heat. Add the orange blossom and/or rose water and cook for 2 minutes longer. Pour into a shallow earthenware ovenproof dish.

Remove the stones from the fruit, if necessary, and halve or core and slice larger fruit. Arrange the fruit on top of the mixture in an attractive pattern, the halved fruit cut side down, and press them in slightly. Bake for about 30 minutes or until the fruit has softened. Serve the clafouti hot, warm or cold.

THE TASTE OF HEALTH

APPLE PUDDING

Mele stufate

SERVES 4   ANTONIO CARLUCCIO

The apple is probably the most common and popular of British fruit. This is a variation on the baked apple with a Mediterranean touch. The pudding is very easy to prepare and is equally good hot or cold. Creamy, strained yoghurt makes a nice accompaniment.

4 cooking apples
3 oranges
5 tablespoons sultanas
½ oz (10 g) pine-nuts (optional)
3 tablespoons runny honey
A pinch of powdered cloves
A pinch of powdered cinnamon
2 oz (50 g) ground almonds

Pre-heat the oven to its highest setting. Peel and core the apples and cut them into ½ inch (1 cm) slices. Grate the rind and squeeze the juice from the oranges. Lay the apple slices in layers, together with the sultanas and pine-nuts, in a shallow ovenproof dish. Pour over the orange juice, spoon over the honey, and sprinkle on the powdered cloves, cinnamon, the grated orange rind and ground almonds. Cover the dish with aluminium foil and bake for 45 minutes. Serve hot or cold.

204

BAKED STUFFED PEACHES

SERVES 4   PAUL LAURENSON AND ETHEL MINOGUE

The art of the patissier and confectioner is arguably the most skilled of all the culinary arts. Nevertheless the most luscious and refreshing end to a meal can often be a simple dessert of sun-ripened fruit. A little chilled low-fat yoghurt or goat's cheese is a very pleasant accompaniment for these peaches.

4 large ripe peaches
6 dried dates
6 oz (175 ml) ground almonds
A small amount of egg white, **or 1 dessertspoonful almond oil**
1 dessertspoon Ratafia or Kirsch (optional)
Oil for greasing
2 oz (50 g) flaked almonds

Pre-heat the oven to gas mark 6, 400°F (200°C). Halve and stone the peaches. Skin the dates if their skins are tough and put the dates into a blender or processor, together with the ground almonds, egg white or almond oil, and liqueur, if using. Process until the mixture is just blended. Spoon this stuffing into the peach halves in firm mounds and place on an oiled baking tray. Scatter the flaked almonds on top and bake the peaches for 20–30 minutes, then serve.

DRIED FRUIT GRATIN

Gratin de Fruits secs

SERVES 4   CHRISTOPHE BUEY

This is an unusual soufflé made from marinated dried fruit and cooked in a shallow gratin dish. It is lovely served with cold Greek yoghurt.

10 oz (250 g) mixed dried fruit, such as prunes, pears, peaches, apricots and apple rings
10 fl oz (250 ml) apple juice
Grated rind and juice of ½ lemon
1 oz (25 g) raisins
4 egg whites
1 oz (25 g) muscovado sugar (optional)

Oil a shallow 10 inch (25 cm) ovenproof gratin dish. Wash the fruit very well 3 times in cold water, then add the apple juice, 10 fl oz (250 ml) water and the grated rind of the lemon. Refrigerate overnight to marinate in the apple juice, or simmer the fruit for 15 minutes, then leave to cool.

Place the fruit and marinade in a saucepan. Bring it slowly to the boil and simmer for 5–10 minutes. Leave it to cool for about 20 minutes, then drain it, reserving 1 tablespoon of the juice. Stone the prunes, if necessary. Set aside the raisins for a moment, then chop the rest of the fruit finely, by hand or in a food processor, and add the lemon juice, the reserved cooking juice and the raisins. Pre-heat the oven to gas mark 4, 350°F (180°C). Whisk the egg whites until they are stiff, add the sugar, if using, and fold this mixture gently into the fruit. Put the mixture into the gratin dish and bake it for 15–20 minutes. Serve immediately.

APRICOT CHEESE

SERVES 4–6   CAROLINE WALDEGRAVE

This pudding is very rich, and most people cannot eat more than a small portion. If you are making it for a dinner party, it can be served in individual ramekins.

12 oz (350 g) dried apricots
6 cardamom pods, cracked
1 cinnamon stick
12 oz (350 g) quark (see page 34)
1 oz (25 g) mixed nuts for decoration

Soak the apricots in cold water for 2 hours, then drain. Put them in a saucepan with 8 fl oz (250 ml) water, the cracked cardamom pods and the cinnamon stick. Bring it gradually to the boil, then lower the heat and simmer slowly for about 20 minutes, or until the apricots are tender.

Remove the cinnamon stick and cardamoms. Return the seeds from 2 of the pods to the saucepan. Process the apricots, the remaining water and the cardamom seeds well in a food processor. Allow the mixture to cool, then add the cheese, beating or pounding well. Pile it into a dish or individual ramekins, cover and refrigerate. To serve, roughly chop the nuts and scatter them over the pudding.

WALNUT-STUFFED PRUNES WITH YOGHURT

SERVES 4   CLAUDIA RODEN

Prunes stuffed with walnuts are an old-fashioned dainty which you can serve with coffee. They keep very well in a jar in the refrigerator, perfect for the unexpected caller. Simmering the prunes briefly, then swirling them with yoghurt turns them into a delightful dessert. As a variation, use red or white wine instead of water, or a mixture of wine and water, and omit the liqueur.

8 oz (225 g) moist, stoned prunes
4 oz (110 g) shelled walnuts
2 tablespoons Grand Marnier or Cointreau (optional)
8 oz (225 g) natural yoghurt

Press a finger in the hole of each prune to enlarge it, then push half a walnut inside. Put the prunes in a saucepan with the Grand Marnier and cover them with about 10 fl oz (300 ml) water. Simmer gently for about 20 minutes or until the prunes are soft and most of the liquid absorbed. You will need some liquid for the sauce, so if the prunes become too dry, add a little more water. Transfer the prunes and remaining liquid to a serving bowl and carefully pour over the yoghurt – it will blend pleasingly with the sauce. Serve chilled.

OUTDOOR EATING

Eating out of doors tends to be a rare pleasure in our unpredictable climate. Nonetheless, barbecues and picnics – at home, in the country or on the beach – are steadily becoming more popular.

We have mostly kept to simplicity in this section. The essential fun of eating out of doors is to enjoy the outdoor experience, not to spend a lot of the time preparing elaborate food, though some of the picnic ideas do involve a little advance preparation. (For information on barbecuing itself see page 13.)

BARBECUE SAUCE

This recipe is for a basic barbecue sauce which can be used for fish or meat. The ingredients can be varied according to your own preference; for instance, if you like 'hot' flavours you could add some cayenne pepper and a fresh chilli. Use the sauce for food that is to be grilled, as well as for barbecueing.

This makes 3 fl oz (75 ml) of sauce, enough to coat 4 large chicken breasts or the equivalent quantity of kebabs, fish or spare ribs.

2 dessertspoons soy sauce
2 tablespoons red wine vinegar
Juice of 1 large lemon
4 cloves garlic, crushed
2 tablespoons tomato purée
1 tablespoon English mustard powder
1 teaspoon black molasses
Freshly ground black pepper
1 tablespoon chopped fresh mixed herbs, **or 1 teaspoon dried herbs**
½ teaspoon dried oregano

Blend all the ingredients in a liquidiser or food processor. Let the sauce stand for 15 minutes or so. Using a pastry brush, coat the food thickly on all sides. Large pieces of meat should be slashed in several places to allow the sauce to penetrate. Chicken should always be skinned, for the same reason. Let the food stand, covered, for another 15–30 minutes before putting it on the barbecue. Add more sauce during cooking if necessary.

CHICKEN DEVIL

SERVES 4   DINAH MORRISON

This recipe is very easy to prepare and cook. Removing the skin from the chicken joints reduces the level of fat and enables the marinade to penetrate the meat. This is a 'hot' marinade most suitable for adults; for children you could omit the chilli powder.

Hot grilled banana is a delicious accompaniment, and so are a green salad and foil-baked potatoes.

4 chicken joints, weighing 5–6 oz (150–175 g) each
1 teaspoon English mustard powder
1 teaspoon chilli powder
1 teaspoon powdered ginger
Juice of 1 lemon
Freshly ground black pepper
5 oz (125 g) yoghurt
A little oil for the grill
4 bananas

Prepare this dish about 3 hours before you wish to cook it. Skin the chicken joints and slash them 2 or 3 times with a sharp knife. Lay them in a flat non-metallic dish. Mix the spices, lemon juice, freshly ground black pepper and the yoghurt and pour this over the chicken, turning the pieces until they are well coated. Marinate in the refrigerator for 2–3 hours, basting the chicken with the marinade 2 or 3 times. Light a charcoal fire and, when it is ready (the charcoal will be hot and coated with grey ash), shake the chicken pieces and cook them on a greased grill for about 10 minutes each side. (The meat may look quite black in places.) If there is some marinade left in the dish it can be used to baste the chicken. Bake the bananas in their skins round the edge of the barbecue while the meat is cooking and serve them with the chicken.

FISH KEBABS

SERVES 4   DINAH MORRISON

Burning fennel stalks or other firm or woody herbs on the coals under these kebabs imparts a wonderful flavour to the fish. This technique is widely used in the South of France.

1 lb 4 oz (550 g) firm fish steaks, such as: cod, halibut, haddock, turbot, swordfish or fresh tuna fish
Juice of 1 lemon
2 tablespoons sunflower oil
1 small bunch fennel, finely chopped
Freshly ground black pepper
2 red or green peppers
Oil for greasing
Fresh or dried fennel stalks for the barbecue

Remove the skin and any bones from the fish and cut it into 1 inch (2·5 cm) cubes. Put the cubes of fish in a shallow non-metallic dish and add the lemon juice, the oil, the finely chopped fennel and some freshly ground black pepper. Marinate the fish in the refrigerator for 1–2 hours, turning the fish in the liquid from time to time. Light the fire in good time and when it is nearly ready cut the peppers into 1 inch (2·5 cm) squares, removing any seeds. Thread the cubes of fish and the squares of pepper onto 4 skewers and cook on a greased grill over the charcoal for about 7–8 minutes with the fennel stalks burning underneath. Serve immediately.

GRILLED GREY MULLET
WITH AVOCADO AND RED PEPPER SAUCE

SERVES 4   DINAH MORRISON

Whole fish can be cooked extremely well on a barbecue; mullet, sea bass or sea bream are all suitable. It does help to use one of the fish-shaped holders, otherwise the cooked fish is sometimes difficult to remove from the barbecue in one piece. The sauce can be made a little ahead of time and refrigerated.

Avocado and Pepper Sauce
2 ripe avocados
1 red pepper
Juice of 1 lemon
Salt
2 tablespoons olive oil

Peel and stone the avocados, cut up and de-seed the red pepper. Put the vegetables in a liquidiser, together with the lemon juice, salt and olive oil, and process until smooth. If you are not going to use the sauce immediately, cover it with a layer of cling-film to prevent it from turning brown.

2 lb 8 oz (1·2 kg) grey mullet
Bunch of thyme or rosemary
Oil for greasing

Have the fish gutted and cleaned but not scaled, as the scales help protect the fish from burning. Grease the grill, whether it is flat or a special fish-shaped holder. Stuff the cavity of the fish with the thyme or rosemary and cook the fish over the fire for 8–10 minutes on each side. Serve with the sauce.

GRILLED VEGETABLES

DINAH MORRISON

The following vegetables can be cooked directly on the barbecue: whole mushrooms, whole tomatoes, slices of fennel cut vertically, onions either whole or sliced in the same way as the fennel (leave the slices attached to a piece of root to stop them falling apart). Pieces of pepper and thick slices of aubergine can also be barbecued, as long as they are well coated with oil. Vegetable kebabs can be made up on skewers, using pieces of any of the above. Put basil or bay leaves between the pieces and paint the kebabs with a little oil before putting them on the barbecue for about 15–20 minutes. Cook vegetables round the edge of the fire, where the heat is less intense, while you cook the meat or fish over the hotter fire in the middle.

GRILLED SWEETCORN

DINAH MORRISON

Fresh young sweetcorn can be cooked in its husk over the fire (but beware of using older sweetcorn – it cannot be given the same treatment). First pull back the green leaves, being careful not to tear them off, and remove the silky tassels. Soak the sweetcorn and leaves in a basin of cold water and when they are thoroughly wet pull the leaves back over to cover the sweetcorn, twist the leaves together at the top and fasten them with a piece of wire. Cook the sweetcorn for about 20 minutes over a low fire, spraying the sweetcorn with water from time to time to prevent the leaves from burning.

VEGETABLES COOKED IN FOIL

DINAH MORRISON

Vegetables are easily cooked in foil over the barbecue or in the oven. They can be prepared in advance and taken out to the barbecue ready to cook. Use a large piece of foil and, for cooking over a barbecue, use a double layer in case the foil snags on the grill.

Brush the foil thinly with oil and put in the cleaned vegetables, sprinkled with a pinch of salt, freshly ground black pepper and some fresh chopped herbs. Fold up the foil and seal it into a neat packet. Cook over the fire or in the oven, gas mark 6, 400°F (200°C), for 30–40 minutes. Many different vegetables can be cooked in this way and it is worth experimenting with different combinations of vegetables and herbs or spices. For instance, baby carrots can be cooked with tarragon or mint, and mushrooms combine well with bay leaves or crushed coriander seeds. You can also add crushed garlic to any of these.

COURGETTES WITH FETA AND MINT

SERVES 4   DINAH MORRISON

Oil for greasing
1 lb (450 g) small courgettes
4 oz (110 g) Greek feta cheese or any other goat's cheese
Salt, freshly ground black pepper
Small bunch of fresh mint or 1 tablespoon dried mint

Prepare the foil as described above. Wash the courgettes and cut off the ends, then cut a thin slit along the length of each courgette, and stuff in slivers of the cheese. Sprinkle with the seasoning and the chopped mint leaves. Seal up the parcel and cook, either in the oven or on the fire, for about 30 minutes.

NEW POTATOES WITH DILL

SERVES 4   DINAH MORRISON

Summer is the time for experimenting with fresh herbs. The potatoes would be equally good combined with fresh mint or caraway seeds instead of the dill.

Oil for greasing
1 lb (450 g) small new potatoes
Salt, freshly ground black pepper
Small bunch of fresh dill, finely chopped, or 1 tablespoon dried dill

Prepare the foil as above. Wash the potatoes but leave their skins on. Put the potatoes in the foil, together with the seasoning and the chopped or dried dill, and cook for 30–40 minutes, depending on the size of the potatoes.

GRILLED AUBERGINE SAUCE OR DIP

SERVES 4   DINAH MORRISON

This sauce or dip can be cooked on the fire when it is first lit, then served as an hors d'oeuvre with slices of bread or as a sauce for the grilled fish or meat that follows.

8 oz (225 g) aubergines
1 clove garlic
3 oz (75 g) curd cheese
2 tablespoons lemon juice
1 tablespoon olive oil
Salt, freshly ground black pepper
1 teaspoon ground coriander
½ teaspoon ground cumin

Cook the aubergines on the grill until they are charred on the outside and soft within. Allow them to cool a little before peeling off the charred skin. Put the flesh into a fine meshed sieve and press hard until the flesh of the aubergine is quite dry. Peel and crush the garlic. Process or blend the aubergine with the rest of the ingredients. Put the purée in a bowl and serve either as a sauce or with slices of bread as a starter.

VEGETABLES IN OLIVE OIL

SERVES 4 GENEROUSLY   CLAUDIA RODEN

Vegetables cooked in olive oil are a common feature of a Middle Eastern meal, served cold as an appetiser, as a side dish or as a course on their own. Aubergines, okra, courgettes, green beans, peppers, spinach, broad beans and artichoke hearts can all be cooked in this way, either alone or in combination with others. The theme is onion and parsley but other flavours are also present: garlic, lemon or vinegar, a touch of sugar, tomatoes, mint and fresh coriander. Served with cheese and a salad, this dish makes a satisfying lunch or light supper.

1 medium-sized aubergine
Salt, freshly ground black pepper
8 oz (225 g) green beans
8 oz (225 g) okra
1 red pepper
1 onion, coarsley chopped
2 tablespoons olive oil
2 cloves garlic, chopped
14 oz (400 g) tinned tomatoes
1 tablespoon vinegar or according to taste
1 teaspoon sugar
4 courgettes
A bunch of mint, chopped (optional)
A bunch of coriander and parsley, chopped

Cut the aubergine into cubes, sprinkle with salt and leave for an hour, then rinse them and pat dry.

Top and tail the green beans and cut them into 3. Trim the okra at the stem end, and cut the red pepper into pieces. Fry the onion in oil in a large pan until it has softened slightly. Add all the prepared vegetables and continue to fry, stirring, for about 10 minutes, adding the garlic towards the end. Add the peeled tomatoes and their juice, and a little water if necessary, and stir in salt and pepper to taste, vinegar and sugar. Simmer gently, uncovered, for about 15 minutes. Thickly slice the courgettes, add them to the pan, and continue to cook until the vegetables are just done. Add the mint, if using, then the fresh coriander and parsley for the last few minutes of cooking. Allow to cool, then serve.

FISH AND SEAFOOD SALAD

SERVES 4   CLAUDIA RODEN

Depending on your choice of fish and seafood, this salad can be as cheap or as grand as you like. The fish must be firm, however. Choose two, three or more from the following: cod, haddock, halibut, sea bream, sea bass, monkfish, salmon trout, baby squid, prawns, scallops, mussels, cooked crab. If you need to feed a lot more people, a marvellous way of making the fish go farther is to combine it with cold pasta or basmati rice with plenty of extra dressing. You can also add chopped raw vegetables, such as tomatoes, olives, peppers, cucumber and celery.

About 2 lb (900 g) of prepared mixed fish and seafood, such as 1 lb (450 g) cod, 8 oz (225 g) squid, 2 pints (1·1 litres) mussels and 2 scallops
Salt, freshly ground black pepper
A large bunch of fresh mixed herbs: parsley, chives, tarragon, coriander and mint
3 tablespoons olive oil
Juice of 1 lemon or more
5–6 spring onions, finely chopped

Clean and skin the fish and seafood. (For detailed information on preparing squid, mussels and scallops see pages 39–41.)

Simply poach the fish in very lightly salted water for as short a time as possible until the flesh is translucent and flaky. It is better to undercook than overcook: scallops need only about a minute. Drain them well. Clean the mussels, then cook them by steaming in a saucepan with a little boiling water and the lid on. Discard any that are open before being steamed and any that remain closed after steaming.

Cut the fish into cubes. Cut the body of the squid into rounds, and the tentacles into pieces. Slice the scallops and take the mussels out of their shells.

Combine the herbs with the rest of the ingredients to make the dressing, and pour it over the fish. Leave it for about 30 minutes so that the flavours develop, then serve.

BULGAR SALAD

Tabbouleth

SERVES 4   DINAH MORRISON

Bulgar is a most useful cereal for last-minute meals as it needs no long cooking (see page 60). This is a slight variation on the traditional Middle Eastern *tabbouleth* – if you like it, experiment with other combinations. It keeps well for several days. Serve it with cold chicken or fish, or for a vegetarian version add some toasted almonds.

4 oz (110 g) bulgar
6 oz (175 g) Spanish or red onions
8 oz (225 g) tomatoes
4 oz (110 g) green or red peppers
Small bunch of fresh coriander or parsley, chopped
3 tablespoons olive oil
3 tablespoons lemon juice
Salt, freshly ground black pepper
1 ripe avocado

Put the bulgar into a large bowl with 2 pints (1·1 litres) of cold water, and leave to soak for 20–30 minutes. (The length of time it needs will depend on the age of the cereal.) Meanwhile, peel and chop the onions, skin and chop the tomatoes and de-seed and chop the peppers very finely.

After 30 minutes strain the bulgar into a colander lined with a piece of muslin or a tea towel. Gather up the corners of the cloth and wring the water out of the bulgar until it is quite dry. Put it into a serving dish and add the vegetables. Stir in the chopped coriander and add the oil, lemon juice and seasoning. Just before serving, peel and chop the avocado and add this to the salad.

PITTA SANDWICHES

DINAH MORRISON

Pitta bread is one of the best breads to use for picnics. It is now widely available in white or wholemeal form. Warm it in a medium oven for a few minutes and cut the pieces widthways in half, then open up each half to form a little pocket to hold the filling: the sandwich won't drip and the filling stays neatly in place to the last bite. Don't fill the pitta too far in advance, however, or it will go soggy. You can take the pittas wrapped in foil and the fillings in plastic boxes, then assemble the sandwiches just before eating. If you have to make them in advance, wrap each one separately in cling-film.

The filling can be any salad or sandwich filling that you like. There are endless variants possible using combinations of meat, fish, vegetables and fruit, with crunchy or smooth textures. No butter or yellow fat spread is necessary, but the filling should be a little moist – there is nothing more horrible than a sandwich that is too dry. Here are a few ideas:

Watercress, orange segments and walnuts

Grated carrot, cheese and apple

Coleslaw and cold chicken

Cheese and tomato with endive or lettuce

Cream cheese with raisins or dates and hazelnuts

Sardines and cucumber

Raw mushrooms with ham and chicory.

SUBMARINES OR HERO SANDWICHES

SERVES 4   DINAH MORRISON

This is a very speedy sandwich to assemble and is easy to carry if you are out walking. It is also ideal food for hungry youngsters during the school holidays when they are often too busy to stop their activities to come inside and sit down at the table. The same filling can be used for individual rolls but these will take longer to make.

1 large French loaf, preferably granary or wholemeal
3 tablespoons olive oil
7 oz (200 g) tinned tuna fish
2 heaped teaspoons capers
3 tablespoons natural yoghurt
1 round lettuce or ½ Iceberg lettuce
6 oz (175 g) tomatoes
½ cucumber

Cut the loaf horizontally in 2. Trickle the olive oil over the cut surfaces of the loaf and allow it to soak in. Drain the tuna fish and mash it with a fork, adding the capers and yoghurt. When the tuna is thoroughly mixed with the other ingredients, spread it on one half of the loaf. Wash and dry the lettuce and shred it with a sharp knife into thin strips. Put this on top of the tuna fish together with the sliced tomatoes and cucumber. Put the top of the loaf over the filling and press it gently together. Cut the loaf into 8 pieces and wrap individually in cling-film or aluminium foil.

APPLE AND APRICOT CAKE

SERVES 8/10   DINAH MORRISON

This is a rich gooey cake with a moist texture. Unlike most cakes it has very little saturated fat and sugar; the sweetness comes from the Apple and Pear Spread which is obtainable from health and wholefood shops. The cake will be easier to cut if it is cooked the day before it is needed.

8 oz (225 g) cooking apples
4 oz (110 g) dried apricots
4 oz (110 g) plain white flour
1 teaspoon bicarbonate of soda
4 oz (110 g) 100% wholemeal flour
2 oz (50 g) soft light brown sugar
6 oz (175 g) Apple and Pear Spread (see page 71)
5 fl oz (150 ml) sunflower oil
3 fl oz (75 ml) buttermilk

Pre-heat the oven to gas mark 4, 350°F (180°C). Prepare an 8 inch (20 cm) cake tin, lining the bottom with baking parchment or greaseproof paper.

Grate the apple and chop the apricots. Sift the white flour together with the bicarbonate of soda and sprinkle 1 tablespoonful over the apricots to prevent them from sinking during cooking. Mix the white and wholemeal flour together, making sure that there are no lumps in the wholemeal flour. Melt the sugar and the Apple and Pear Spread together over a low heat until just blended. Transfer this mixture to a large bowl and beat in the oil. Mix in the fruit and the flour, then the buttermilk, stirring very quickly. Transfer the stiffish mixture to the prepared tin, then bake for 45 minutes. Cool in the tin for 10 minutes and then turn out onto a cake rack to finish cooling. When the cake is cold, put it in an air-tight container until needed.

FRUIT AND YOGHURT ICE

DINAH MORRISON

Most of us love ice-cream but it usually has a very high fat and sugar content. These refreshing ices are low in both and, as a result, they freeze very hard. This is an advantage when it comes to picnics. Kept in a large wide-necked thermos for a couple of hours they will have melted just enough to make them easy to eat. The texture will be improved if the ices are beaten hard with a fork or put in a food processor two or three times during the freezing process. For children, these ices are also very popular made on sticks in ice-lolly moulds.

BANANA AND YOGHURT ICE

SERVES 4

5 oz (150 g) natural yoghurt
12 oz (350 g) ripe bananas
1 teaspoon vanilla flavouring
2 egg whites
2 tablespoons toasted almonds, crushed

Process the yoghurt, peeled banana and vanilla, until they form a liquid. Freeze the mixture until it is slushy, then whip the egg whites until soft peaks form and fold them into the semi-frozen mixture. Return the mixture to the freezer. When it has solidified around the edges, beat it well. Repeat this process and, after this second beating, fold in the crushed toasted almonds. Freeze until solid.

MANGO AND YOGHURT ICE

SERVES 4

12 oz (350 g) mango
5 oz (150 g) natural yoghurt
2 egg whites

Peel the mango and scrape away all the flesh from the large stone in the middle. Make the ice in the same way as for Banana and Yoghurt Ice.

PINEAPPLE AND YOGHURT ICE

SERVES 4

12 oz (350 g) pineapple

5 oz (150 g) natural yoghurt

Cut the skin from the pineapple and cube the flesh, discarding the hard core. Make the ice in the same way as for Banana and Yoghurt Ice.

DINNER PARTIES

In planning this section, we have assumed that giving a dinner party is one occasion when many people are willing to spend more money and more time than usual. The two distinguished chefs who devised the menus have put the emphasis on good-quality, fresh ingredients presented in original ways.

Their recipes enhance the natural flavours of the ingredients rather than disguising them with heavy sauces. The meals should leave your guests feeling that they have eaten well and even adventurously. Our aim is to avoid that bloated feeling that so often follows meals where rich sauces and sweet creamy puddings predominate. The chefs also make suggestions about presentation which is an important part of enjoying food. Care taken in trimming a vegetable or using colours imaginatively can turn an ordinary-looking dish into a beautiful one.

Menu 1

Menu for 6

Little Cheese Soufflés
Turbot and Salmon Papillote
Terrine with a Purée of Mango

LITTLE CHEESE SOUFFLÉS

Petit Soufflés au Fromage

SERVES 6   RAYMOND BLANC

This light fluffy soufflé is easy to prepare. Unlike many soufflés, it uses
low-fat ingredients and can also be prepared in advance, then reheated.
Cooked in individual ramekins it makes a wonderful first course for any
dinner party.

Soufflé mixture:
Melted butter for greasing
A little flour
4½ fl oz (125 ml) skimmed milk
½ onion, finely chopped
Pinch of nutmeg
6 turns of the pepper mill
1 teaspoon arrowroot
3½ oz (90 g) Gruyère or Edam cheese, grated
1 egg, separated
A dash of lemon juice
4 oz (110 g) fine wholemeal breadcrumbs
Salad mixture:
4 oz (110 g) French beans
4 oz (110 g) button mushrooms
A little lemon juice
4 handfuls of mixed salad lettuces, such as batavia, frilly endive, cos

Vinaigrette:
1 fl oz (25 ml) walnut oil
2 fl oz (50 ml) sunflower oil
½ fl oz (10 ml) white wine vinegar

Garnish:
6 slices of brown bread
2 tablespoons chives, finely chopped

Pre-heat the oven to gas mark 7, 425°F (220°C). First prepare the ramekins. Brush the insides with melted butter and dust them finely with flour, shaking out any excess. Put a circle of buttered greaseproof paper on the bottom to help you remove the soufflé later.

To make the soufflé base, bring the milk, chopped onion, nutmeg and pepper to the boil, and simmer gently for 5 minutes so that the onion flavours the milk. Mix the arrowroot with 2 tablespoons of water, then gradually add it to the milk and bring it to the boil, whisking constantly to obtain a smooth sauce. Pass this through a fine sieve into a bowl, leave to cool for a few minutes, then mix in the grated cheese and the egg yolk. Whisk the egg white until peaks form, then add the lemon juice (to help the coagulation of the egg white) and continue whisking until it is stiff. Add a quarter of the white to the cheese sauce and mix thoroughly. Fold in the remaining egg white, using a gentle cutting and lifting motion. Fill the ramekins nearly to the top, then place them in a roasting tray. Pour in boiling water to reach a third of the way up their sides and bake them in the oven for 8 minutes. Remove from the oven and leave to cool for 5 minutes, then gently turn them out (discarding the greaseproof paper) and roll them in the breadcrumbs. (All this can be done up to a day in advance.)

To prepare the salad mixture, top and tail the beans, blanch them for 3 minutes, then plunge them under cold water and dry them. Wash the mushrooms, trim the stalks and cut them into ⅛ inch (3 mm) slices. Sprinkle them with lemon juice to prevent discolouration. Wash and dry the lettuces and mix the vinaigrette. Cut little croûtons (cubes) from the brown bread and bake them in the oven until they are golden.

Put the soufflés, already rolled in breadcrumbs, onto a lightly oiled baking tray, and put them back in the oven for 5 minutes. They will puff up. Meanwhile mix the lettuces, mushrooms, beans and cheese with the vinaigrette and arrange round each plate, together with the croûtons. Sprinkle with the chives, then place the soufflé in the middle of each plate and serve.

TURBOT AND SALMON PAPILLOTE

Papillote de Turbot et Saumon au Poivrons doux

SERVES 6   RAYMOND BLANC

In this dish, the cabbage wrapping is edible and the contents are a delight to the eye – a pink and white sandwich of just-cooked turbot and salmon. The parcels sit on a brilliant red pepper *coulis*.

2 red peppers
1 tablespoon olive oil
12 oz (350 g) fresh salmon fillet, farmed or wild
1 lb 8 oz (700 g) turbot fillet
Juice of ½ lemon
Freshly ground black pepper
1 small bunch fresh dill
12 leaves of white cabbage, boiled for 5 minutes then refreshed under cold water
A few sprigs of chervil (optional)

First make the sauce. Pre-heat the oven to gas mark 4, 350°F (180°C). Cut the red peppers in half, then core, de-seed and dice them. Warm the olive oil in a casserole on top of the stove, and sauté the peppers for 1 minute. Cover the casserole and put it in the oven for 30 minutes or until the peppers are soft. Liquidise the peppers in 1 pint (570 ml) water, and pass them through a sieve to obtain a fine purée. Keep aside.

With a pair of tweezers, pick out any bones left in the fish. Cut 12 2 inch (5 cm) squares of turbot fillet and six 2 inch (5 cm) squares of salmon fillet. Squeeze the lemon juice over each piece and season them with black pepper. Place a sprig of dill on each salmon square and sandwich these between two squares of turbot each.

Pat the cabbage leaves dry with kitchen paper and place each of the fish 'sandwiches' in the middle of a leaf. Wrap the leaf round the fish and cover with another leaf to seal the fish in completely. Tie the parcels up with string to secure the cabbage leaves. Steam them for 3 minutes (see page 22), then remove the pan from the heat and leave it, covered, for another 3 minutes. The salmon should be barely cooked, but warm right through.

To serve, warm the red pepper sauce and place a ladleful on 6 plates. Remove the strings from the parcels and place a parcel in the middle of each plate on top of the coulis and decorate with the chervil, if using. With a sharp knife open the parcel down the middle to show the colours.

FRUIT TERRINE WITH A PURÉE OF MANGO

Terrine de Fruits au Coulis de Mangue

SERVES 6–8   RAYMOND BLANC

This colourful, fresh-tasting dish illustrates the generosity of summer. The dessert is light, inexpensive and easy to make, three more reasons to try it. You can use any other combinations of seasonal fruit – apples, pears and peaches, for instance. Note that it takes 4 hours for the gelatine to set, so begin preparations well in advance of serving.

Selection of fresh fruit – for example: **2 bananas; 4 oz melon; 1 peach or kiwi fruit, peeled;** **4 eating plums; approximately 4 oz (110 g) each of** **raspberries and strawberries; 2 oranges**
5½ leaves of gelatine or ½ oz (10 g) powdered gelatine
10 fl oz (300 ml) orange juice, freshly squeezed **(approximately 8 oranges)**
For the purée:
2 ripe mangoes
4 passion fruit
2 oranges

Cut the bananas into 4 slices lengthways. Cut the melon into little cubes, the peach or kiwi fruit into slices, the plums in half, discarding any stones, and the oranges into segments. Layer these ingredients with the raspberries and strawberries neatly in a dish so that it is three-quarters full.

To make the jelly, soak the gelatine in a little water and put aside. Strain the orange juice into a pan, bring it to the boil and skim the surface to obtain a clear liquid. Add the soaked gelatine and whisk. Cool the liquid jelly and when it is tepid, pour as much over the fruit as is necessary to fill the dish completely. (The liquid should be tepid to absorb the flavour of the fruit.) Refrigerate for at least 4 hours to set the jelly.

For the purée, peel the mangoes and remove the flesh with a knife. Cut the passion fruit in half, scoop out the seeds and flesh and mix these with the juice of the 2 oranges. Pass all the fruit and juice through a fine sieve and refrigerate.

To serve, cut portions of terrine about ¾ inch (2 cm) thick, place them on individual plates and pour the mango and passion fruit purée around each portion.

Menu 2

Menu for 6

Marinade of Little Mackerel
Roast Guinea Fowl with Lime Sauce
Banana Soufflé with Rum

MARINADE OF LITTLE MACKEREL

Marinade de petits Maquereaux de Ligne

SERVES 6   RAYMOND BLANC

We all have childhood souvenirs, and this is one of mine. And what a feast it was – a perfect hors d'oeuvre for a warm lazy summer's day.

This dish also has the advantage of being cheap, its ingredients are easy to find, and it is simple to make. The raw mackerel is steeped overnight in a fragrant marinade.

1 clove garlic
1 small bunch parsley
1 small bunch fresh dill, or 1 teaspoon dried dill
4 sprigs fresh coriander
4 carrots
4 leeks
3 medium-sized onions
2 celery stalks
2 fennel bulbs
2 juniper berries
¼ orange
¼ lemon
6 small, or 3 large, mackerel
1 pint (570 ml) good white wine vinegar
2 fl oz (50 ml) white wine
2 sprigs thyme, or 1 teaspoon dried thyme
1 teaspoon crushed peppercorns
2 tablespoons olive oil

First prepare the marinade. Peel the clove of garlic, and remove the stalks from the parsley, dill and coriander leaves. Peel the carrots and cut them into fine matchstick strips. Discard the outer leaves and coarse tops from the leeks and chop them finely. Peel and slice the onions finely. Use a potato peeler to remove the outer fibres from the celery stalks and fennel bulbs, then cut them into little strips. Crush the juniper berries. Peel the rind from the orange and lemon quarters, cut it into fine strips, then blanch them to remove the bitterness by boiling briefly in water.

If the fish has not been filleted for you, remove the fins, and wash and dry the fish on kitchen paper. Fillet the mackerel by cutting off the head, then, holding your knife horizontally, slice down between the flesh and the bone towards the tail. Turn the fish over and slice off the other fillet. Wash off any traces of blood and dry the fillets.

Pour the wine vinegar, the wine and all the chopped vegetables, herbs and other flavourings into a glass or china bowl, then place the mackerel fillets in the bowl so that they are fully covered. Pour over the olive oil, seal the dish with cling-film and place in the refrigerator for 24 hours. The dish is then ready to be served. Remove the fillets from the marinade, arrange them on a plate, then spoon a little of the marinade over the fish.

ROAST GUINEA FOWL WITH LIME SAUCE

Pintadeau rôti au Citron vert

SERVES 6   RAYMOND BLANC

Guinea fowl deserves to be better known: its flesh is so much more attractive than that of chicken, especially when hung for a few days so that it develops the most delicate scent and becomes tender. The association with lime is a complete success and the flavours will surprise your guests.

2 large or 3 small guinea fowl
1 tablespoon sunflower oil
1 ½ oz (40 g) shallots, finely chopped
2 fl oz (50 ml) red wine vinegar
4 oz (110 g) button mushrooms, sliced
1 small-sized carrot, finely diced
1 sprig thyme
4 fl oz (110 ml) white wine
5 fl oz (150 ml) medium dry Madeira
8 fl oz (110 ml) port
1 pint (570 ml) chicken stock
1 lime
20 small redcurrants
Freshly ground black pepper

Continued overleaf

231

Pre-heat the oven to gas mark 8, 450°F (230°C). Remove the wishbone and any feathers from the guinea fowl. Lightly brush a frying-pan with oil, season the guinea fowl with pepper and sauté for about 3 minutes on all sides until they are brown all over. Transfer to a roasting tin and roast them on their side in the oven for 8 minutes each side. Remove from the oven, cut off the legs and thighs, put them in a small dish and return them to the oven for another 5 minutes. Carve the breast and keep it warm on a serving plate. When the legs and thighs are cooked, transfer them to the serving plate using a slotted spoon. Pour any juices into the roasting tin.

Cut the carcasses into small pieces and sweat them in the roasting tin over a low heat with the roasting juices. Add the shallots and carrots and the wine vinegar, bring to the boil and boil quickly until the liquid has reduced. Once the liquid has almost disappeared add the mushrooms, thyme, port and white wine. Bring to the boil, then reduce the liquid again by almost half. (This removes the acidity and alcohol of the wine but keeps its flavour.) Add the Madeira and chicken stock. Bring to the boil again, remove any scum, then simmer for 10 minutes. Pass the stock through a sieve and reduce it again until you have a light, well-scented sauce.

Peel all the rind from the lime, cut the rind into thin strips and blanch these for 10 minutes in boiling water. Plunge them in cold water, then pat dry. Remove the pith from the lime with a sharp knife, and cut the flesh into segments, reserving the juice.

Remove the skin from the carved guinea fowl and return all the meat to the oven for 2 to 3 minutes so that it is very hot. Taste the sauce, adding no more than a tablespoon of the lime juice to it, then pour some of the sauce around the meat and garnish it with the lime segments, strips of peel and redcurrants. Put the remaining sauce into a sauceboat and hand separately.

BANANA SOUFFLÉ WITH RUM

Soufflé à la Banane et Rhum

SERVES 6   RAYMOND BLANC

A soufflé seems to be, in many people's minds, the ultimate culinary achievement, and they often therefore do not make the attempt for fear of failure. But there is nothing magical about making soufflé, and I intend to try and shatter the old myth so that you can indulge in this delectable, feathery sweet.

The basic lifting power in a soufflé is provided by egg white. When this is beaten, small bubbles of air are introduced which expand during cooking, causing the soufflé to rise. The heat also alters the 'walls' of the bubbles, making them tougher, and this gives the soufflé its texture. Coating the soufflé dish or ramekins with a film of butter and sugar will help the soufflé to rise freely.

Although banana is used for the fruit flavouring here, there are other naturally sweet fruit, such as apples, pears and blackberries, that would suit the recipe. The fruit must be puréed first and then dried out over a high heat. In this version I have used pastry cream to add flavour, to help remove some of the moisture content of the fruit used, and to help to bind the fruit and egg white together for a smoother result.

6 fl oz (175 ml) milk
1 vanilla pod
½ oz (10 g) sugar
1 egg yolk
¾ oz (15 g) plain flour
3 over-ripe bananas
1 fl oz (25 ml) rum
Juice of ½ lemon
Melted butter
Caster sugar
7 egg whites

Pre-heat the oven to gas mark 5, 375°F (190°C). Prepare a pastry cream by simmering the vanilla pod (which should be split to give out all its flavour) in the milk for a few minutes. Mix the sugar and egg yolk together, then add the flour, making sure it is well blended. Pour in the boiling milk gradually, whisking constantly so that you obtain a smooth consistency, then simmer it without boiling for a further 3 minutes. Remove the pod.

Process or liquidise the bananas and mix them into the pastry cream. Then add the rum and half the lemon juice, and transfer the mixture into a large round bowl. Prepare 6 ramekins by brushing the insides with melted butter. Place some caster sugar in each ramekin, and tip it round so that the sugar is evenly distributed over the bottoms and sides.

Put the egg whites into a dry mixing bowl and whisk them at a low speed to start with, then increase the speed gradually until they stiffen. Add the remaining lemon juice. As quickly as possible, mix a quarter of the egg whites into the pastry cream. Then fold in the remaining egg white carefully by lifting and cutting it in with a spatula (do not try to achieve a perfectly homogeneous result). Pour the mixture into the ramekins. Smooth the surface of each soufflé with a knife and, using your thumb, push the mixture away from the sides to help it to rise. Place the soufflés on a baking tray and bake for 12 minutes. Serve immediately.

Menu 3

Menu for 6

Crab and Spinach Parcels
Served with a warm Green Bean Salad
Calves' Sweetbreads with Fresh Herbs and Baby Onions
Iced Soup of Pears and Guava

CRAB AND SPINACH PARCELS

SERVES 6   NICK GILL

Crabs have long been the understudy of the lobster, but this is not always
fair. Their meat can be sweeter and more succulent, and has the contrast
of the white with the dark meat. In this dish the white meat is wrapped up
in spinach leaves, and the dark meat is used to make a creamy sauce. The
bright red, yellow and light green of the peppers make a pretty combination with the dark green spinach parcels.

2 each of small, red, yellow and green peppers
3 fresh crabs
Juice of ½ lemon (or to taste)
Fish or chicken stock (optional)
12 large perfect spinach leaves
1 tablespoon olive oil
Salt, freshly ground black pepper
Chopped fresh chives for garnish

First prepare the peppers. Cut them in half lengthways, and remove the
seeds. Place cut side down under a hot grill for about 8 minutes to blister
the skins. Allow them to cool, then peel off the skin. Slice each pepper into
thin strips, keeping the colours separate, and set them aside.

Remove the meat from the crabs (see page 39). Purée the dark meat in
a blender or food processor, and add a little lemon juice, tasting carefully,
to create a smooth, creamy sauce. If more liquid is needed to obtain the
right consistency, add more lemon juice or a little fish or chicken stock.
Pass the sauce through a fine sieve into a saucepan and keep it warm.

Next, cut out the thick stalk from the base of each spinach leaf. Blanch

234

the leaves for a moment in boiling water, then plunge them immediately into ice-cold water for about 30 seconds, and dry them. Lay the leaves out and place an equal quantity of white crabmeat on each. Fold the sides of the leaves over to make a small parcel, and steam the parcels for about 30 seconds to warm the crab through.

Meanwhile warm up the pepper strips (keeping the colours separate) in the olive oil, adding a little salt and pepper.

To assemble the dish, coat the base of 6 warmed plates with the crab sauce. In the middle of each place a crab parcel and surround it with 3 clusters of the pepper strips in their separate colours. Sprinkle over the chopped chives and serve immediately accompanied by the Green Bean Salad (see below).

GREEN BEAN SALAD

SERVES 6   NICK GILL

| 1 lb (450 g) French beans |
| 1 fl oz (25 ml) sherry vinegar |
| 1 teaspoon Dijon mustard |
| 1 shallot, finely chopped |
| 2 fl oz (50 ml) olive oil |
| 2 fl oz (50 ml) walnut oil |
| Juice of 1 lemon |
| 1 tablespoon fresh tarragon, chopped |

Top and tail the French beans and boil them, fast, for about 5 minutes or until they are just cooked. Meanwhile, combine the remaining ingredients to form a vinaigrette. Drain the beans and put them into a salad bowl. Pour over the vinaigrette immediately and toss the beans until evenly coated.

CALVES' SWEETBREADS WITH FRESH HERBS AND BABY ONIONS

SERVES 6   NICK GILL

Sweetbreads have a delicate flavour and a beautiful creamy texture. Calves' sweetbreads are considered a great delicacy, but lambs' sweetbreads are a close rival. In old recipes sweetbreads are usually braised for about 2 hours, which is far too long and quite unnecessary. This recipe retains the sweetbread's own juices and adds the sweetness of onions, and the subtle taste of fresh herbs. You can also cook sweetbreads very simply by frying them gently in olive oil, with garlic and herbs. Serve this dish with lightly cooked mange-tout peas.

1 lb 8 oz (700 g) calves' or lamb's sweetbreads
1 carrot
1 onion
1 celery stalk
A few parsley stalks
14 oz (400 g) baby onions
4 oz (110 g) lean bacon
6 oz (175 g) button mushrooms
1 tablespoon olive oil
8 fl oz (225 ml) dry white wine
8 fl oz (225 ml) chicken stock
2 oz (50 g) mixed fresh herbs, left whole: eg tarragon, chervil, parsley, basil, chives, thyme
1 bay leaf
Salt, freshly ground black pepper

First prepare the sweetbreads. Put them in a pan and cover them with cold water. Roughly chop the carrot, onion and celery with the parsley stalks and add them to the pan. Bring the sweetbreads to the boil, then immediately take them off the heat. Let the sweetbreads cool in the water. Remove the membrane, then cut them into thick diagonal slices.

To skin the baby onions, plunge them into boiling water for a minute and then put them into cold water. Cut off their tops and roots and peel

Continued overleaf

OPPOSITE: FROM TOP TO BOTTOM
Calves' Sweetbreads with Fresh Herbs and Baby Onions (*page 236*)
Crab and Spinach Parcels (*page 234*)
Green Bean Salad (*page 235*)
Summer Berries and Sabayon (*page 230*)

away the skin. Remove the rind from the bacon and dice it. Wipe and slice the mushrooms. Put the oil into a heated, shallow casserole and fry the onions and bacon for a few minutes. Add the mushrooms and continue cooking for a minute or two until they soften. Then add the sweetbreads, white wine, stock, whole herbs (reserving some for garnish), bay leaf, salt and pepper and simmer them gently for 10 minutes. Sprinkle the dish with the remaining whole herbs and serve.

ICED SOUP OF PEARS AND GUAVAS

SERVES 6   NICK GILL

This is a light and refreshing end to the meal. The fruit must be really ripe, so that the soup is sweet enough. You could substitute quince for the guavas, or even rhubarb.

6 ripe pears
4 guavas
A little Cointreau
1 tablespoon sugar
1 tablespoon lemon juice
2 tablespoons fresh orange juice (optional)

Peel and core the pears, and peel the guavas. Pick out the best pear and guava, remove the pips from the guava, and slice both fruits neatly into small dice for 'croûtons'. Marinate the dice in Cointreau.

Now roughly chop the rest of the fruit and cook it, covered, in the sugar, lemon juice and 4 tablespoons of water for about 10 minutes or until the fruit is soft. Purée the cooked fruit in a blender or food processor, adding the orange juice as necessary to obtain a smooth creamy consistency. Push the purée through a fine sieve. The soup should now have the consistency of double cream, just coating the back of a spoon. If it is too thick, thin it down with fresh orange juice. Refrigerate the soup for at least 2 hours to make sure it is well chilled.

Pour the soup into the soup plates and sprinkle generously with the reserved fruit 'croûtons' and a splash of Cointreau.

OPPOSITE: FROM BOTTOM TO TOP
Salmon and Scallop Salad (*page 246*)
Fillet of Lamb Baked in a Rosemary-scented Salt Crust (*page 248*)
Summer Fruit Parcels (*page 249*)

Menu 4

Menu for 6

Sliced Pigeon Breast Salad
Hot Pot of the Sea
Young Vegetables in Fresh Herb Broth
Summer Berries and Sabayon

SLICED PIGEON BREAST SALAD

SERVES 6   NICK GILL

This is a most delicious first course for a party, served with hot crusty bread. The salad combines the crispness and freshness of leaves with warm pink pigeon breast. The walnut sauce which covers the salad contains the essentials in good cooking: a perfect balance between the rich pigeon juices, the sharp vinegar and the sweet redcurrant jelly. Try to find young wood pigeons or squabs, preferably still in feather. A good substitute would be a brace of fresh quail.

12 oz (350 g) mixed salad (a selection of the following: lettuce, baby spinach, corn salad, radicchio, chicory, batavia frisée, red oakleaf lettuce, dandelion leaves)
3 wood pigeons
1 carrot
1 celery stalk
2 cloves
1 onion, peeled
1 tablespoon sunflower oil
2 fl oz (50 ml) white wine
2 cloves garlic
1 bay leaf
1 sprig fresh thyme, or ½ teaspoon dried thyme
Up to 1 pint (570 ml) chicken or veal stock (optional)
3 shallots
3 fl oz (75 ml) dry sherry
1 fl oz (25 ml) white wine vinegar
1–2 teaspoons (5–10 ml) redcurrant jelly
2 tablespoons walnut oil, plus extra for frying
Salt, freshly ground black pepper
1 oz (25 g) pine-nuts
Sprigs of flat-leafed parsley

Wash and dry the salads well, then cover and refrigerate them.

Remove the breasts from the pigeons by sliding a sharp knife down either side of the breastbone; set these aside. Remove and discard all the innards, then roughly chop the carcasses. Roughly chop the carrot and the celery. Stick the 2 cloves into the peeled onion. Heat the oil in a large saucepan, and fry the vegetables and the chopped carcasses for 2 minutes. Add the white wine, garlic, bay leaf and most of the thyme, and just cover with chicken or veal stock, or water. Cover and simmer gently for 2 hours.

Strain the stock into a clean saucepan, pressing the solids with a spoon to extract all the juices. Bring the stock to a simmer, skimming off any impurities with a ladle, then bring to the boil. Boil the stock fast for about 30 minutes or until it has reduced to about a cupful, and has a syrupy consistency. Meanwhile chop the shallots very finely, and put them in a saucepan, together with the sherry and the vinegar. Boil them until the acidic taste of the vinegar has almost disappeared and the liquid has reduced by half. Add the reduced stock and a little redcurrant jelly to taste, then whisk in the walnut oil.

On a serving plate, build up the different salad leaves to make a pretty mound. Put a little walnut oil into a frying-pan. Season the pigeon breasts with salt, pepper and the reserved thyme and fry the breasts very gently for about 4 minutes on each side. They should still be pink inside. Using a sharp knife, slice the pigeon breasts as thinly as possible. You should be able to cut 15 slices in all.

Sprinkle the salad with pine-nuts and then carefully arrange the slices of pigeon breast over the top of the salad. Spoon over the sauce to coat both the salad and the pigeon.

Finally plant sprigs of flat-leaved parsley here and there to heighten the salad still further. Serve immediately.

HOT POT OF THE SEA

SERVES 6   NICK GILL

This is a light, delicate way of presenting a variety of fish by steaming and serving them in a mosaic pattern on the plate. Try to include white and pink fish, and some shellfish in your selection, and make sure that all the fish is really fresh (see page 38).

To serve with the fish, try to find fresh samphire, a marshland and sea plant which has a fresh, slightly salty crispness. If you cannot obtain it, leeks would be a good substitute in the winter, or French beans in the summer.

2 lb (900 g) skinned and filleted fish and prepared shellfish, preferably 5 of the following: John Dorey, monkfish, turbot, brill, scallops, Dublin Bay prawns, sole, red mullet, sea bass, grey mullet, salmon, sea trout (keep the trimmings)
1 onion
1 carrot
1 celery stalk
1 glass white wine
A few parsley stalks
A sprig of thyme
1 bay leaf
5 peppercorns
Salt, freshly ground black pepper
12 oz (350 g) samphire, or 1 lb (450 g) leeks or French beans
1 tablespoon fresh chervil or tarragon, chopped
2 shallots
1 dessertspoon olive oil
½ glass dry vermouth
1–2 tablespoons olive or walnut oil
Parsley or chervil sprigs for garnish

Put all the fish trimmings into a saucepan. Roughly chop the onion, carrot and celery. Add these to the saucepan, together with the white wine, and sweat for 5 minutes with the lid on. Pour in enough cold water to cover them, and add the parsley stalks, herbs and peppercorns. Bring this to the boil and skim off any impurities using a spoon. Reduce the heat and simmer the stock gently for 20 minutes, then strain through a fine sieve.

Meanwhile slice the fish with a sharp knife into neat, bite-sized pieces all of uniform thickness. Season them lightly with salt and pepper and set aside. If you are using leeks, remove any tough leaves, wash them thoroughly and with a very sharp knife cut them into thin strips (julienne) about 3 inches (7·5 cm) long. If you are using beans, top and tail them and cut them into 3 inch (7.5 cm) lengths.

Chop the shallots very finely and sweat them briefly in the olive oil. Add the vermouth and boil hard until it is almost dry, then add the fish stock and boil hard again until the stock has reduced to about a cupful and has a syrupy texture. Whisk in the herbs and olive or walnut oil and keep the sauce warm.

Place all the pieces of fish in a steamer (see page 22) with the samphire, leeks or beans. Steam them quickly for about 1–2 minutes or until the fish is just cooked.

To serve, pour a little sauce onto each warmed plate. Arrange the fish on top of this with the vegetables. Finally add little sprigs of chervil or parsley and serve immediately.

YOUNG VEGETABLES IN FRESH HERB BROTH

SERVES 6   NICK GILL

Vegetables are too often treated as second-class citizens in the culinary world, and merely as an accompaniment to meat or fish. In this menu they have been elevated to a course all of their own.

Here, baby vegetables are cooked in a flavoured broth rather than in water. They take on a succulence from the chicken stock and herbs, and the accompanying sauce has a light creamy texture.

It is important that time is taken to prepare each of the vegetables carefully and to cut them into uniform shapes for equal cooking. The cooking time itself is only a few minutes.

1 lb 4 oz (550 g) of 6 young vegetables, half root, half green, from the following: carrots, leeks, courgettes, French beans, mange-tout peas, cauliflower, broccoli, asparagus, broad beans, peas, parsnips, swedes, beetroot, cucumber
1 lb (450 g) Jerusalem artichokes
1 shallot
2 pints (1·1 litres) strong chicken stock
Salt, freshly ground black pepper
1 lb (450 g) spinach
Small bunch of chervil
Few sprigs of tarragon
Small bunch of parsley
Small bunch of chives

Prepare the baby vegetables. Wash, peel and trim them as necessary, cut them into uniform pieces and set aside.

Next peel and roughly chop the artichokes and shallot, and cook them in just enough chicken stock to cover them, adding some salt and pepper. Then purée them in a food processor or blender, gradually adding a little more stock until the mixture is smooth and creamy. Remove the stalks from the spinach, wash the leaves, and cook them in a heavy-bottomed pan without water for about 2 minutes until they have wilted. Drain and purée the spinach, add it to the artichokes and stir well. The consistency should be just thick enough to coat the back of a spoon; if the sauce is too thick, add a little more chicken stock. Keep the sauce warm.

Put the remaining stock into a large pan and add most of the whole herbs, reserving some for garnish. Bring the stock to the boil. Now cook the vegetables in the stock. The easiest way to do this is to suspend a colander in the stock and place the vegetables in the colander. The colander should sit just low enough in the stock for the liquid to cover the vegetables. Each vegetable should be cooked *al dente* – with a 'bite' to it – so put the ones which need the longest cooking time in first, and remove them and keep them warm if necessary while the others finish cooking. You may need to top up the stock during this process. Once the vegetables are cooked, strain off the broth and use it for a soup or casserole.

To assemble the dish, coat the base of each plate with the artichoke and spinach sauce. Place the vegetables on top, each type in a small cluster, garnish them with the remaining fresh herbs, and serve.

SUMMER BERRIES AND SABAYON

SERVES 6   NICK GILL

Summer berries are almost always served with thick double cream, which is delicious but heavy at the end of a meal and not terribly good for you. Instead, the cream I have devised here is far lighter and has a delicate flavour of oranges. The fruit is served inside light, airy baskets made from filo pastry, which can be bought ready-made in Greek shops or delicatessens. The filo pastry baskets can be made a few days in advance, and kept in an airtight tin.

1 lb (450 g) filo pastry
8 oz (225 g) fresh or frozen raspberries
Juice and rind of 2 oranges (blood oranges if possible)
A little caster sugar
3 egg yolks
A dash of orange liqueur
12 oz (350 g) of 2 or 3 types of ripe soft fruit from the following: strawberries, raspberries, blackberries, redcurrants, loganberries, blackcurrants, blueberries
Sprigs of fresh mint

Pre-heat the oven to gas mark 5, 375°F (190°C). Cut the filo pastry into 18 squares of approximately 4 × 4 inches (10 cm). Very lightly grease the outside of 6 upturned dariole moulds or ovenproof cups, then carefully drape 3 leaves over each to form a shape similar to an open lily; do not press them down towards the side of the cup, otherwise they will stick to it. *Note:* The base of the moulds must be flat so that the pastry cases will sit properly on a plate when inverted.) Bake them on their moulds in the oven for 10–12 minutes or until they are crisp and golden brown. Keep a careful eye on them to ensure they do not burn. Allow them to cool, then remove them carefully from the moulds and turn them onto their bases. Purée the raspberries in a blender or food processor, then sieve the purée to remove the pips. Set this sauce aside.

To make the sabayon, bring the orange juice and zest to the boil, then remove it from the heat immediately. Add the egg yolks and whisk vigorously until the mixture is creamy. Add a dash of orange liqueur with a little caster sugar to taste. Place the mixture in a pudding basin. Set over a pan of hot water over a low heat and keep whisking until the mixture has thickened. Let it cool completely.

No more than 15 minutes before serving (or the pastry will go soggy), fill each pastry case with the sabayon and sprinkle generously with the different berries. Put a sprig of fresh mint on the top. Coat the base of 6 large plates with raspberry sauce and place a pastry basket in the middle of each. Arrange little clusters of berries around each basket in the sauce, then serve.

Menu 5

Menu for 6

Salmon and Scallop Salad
Fillets of Lamb Baked in a Rosemary-scented Salt Crust
Summer Fruit Parcels

SALMON AND SCALLOP SALAD

*Salade de Coquilles St Jacques et
Saumon sauvage mariné à l'Aneth*

SERVES 6   RAYMOND BLANC

This is a stunning way to start a meal, with a delicious complexity of tastes and textures. The success of any dish depends on the quality of the ingredients, so although it is possible to substitute farmed salmon for wild salmon, the final taste will, of course, be affected, as it would if you used frozen scallops instead of fresh.

Although the number of ingredients may seem high, the dish itself does not represent a lot of work, as there is virtually no 'cooking' involved. All the preparation can be done beforehand and the dish assembled at the last minute. The salmon is first 'cured' in a salt, dill, lemon rind and sugar mixture for about 16 hours.

1 lemon
10 oz (275 g) fillet of wild salmon
Salt, freshly ground black pepper
2 teaspoons sugar
1 bunch fresh dill, finely chopped, or 1 teaspoon dried dill
1 small-sized carrot
¼ celery stalk
¼ large fennel bulb
2 shallots
1 tomato
4 handfuls mixed salad leaves (such as radicchio, lettuce, batavia, frilly endive)
6 fresh scallops with their corals
Olive oil for frying
12 leaves fresh coriander, finely chopped

For vinaigrette:
2 fl oz (50 ml) olive oil
1 fl oz (25 ml) sunflower oil
Salt, freshly ground black pepper
3 tablespoons white wine vinegar
Juice of ¼ lemon

First pare 3 strips of rind from the lemon (top to bottom). Squeeze the juice from the lemon and reserve. Blanch the strips for 3 minutes in boiling water, then plunge them into cold water. Pat them dry and slice them finely into threads. Set aside a few strips for decoration.

Spread a large sheet of cling-film on your work surface. Put the salmon fillet in the middle. Using tweezers, carefully remove any bones left in the fish. Mix 2 teaspoons of salt, the sugar, the dill and freshly ground pepper and scatter this over the surface of the fish. Then put the remaining lemon strips on the fish. Wrap it tightly in the cling-film and place it in the refrigerator to marinate for 16 hours.

Peel the carrots, celery stalk and fennel bulb, and cut them into thin strips of ⅛ inch (3 mm) thick. Chop the shallots finely. Plunge the tomatoes into boiling water for 5 seconds, then drain, cool and skin them. Remove the seeds and cube the flesh. Mix all the prepared vegetables together. Remove any wilted leaves from the salads and cut out the cores. Rinse and dry the salads and put them in the refrigerator, together with the vegetables. To make the vinaigrette, whisk together the olive oil, sunflower oil, salt, pepper, white wine vinegar and the juice of ¼ lemon.

Remove the salmon from the refrigerator and wash off the marinade under cold running water. Pat the fish dry with kitchen paper and cut 3 thin slices per person diagonally through the flesh. Take 6 dinner plates and arrange the slices around the edge of each plate. Brush each slice with the reserved lemon juice. Mix half the vinaigrette with the chopped vegetables, and place 3 little mounds between the salmon slices. Mix the remaining vinaigrette with the salad leaves and place a little mound of salad in the middle of each plate.

Separate the corals from the scallops and poach the corals for 1 minute. Plunge them into cold water, then dry and cut, into fine slices. Brush a non-stick pan with olive oil and sauté the coral slices over a high heat for 1 minute, then put them aside in a small dish. Cut each scallop into 4 slices. Heat the pan again and sear the scallops for about 10 seconds on each side. Remove them from the heat, add a tablespoon of lemon juice and the coriander leaves and mix gently. Place 4 tepid scallop slices on each plate on top of the salads. Give 2 turns of the pepper mill and scatter the reserved lemon zests on top. Garnish with the coral and serve.

FILLETS OF LAMB BAKED IN A ROSEMARY-SCENTED SALT CRUST

Filet d'Agneau de Lait rôti en Croûte de Sel

SERVES 6   RAYMOND BLANC

A fillet of tender, new-season lamb wrapped and cooked in a salt paste scented with rosemary is the perfect way to preserve and intensify its flavours, and the tenderness of the meat will surprise you. Try to buy a loin of milk-fed English lamb, hung for 8 or 9 days so that the meat is well flavoured and tender. The salt paste is not meant to be eaten, so don't be alarmed by the amount of salt. It simply hardens the crust, keeps the lamb succulent and allows the rosemary to flavour it. Also, the presentation will puzzle and charm your guests. The ideal accompaniment for this dish is ratatouille.

1 loin of lamb, boned, with bones reserved and broken into small pieces (ask your butcher to do this for you)
12 oz (350 g) plain flour
6 oz (175 g) salt
3 egg whites
1 tablespoon dried rosemary, powdered in a grinder
1 dessertspoon olive oil, plus extra for frying
1 onion, thinly sliced
1 large clove garlic, cut in half
2 sprigs thyme
7 sprigs rosemary
6 spinach leaves
Small bunch of fresh mixed herbs for garnish

Remove any remaining nerves or fibres from the lamb and set it aside.

To make the salt paste, put the flour and salt in an electric mixer and mix them slowly. Gradually add 4½ fl oz (130 ml) water, then the egg whites and powdered rosemary. The paste should be quite firm; if it is too wet, add a little flour. Wrap in cling-film and let it relax for 1–2 hours.

Meanwhile, make the sauce. Heat the olive oil and when it is very hot add the broken lamb bones and brown them lightly. Add the onion, garlic, thyme, and 1 sprig of rosemary and sweat them for 5 minutes. Add 1 pint (570 ml) cold water and bring it to the boil, skimming off any impurities. Simmer for 20 minutes, then pass the liquid through a fine sieve and boil it fast to reduce it by two thirds, until it is a brown-coloured, herb-scented juice. Season with pepper and keep it warm.

Pre-heat the oven to its maximum setting. Divide the salt paste into 6 equal portions, then roll each out into a rectangle ¼ inch (5 mm) thick.

Cut the filleted lamb into 6 equal pieces and fry these in very hot olive oil for 2 minutes or until they are golden all over. Blanch the spinach leaves in boiling water for a few seconds, then squeeze all the water out of them and pat them completely dry. When the lamb and spinach are cool, wrap up each fillet of lamb in a piece of spinach, then enclose each piece in a salt paste rectangle, together with a little sprig of rosemary, brushing the outer edges with water to help seal the parcels. Place them on a baking tray brushed with olive oil and bake in the oven for only 8 minutes, then remove them from the oven and rest them for 5 minutes. This may seem a very short cooking time, but lamb in a crust cooks very quickly.

To serve, place the 6 parcels on a serving dish covered with a white napkin. Garnish with a bunch of mixed herbs and present the dish to your guests. The golden salt crust will look so pretty and so mysterious. On a cutting board cut through the paste and remove the fillets (discarding the crust and the now-salty spinach leaves). Place each fillet on a dinner plate, pouring the sauce around it, and enjoy the enticing aroma of meat and herbs.

SUMMER FRUIT PARCELS

Papillote de Fruits d'Eté

SERVES 6   RAYMOND BLANC

This is a dessert of fresh summer fruit resting on a purée of melon and peach, scented with bitter almond essence and a vanilla pod, wrapped in a foil parcel and baked briefly. It is absolutely essential for the fruit to be at a peak of ripeness for each piece to cook equally. If you cannot find the fruit listed below, feel free to use other ripe fruits. However, you should avoid acidic fruit such as pineapple. Place each parcel or *papillote* on a large plate and let your guests have the pleasure of opening them.

For the fruit purée:
¼ melon, about 7 oz (200 g)
4 peaches
2 apricots
Dash of bitter almond essence
2 vanilla pods

Continued overleaf

For the parcels:
2 bananas
1 orange
8 greengages
8 Victoria plums
24 raspberries
1 pear
Fresh mint leaves
2 fl oz (50 ml) Grand Marnier (optional)
Oil for brushing

Pre-heat the oven to its highest setting. Prepare the fruit purée. Cube the melon flesh; halve and stone the peaches and apricots, and cut the flesh into cubes. Put the fruit in a small saucepan, add 4 fl oz (110 ml) of water, a dash of almond essence and 2 split vanilla pods. Cover and simmer the fruit for 10 minutes or until a light purée is formed; if it is too thick, add more water. Remove the vanilla pods, wash and set them aside. Liquidise the purée and then, if you have time, pass the purée through a fine sieve. You should have about 11 fl oz (325 ml) purée.

Prepare the remaining fruit. Make sure you use a stainless steel knife to prevent the fruit from discolouring. Peel the bananas, cut them lengthways and then in half. Peel and cut the pith off the orange, then remove the segments. Cut the greengages in 2, remove the stones and keep aside. Do the same with the Victoria plums. Remove any stalks from the raspberries. Peel the pear, cut it in half, remove the core and cut the flesh into 8.

Cut 6 sheets of foil each 14 inches (35 cm) square, checking them carefully to ensure there are no holes in them. Place 3 tablespoons of purée on each piece of foil and arrange the fruit attractively on top. Add ½ vanilla pod per papillote and 2 or 3 little mint leaves. A dash of Grand Marnier is a delicious addition. Fold up the edges of the foil very carefully to seal the papillotes completely. Place them on oiled baking trays very carefully and bake in the oven for 7 minutes. Serve immediately on individual plates.

CELEBRATIONS

Birthday parties, weddings, christenings, housewarmings
. . . they all should be delightful occasions for both hosts
and guests. Sometimes, however, parties can also be a
cook's nightmare. Will there be enough food? How can
you provide for people whose tastes might be conservative
as well as for those who might expect something a little
more adventurous? Some people may be vegetarians and
may scan your food apprehensively, hoping there will be
something they can eat. Usually, food has to be eaten
standing up or, at best, with plates balanced on laps, so it
must be easy to eat with a fork or just using fingers.

We have tried to anticipate many of these difficulties
in this section. Most of the food is cold and can be
prepared well in advance. The quantities given are correct
for a buffet where there are 20 guests and where several
dishes will be served together.

Use this section to plan a menu which will have
between two and four contrasting main dishes together
with a range of salads and two puddings. It is always a
good idea to serve a selection of excellent breads and fresh
fruit at a buffet, perhaps with a bowl of fresh soft cheese on
the side.

SPINACH ROULADE WITH FRESH TOMATO SAUCE

SERVES 20 (SEE PAGE 251)   LYN HALL

This fresh, green roulade, with its delicate tracing of white filling and a rich red sauce, has a gentle flavour and soft texture, making it easy to eat with a fork. The sauce is slightly sweet which contrasts nicely with the spicier dishes in this section. Easy to make well in advance and simple to slice into dainty ovals, the roulade would also suit a late supper after the theatre, or a picnic. It can be served hot or cold.

The stuffing (for 2 roulades):
1 fl oz (25 ml) safflower oil
6 oz (175 g) shallots, finely chopped
12 oz (350 g) fromage blanc (see page 34)
A dash of lemon juice
Nutmeg, freshly grated
Salt, freshly ground black pepper
The roulades
1 lb 10 oz (760 g) spinach, with stalks removed
4 egg yolks
4 tablespoons Parmesan cheese, freshly grated
Salt, freshly ground black pepper
8 egg whites
Nutmeg, freshly grated

Pre-heat the oven to gas mark 5, 375°F (190°C).

To make the stuffing, heat a non-stick pan and pour in the oil. Add the shallots and cook them gently; do not allow them to colour. When the shallots are transparent, remove the pan from the heat, drain off the oil and allow the shallots to cool a little, then add the fromage blanc. Season with lemon juice, plenty of freshly grated nutmeg, and salt and black pepper. Put on one side.

To make the roulades, blanch the spinach (see page 15) and squeeze out all the liquid, either in a clean tea towel or between 2 plates. Place the spinach in a food processor, together with the egg yolks, Parmesan cheese, salt and pepper. Have ready 2 straight-sided Swiss roll tins 10 × 13 inches (25 × 33 cm) lined with cling-film. Press the film into the corners firmly.

Beat the egg whites until they are stiff, then fold them into the spinach mixture gently, using a balloon whisk. Check the seasoning again, and stir in a generous grating of nutmeg.

Pour the mixture into the tins, smooth it level with a palette knife to the depth of just over ½ inch (1 cm), then place them in the oven. Bake the roulades for 12 minutes or until they are set and springy, then allow them to cool for 5 minutes on the trays. Spread one with half the stuffing. Take hold of the cling-film along the longer side of the roulade, and roll it up pulling away the cling-film as you do so. Repeat with the second roulade. To serve, cut the roulades into diagonal slices and hand the tomato sauce separately.

TOMATO SAUCE

MAKES 1 PINT 10 FL OZ (850 ML)   LYN HALL

2 lb (900 g) ripe tomatoes
2 small red peppers
2 medium-sized onions
8 celery leaves
6 fl oz (175 ml) red wine
2 oz (50 g) brown sugar
2 fl oz (50 ml) red wine vinegar
2 teaspoons each of fresh mixed herbs (eg parsley, marjoram, basil), chopped, or 2 teaspoons dried mixed herbs
2 teaspoons dried oregano
2 sprigs of thyme, or a pinch of dried thyme
Salt, freshly ground black pepper

Peel, de-seed and chop the tomatoes. Core and de-seed the red peppers and chop them. Roughly chop the onions and celery leaves. Put all these vegetables into a saucepan, then add the remaining ingredients. Bring the sauce to the boil, then immediately reduce the heat. Cover the pan, and simmer the sauce for 30 minutes, then liquidise it in a blender or food processor. Sieving it after this will produce a smoother texture. You could also boil the sauce down a little to produce a thicker sauce with more concentrated flavour.

CHICKEN AND SPINACH TERRINE WITH WATERCRESS SAUCE

SERVES 20 (SEE PAGE 251)   CAROLINE WALDEGRAVE

This is an exceptionally simple dish which looks beautiful. It is fairly extravagant in that it only uses chicken breasts. Most supermarkets do sell packets of chicken breasts, or you could use the breast meat from four whole chickens and make a stir-fried dish with the remaining brown meat. Try using the yellow corn-fed chickens – they have a truly excellent flavour. You will need two 2 lb (900 g) loaf tins or terrines for baking; the lemony watercress sauce should be made at the last minute.

8 very large chicken breasts
4 lb (1·8 kg) fresh spinach
2 bunches fresh tarragon, or 2 teaspoons dried tarragon
Oil for greasing
Salt, freshly ground black pepper
4 fl oz (110 ml) chicken stock
Nutmeg
2 bunches of watercress for garnish

Pre-heat the oven to gas mark 4, 350°F (180°C).

Remove the skin and bones from the chicken breasts and cut them horizontally into several paper-thin slices. Remove the stalks from the spinach, wash the leaves thoroughly and put them in a pan without water. Cover and cook gently, shaking the pan frequently, for about 2 minutes or until the spinach has wilted. Drain it well by squeezing it between two plates. Turn it onto a board and chop it roughly. Chop the fresh tarragon roughly, if using.

Lightly oil the loaf tins. Spread a layer of spinach, then tarragon, then chicken breast in each tin, seasoning as you go. Repeat until you have almost filled the tins or terrines. You should end up with a layer of spinach on the top. Pour in a little chicken stock. Cover each tin with a piece of

damp greaseproof paper. (Do not use tin foil as it can corrode on contact with the spinach and is in any case much more expensive than greaseproof paper.) Half-fill a roasting tin with hot water, place the loaf tins in this and bake for 1 hour. Remove from the roasting pan and carefully pour away the juices (save them for soup). Refrigerate with a weight on top before turning them out.

To serve, slice thinly and garnish with watercress. Hand the watercress sauce separately.

WATERCRESS SAUCE

CAROLINE WALDEGRAVE

2 bunches of watercress

14 oz (400 g) low-fat natural yoghurt

Juice of 1 lemon

2 cloves garlic

Salt, freshly ground black pepper

Bring a pan of water to the boil, add the watercress and let it cook for 1 minute. Drain the watercress, plunge it into cold water, drain it again and pat it dry. Now process or liquidise the watercress, together with all the other ingredients, to produce a green speckled sauce. It will retain its bright green colour for about an hour.

OPPOSITE: FROM TOP TO BOTTOM
Breakfast Nog (*page 187*)
The Alternative Breakfast (*page 186*)
Wholemeal Toast with Dried Fruit Conserves (*page 189*)
Wholemeal Pancakes with Low-fat Cheese and Dried Fruit Conserve (*page 188*)

STUFFED SEA BASS IN BLACK BEAN SAUCE

SERVES 20 (SEE PAGE 251)   LYN HALL

Sea bass is expensive, but the flavour is special. This recipe is adapted from one of my favourite Chinese dishes, with its earthy flavour redolent of fermented black beans, garlic and ginger, and lends itself well to a buffet. The sea bass is stuffed with brown rice and sesame seeds and baked in the oven. You can prepare the fish in the morning and slip it into the oven just before serving; the sauce and stuffing improve in flavour if prepared in advance.

2 sea bass, weighing 4 lb (1·8 kg) each
1 lemon
8 tablespoons fermented black beans
4½ oz (120 g) brown rice
22 spring onions
3 tablespoons safflower oil
4 large cloves garlic, coarsely chopped
3 tablespoons ginger, coarsely chopped
4 tablespoons dark soy sauce
4 tablespoons dry sherry
1 dessertspoon sugar
2 dessertspoons cornflour
3 dessertspoons sesame seed oil (approximately)
6 shallots
1 oz (25 g) fresh chives
4 tablespoons sesame seed oil, plus extra for greasing
4 tablespoons toasted sesame seeds

Have the fishmonger scale, gut and bone the sea bass, but leave the heads and tails on. Cut the lemon in half, and rub the cavities of the fish with it.

Pre-heat the oven to gas mark 2, 300°F (150°C).

For the stuffing and sauce, soak the black beans for at least 30 minutes, then rinse them thoroughly under the tap in a sieve, or else wash them in several changes of water. (Fermented black beans are very salty, so it is important to do this thoroughly.) Chop them coarsely and set aside. Cook the brown rice (see page 59).

Use 20 of the spring onions to make 'tassels' for the garnish, reserving the other 2 for the sauce. To do this, chop off the ends of the green tops and slice off the roots. Carefully make cuts at narrow intervals vertically down both ends of the prepared onions with the point of a sharp knife. Put them

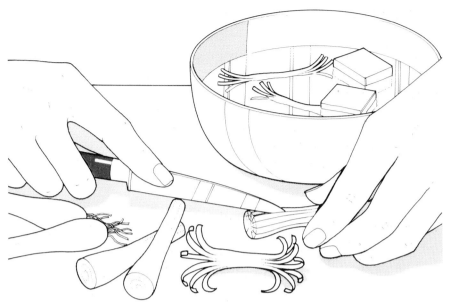

into a bowl of ice-cold water. They will open out like tassels (see illustration).

Make the sauce before you cook the fish. Chop the 2 reserved spring onions finely. Heat a large frying-pan, wok or sauté pan until very hot and then add the safflower oil. When the oil is hot add the garlic, 5 tablespoons of the black beans, the ginger and the chopped spring onions. Stir and toss to bring out the flavours. Mix the soy sauce, dry sherry, sugar and 16 fl oz (450 ml) water together, and stir gently to dissolve the sugar. Add all this liquid to the pan, bring it to the boil, then cover and simmer for 15 minutes. Mix the cornflour with the 3 dessertspoons of sesame oil and 4 tablespoons of water, and give it a good stir, scraping round the base of the bowl. Add this to the sauce, whisking well, until the sauce is thick and smooth. Set on one side.

Now make the stuffing. Finely chop the shallots and chives. Heat the 4 tablespoons of sesame oil in a frying-pan, and gently fry the shallots until they are transparent, but not coloured. Mix the cooked rice, the chives and shallots, the sesame seeds and the remaining black beans. Divide the stuffing into two, and stuff the cavities of the fish. Pin the sides of the fish together with small skewers or toothpicks to secure the stuffing. Do not use too much stuffing, or it may swell and split the flesh of the fish during cooking. Alternatively, you can sew the sides together using stout thread.

Brush some Bakewell paper with a little sesame oil, and wrap each fish up loosely. Place the fish in the oven and bake for 30 minutes.

To serve, place the fish on a serving dish, re-heat the sauce and pour it over the fish. Garnish with the spring onion tassels.

BONED SALMON WITH TOMATOES

SERVES 20 (SEE PAGE 251)   CAROLINE WALDEGRAVE

I am very fond of salmon (or salmon trout depending on the state of my purse) but at a buffet, bones are rather a bore. In this recipe the fish is boned after cooking in order to make it easier both to serve and to eat. A fish kettle makes the cooking easier (they can be hired from small catering companies).

If you do not possess a large fish kettle or large oven casserole, the fish can be wrapped in tin foil with lots of lemon, onions, parsley and bay leaves and baked at a low temperature, gas mark 2, 300°F (150°C), for 1 hour. The advantage of cooking fish in a fish kettle is that you get a wonderfully moist and tender result.

4 lb 8 oz (2 kg) salmon or salmon trout, cleaned
1 onion
1 bay leaf
1 parsley stalk
6 peppercorns
5 fl oz (150 ml) white wine vinegar
For the stuffing:
2 onions
20 medium-sized tomatoes
2 tablespoons olive oil
Freshly ground black pepper
1 teaspoon fresh thyme leaves
For the garnish:
1 cucumber
2 lemons, cut into wedges
Bunch of watercress

Make sure that the salmon has been well cleaned by your fishmonger. If not, run it under the cold tap and scrape along the backbone to remove any remaining blood which would otherwise give the fish a bitter flavour. Slice the onion and put it in a large fish kettle with the bay leaf, bruised parsley stalk, peppercorns and vinegar. Lay the salmon flat in the bottom of the kettle and pour in enough water to cover it. Bring it slowly to the boil, reduce the heat and poach for 2 minutes, then turn off the heat. The idea is that the fish should cook in the cooling *court bouillon* (the well flavoured liquid surrounding the fish). Both should become cold at about the same time. Check the fish every so often to make sure that it is not overcooking.

The salmon is cooked when the dorsal fin (the large fin in the middle of the backbone) pulls out easily, the skin lifts off in large pieces and the flesh looks opaque rather than glossy. While the salmon cooks, prepare the tomato stuffing. Chop the onions finely and peel, de-seed and quarter the tomatoes. Cook the onions in the oil for 3 minutes. Add the tomatoes and cook for a further 25 minutes or until it is a fairly thick purée. Stir every so often to prevent it sticking. Season with freshly ground black pepper and allow to cool. Stir in the fresh thyme.

When the salmon is cold, skin it, leaving the head and tail intact. Carefully remove the 2 top fillets and lift off the backbone. Sandwich the fillets back in place with some of the thick tomato purée.

Peel the cucumber along its length and cut the peel into fine strips, each about 10 inches (25 cm) long. Blanch the strips in boiling water for 1 minute. Refresh (to prevent further cooking and to set the colour) by placing them in a colander and allowing them to cool under running cold water. Drain well on absorbent paper.

Garnish the salmon with a lattice work of cucumber skin, lemon wedges and a bunch of watercress. If there is any tomato stuffing left over it can be thinned to the consistency of a sauce with a little chicken or fish stock and served as an accompaniment.

SEA TROUT WRAPPED IN LETTUCE

Truite en Chemise

SERVES 20 (SEE PAGE 251)   CHRISTOPHE BUEY

This sea trout looks beautiful on a buffet with its lettuce 'shirt' on. It is delicious cold. In France, we like to keep the head of the fish on and we put a little parsley or a piece of black olive in place of the eye. If you decide to keep the head on, put a little oil all over it before cooking to prevent it from drying up and sticking to the foil.

3 sea trout, salmon or sea bass, weighing 2 lb (900 g) each
Salt
4 large lettuces
3 lb (1·4 kg) spinach
8 oz (225 g) sorrel
8 oz (225 g) fresh mixed herbs (eg parsley, chervil, tarragon), chopped, or 1 tablespoon dried mixed herbs
4 oz (110 g) wholemeal breadcrumbs
4 eggs
4 fl oz (110 ml) dry vermouth
Oil for greasing
8 fl oz (225 ml) dry white wine
4 lemons, sliced
Parsley and olives for garnish

Ask your fishmonger to bone the fish completely, or do it yourself if you have time.

Pre-heat the oven to gas mark 6, 400°F (200°C). Scale the fish very carefully as the skin itself will be eaten (see page 00). Bring a large saucepan of salted water to the boil and throw the whole lettuces in. Leave them for a minute, then transfer them to a bowl of cold water. Add the spinach to the same boiling water, leave it for 2 minutes, then plunge it into a bowl of cold water. Drain it and chop it finely. Separate all the lettuce leaves and lay them carefully on a board. Finely chop the sorrel and the herbs.

In a bowl combine the sorrel, herbs, spinach and breadcrumbs. Season them, add the eggs and a dash of the vermouth, and mix well. Put the stuffing into the belly of each fish, then wrap the fish entirely in the lettuce leaves making sure that they overlap each other. Oil a large piece of foil, place it on a baking tray and transfer the fish onto it. Dribble the rest of the vermouth and the wine all over the fish, then wrap the foil around it to seal it. Reduce the oven heat to gas mark 4, 350°F (180°C) and bake the fish for 15 minutes. Turn the oven off, partially unwrap the fish, then leave them in the oven with the door ajar for another 10 minutes, basting them as they cool. Transfer them at the last moment onto serving dishes and garnish them with the lemon, parsley and olives.

Variation: This fish is also delicious hot with a refreshing sauce (see below). Make the fish exactly as above until the final stage when it is resting in the hot oven.

Sauce:
4 shallots
A little olive oil
16 fl oz (425 ml) white wine
Dash of dry vermouth
1 lb (450 g) natural yoghurt
Salt, freshly ground black pepper

Sweat the chopped shallot in the olive oil for about 5 minutes. Transfer the fish juices to this pan, add the wine and the vermouth, bring it to the boil and let it reduce to half its volume. Let it cool down a little, then whisk in the yoghurt. Add seasoning to taste, then serve with the still-hot fish.

CHICKEN IN VINEGAR SAUCE

SERVES 20 (SEE PAGE 251)   LYN HALL WITH ANTON MOSIMANN

I was first taught to cook this dish in Persia, over a simple fire stove, by the mother of a Persian noble. Unable to communicate, except by our love of cooking, we spent many afternoons together sharing the delights of this fascinating cuisine. It is the perfect dish for a large party as it is low in cost, the ingredients are readily obtainable, and it can be made in advance and gently re-heated. The enticing sweet-sour aroma as it steams on the hot-plate will soon draw your guests to the buffet-table. When you make a casserole, never boil the meat; the secret of tender succulence is a slow simmer – the surface of the liquid should merely tremble. Always begin with more sauce than you need, then boil it down slowly in a wide pan, skimming occasionally, to concentrate the flavour and thicken the consistency.

The red wine vinegar should not be too acid: if it makes you choke when you taste it, dilute it with a little water. Vinegars sold in Britain are often much more acid than those sold elsewhere.

Serve this dish with soft and creamy mashed potatoes or fresh noodles, turned in a little safflower oil with plenty of chopped fresh herbs and ground black pepper.

4 chickens, weighing 2 lb 8 oz (1·1 kg) each
15 cloves garlic
5 large tomatoes
1 dessertspoon peppercorns
16 fl oz (425 ml) red wine vinegar
1 pint 10 fl oz (900 ml) chicken stock
Salt, freshly ground black pepper
14 oz (400 g) fromage blanc (optional)
5 tablespoons chopped chives (optional)

First divide each chicken into 10 portions. To do this separate the leg from the thigh, cut off the wing with a little breast, and cut each breast, on the bone, in half. Carefully remove the skin and discard it. Remove the wing-tips and reserve them for the stock. Skin and crush the garlic. Skin and de-seed the tomatoes, and chop the flesh.

Heat a non-stick frying-pan: there is no need for any oil. In small batches, brown the chicken portions on all sides for about 6 minutes. Remove the chicken pieces and transfer to wire cake racks set over trays until the chicken has cooled. This prevents the chicken stewing in its own juices and cooking further in its own residual heat.

Transfer the chicken pieces to a large casserole. (You may need to use 2 casseroles.) Add the garlic, peppercorns and tomato and cook for 1 minute. Add the vinegar and boil for 5 minutes to reduce the liquid. Add the chicken stock, cover and simmer for about 10 minutes until the chicken is tender. Remove the chicken from the casserole, and allow it to cool again on the wire cake racks.

Bring the liquid in the casserole to the boil again and simmer it gently until it has the consistency of thin sauce, skimming off the fat and froth from time to time. When you have 1 pint 15 fl oz (1 litre), push the sauce through a sieve with the back of a ladle and season it to taste with pepper and, if required, a little salt. If the sauce is too thin, boil it down further. Return the chicken pieces and sauce to the casserole. The chicken should be visible, not swamped by the sauce, though this depends on the size of your serving vessel and the amount of your sauce. Gently re-heat the casserole when required.

ROAST PORK WITH APPLES

Rôti de Porc aux Pommes

SERVES 20 (SEE PAGE 251)   CHRISTOPHE BUEY

Pork can be a fatty joint. In this recipe, a robust fruit stuffing gives a less fatty, but very succulent result, and also provides a fragrant complement to the meat. This joint can be served hot or cold. If you serve it hot it is delicious with a purée of swedes or celeriac.

12 dessert apples, preferably Cox's
1 lemon
4 ounces (110 g) dried apricots
4 lb (1·8 kg) boned loin of pork
2 onions
2 carrots
2 celery stalks
8 fl oz (225 ml) white wine
15 fl oz (400 ml) chicken stock

Peel, core and chop 4 of the apples. Grate the lemon rind and squeeze the juice. Put the apples, lemon rind and juice into a small saucepan. Cover and simmer them gently until the apples have reduced to a thick purée. Chop the apricots roughly and add them to the apple purée.

Make a slit in the joint large enough to hold all the stuffing. Stuff the meat, then roll it up and tie it with string. Place the meat in a steamer (see page 22) and steam it over a high heat for 20 minutes, turning it over twice.

Pre-heat the oven to its highest setting. Transfer the joint to a roasting tin, reduce the oven temperature to gas mark 8, 450°F (230°C), and roast it at this heat for 10 minutes. Meanwhile, finely chop the onions, and cut the carrots and celery into small dice; peel, core and slice the remaining apples into rings. Add the chopped vegetables, the apples and the wine to the roasting tin. Reduce the heat to gas mark 4, 350°F (180°C), and cook for a further 45 minutes. Baste the joints, then turn the oven off. Leave the door closed and let the joints rest for a further 10 minutes.

Transfer the meat to a warmed serving dish. Discard the vegetables, but use the apples for garnish. Add the chicken stock to the pan and boil it fast to reduce it to a sauce consistency. Let it stand for a few minutes, then spoon off the fat. Bring the sauce back to the boil, then transfer it to a sauceboat. Serve the pork with the sauce handed separately.

VEGETABLES PROVENÇAL STYLE WITH LEMON

Gratin provençal au Citron

SERVES 20 (SEE PAGE 251)   CHRISTOPHE BUEY

In this vegetable dish, the juice of the tomatoes softens and flavours the other vegetables, and the lemon gives them a fresh taste. It is particularly good with fish and can be served hot or cold.

2 lb (900 g) aubergines
3 lb (1·4 kg) courgettes
1 lb 8 oz (700 g) button mushrooms
5 lb (2·3 kg) tomatoes
4 dessertspoons olive oil
4 cloves garlic
4 lemons

Pre-heat the oven to gas mark 6, 400°F (200°C).

Wash all the vegetables and pat them dry with kitchen paper. Prepare 4 shallow 10 inch (25 cm) ovenproof gratin dishes. Rub each with some of the olive oil and the crushed cloves of garlic. Divide the vegetables equally among the 4 dishes. Slice the aubergines and arrange the slices at the bottom of the dishes, then squeeze a little lemon juice over them. Repeat this operation with the courgettes, then the mushrooms and finish with the sliced tomatoes, carefully arranged to overlap each other.

Cover each dish with a piece of kitchen foil which should be greased with olive oil to prevent the tomatoes from sticking to it. Bake the covered vegetables for 30–35 minutes. When the vegetables are cooked, carefully drain the juices from the dishes into a saucepan, using a plate or large fish slice to hold back the vegetables. Bring the juices to the boil and reduce them to a syrupy consistency. Pour this over the vegetables in the dishes or serve it separately.

STUFFED CABBAGE BUNDLES

Paupiettes de Choux

SERVES 20 (SEE PAGE 251)   CHRISTOPHE BUEY

These little stuffed cabbage parcels make a delicious bite-sized savoury for a buffet. They can be prepared ahead of time and left to marinate.

Salt, freshly ground black pepper
3 savoy cabbages
4 leeks
12 spring onions
1 lb (450 g) Swiss chard or spinach
8 tomatoes
2 dessertspoons safflower oil
8 oz (225 g) cooked brown rice
2 dessertspoons Dijon mustard
4 tablespoons tarragon or white wine vinegar
4 tablespoons olive oil
5 oz (150 g) low-fat natural yoghurt
2 dessertspoons fresh herbs (eg parsley, chervil, tarragon), finely chopped, or 1 teaspoon of dried mixed herbs
4 carrots

Bring a very large saucepan of salted water to the boil, detach all the leaves from the cabbage and cook them for 10–15 minutes or until they are tender. Refresh them under the cold tap and lay them on a tea towel to dry.

To make the stuffing, slice the leeks thinly, chop the spring onions and the Swiss chard or spinach. Peel and de-seed the tomatoes, and chop the flesh. Heat the oil and sweat the chopped leek and onion until they are transparent, then add the chard or spinach and cook gently for a further 5 minutes. Mix in the cooked rice and set the stuffing aside to cool.

Make the vinaigrette by mixing the mustard, salt, pepper and vinegar, then beating in the olive oil, yoghurt and herbs. Add the vinaigrette, together with the chopped tomatoes, to the stuffing and leave it to marinate for several hours, tossing it frequently.

Slice the carrots thinly and set them aside for a moment. Take the cabbage leaves and fill each one with a generous spoonful of the marinated stuffing. Roll each one into a neat cigar-shaped parcel. Cut each one in half, pierce it with a cocktail stick and use a slice of carrot to stop the stuffing falling out. Arrange the parcels on a serving dish and serve.

GREEK-STYLE VEGETABLES
Legumes à la Greque

SERVES 20 (SEE PAGE 251)   CHRISTOPHE BUEY

This is a French adaptation of a wonderfully refreshing Greek vegetable salad which is usually prepared the day before. There is no limit to the possibilities as far as the variety of vegetables is concerned.

2 pints (1·1 litres) dry white wine
2 pints (1·1 litres) vegetable stock (optional)
1 dessertspoon black peppercorns
1 dessertspoon coriander seeds
1 dessertspoon fennel seeds
1 dessertspoon fresh sage, chopped, or 1 teaspoon dried sage
A pinch of saffron
8 parsley stalks
Juice of 4 lemons
Salt
4 artichoke hearts (fresh or tinned)
2 celery stalks
1 lb (450 g) button mushrooms
4 bulbs fennel, quartered
1 lb (450 g) green Kenya beans
1 lb (450 g) carrots
16 baby onions
4 leeks
2 cauliflowers
1 lb 8 oz (700 g) broccoli
2 lb (900 g) tomatoes
4 dessertspoons olive oil

In a large saucepan combine the wine, vegetable stock or the same amount of water, the seeds and herbs, lemon juice and a little salt. Bring it slowly to the boil, simmer for 10 minutes, then strain it through a small piece of muslin. Tie up all the seeds and herbs in the muslin, then return the bag to the reserved stock. Meanwhile, prepare all the vegetables as necessary.

One by one, cook each type of vegetable in the stock (see page 243) until all the vegetables are just done (and still *al dente*). Combine them all in a large bowl and pour the remainder of the stock over them. Add a dash of olive oil. Leave the vegetables to marinate overnight. Remove the muslin bag before serving.

PICKLED CABBAGE PEKING STYLE

SERVES 20 (SEE PAGE 251)   LYN HALL WITH ANTON MOSIMANN

I would never have believed I would serve raw cabbage at a buffet, until I learned this dish from the distinguished Chinese cook, Yan-kit So. Wilted with salt, and polished by a little oil, the spices and peppers give the cabbage an exciting and unforgettable flavour. It is deceptively cool and slippery in the beginning, becomes salty and sweet, is simultaneously sharp and smooth, and finally explosively fiery. It is then necessary to try another mouthful to see if it happens again!

This dish keeps for several days in the refrigerator and, to my mind, this improves its flavour. Serve with oriental dishes and barbecues.

1 lb 4 oz (550 g) white cabbage
2 dessertspoons salt
½ inch (1 cm) fresh ginger root, peeled and cut into fine strips
3 tablespoons sugar
2 tablespoons sunflower oil
2 tablespoons sesame oil
1½ dried chillies, de-seeded and chopped
½ teaspoon Szechwan peppercorns (optional)
3 tablespoons rice vinegar or white wine vinegar

Shred the cabbage as finely as possible either in a food processor or with a knife. Transfer to a very large mixing bowl. Sprinkle in the salt and mix well. Leave it to stand at room temperature for 2–3 hours; the cabbage will decrease in bulk because the salt draws out some of its water content. Rinse the cabbage thoroughly. Then take a handful of cabbage at a time and, using both hands, squeeze out the excess water (but leave the cabbage damp). Transfer it to a clean bowl.

Place the ginger on top of the cabbage in the centre of the bowl. Sprinkle in the sugar, taking care not to put it over the ginger.

Heat the oil and sesame oil in a small saucepan over a high heat until smoke rises. Remove the pan from the heat, then add the chopped chillies and the peppercorns. Pour the mixture over the ginger first and then the surrounding cabbage in the bowl. The sizzling oil partially cooks the ginger, enhancing the flavour.

Add the vinegar and mix everything well. Leave it to stand at room temperature for 2–3 hours, then serve. If made in advance, refrigerate until an hour or 2 before needed, then remove from the refrigerator so that the dish reaches room temperature before serving.

SALADS

CAROLINE WALDEGRAVE

Salad recipes can be endless so I have just included a selection of ideas and a recipe for a dressing. On the whole I would allow a total of 1½ portions of salad per person; if you have 50 people to your party, you should provide 75 portions of salad. If you were planning to make 5 salads, each should be enough for about 15 people whereas if you were only going to do 3, each salad should be for about 25 people. Remember the fewer the types of salad you make, the more generous the portions have to be – that is why the quantities below are fairly vague.

Basic salad dressing:

This dressing uses yoghurt instead of oil.

3 tablespoons low-fat natural yoghurt
1 dessertspoon lemon juice
Freshly ground black pepper

Mix well and check the seasoning, adding more pepper if necessary.

This is the basic dressing to which any of the following can be added:

Mustard
Ground cumin
Fresh herbs, chopped
Vinegar (instead of lemon juice – many different flavours are available or you can make your own (see page 72))
Crushed garlic
Chopped shallot
Orange juice (instead of lemon juice – this is particularly good with chopped mint)

CUCUMBER AND DILL SALAD

Peeled, sliced cucumber served with white wine vinegar and masses of fresh dill. 1 large cucumber will be enough for 8 portions of salad.

TOMATO SALAD

Allow 1 ½ peeled tomatoes per head. Serve with a dressing to which either fresh basil or fresh thyme has been added. Season well with freshly ground black pepper. (There are approximately 6 medium-sized tomatoes to the pound.)

SPINACH SALAD

Raw young spinach tossed with sliced raw mushrooms is an unusual but delicious combination.

FENNEL AND RED PEPPER SALAD

Many markets and greengrocers now sell fennel. Its aniseed-like flavour goes well with raw red pepper, so mix sliced raw fennel and raw red pepper, toss them in a plain dressing and decorate with the fennel tops for an excellent salad. I find 2 bulbs of fennel and 1 red pepper are enough for 6–8 people.

CARROT, MINT AND CUMIN SALAD

Grated carrots, mixed with a French dressing made with masses of chopped mint and ground cumin, are very refreshing. Allow 1 large carrot per person. Do not add the dressing too far ahead of time as the carrots will lose bulk.

CUCUMBER AND CHICK PEA SALAD

1 chopped cucumber mixed with 8 oz (225 g) cooked chick peas and tossed in a yoghurt dressing seasoned with freshly ground black pepper and roughly chopped coriander will make enough salad for 8–10 people.

ORANGE AND WATERCRESS SALAD

A pretty arrangement of peeled sliced oranges and washed watercress can make a most refreshing salad. It needs no dressing. 4 large oranges and 1 bunch of watercress would probably be enough for 6 people.

NEW POTATO AND MINT SALAD

Allow 4 oz (110 g) well scrubbed, barely cooked new potatoes per person. While the potatoes are still warm toss them in a salad dressing to which masses of roughly chopped mint has been added. If you have no mint, chives are an excellent substitute. Serve immediately.

WATERMELON SALAD

SERVES 20 (SEE PAGE 251)   CAROLINE WALDEGRAVE

There could not be a simpler recipe but it looks so pretty and will 'sit' perfectly happily if your guests are late.

2 small watermelons, weighing 9 lb (4 kg) together
1 lb (450 g) strawberries
2 tablespoons rose water, or to taste
Flowers such as gypsophila for decoration

Cut off the top quarter of the watermelons. Reserve these to make 'lids' later. Scoop out the rest of the watermelons with a melon baller. You will not be able to make very neat balls but try to get a couple of cupfuls. Cut the rest of the flesh into dice, discarding the pips. Clean out the shells. Hull and halve the strawberries. Toss all but 6 of the strawberries and all the diced melon in three quarters of the rose water and pile into the empty shells. Toss the remaining strawberries with the melon balls and rose water and arrange in the melon shells. Replace the lids at a jaunty angle and refrigerate.

When ready to serve, decorate with gypsophila flowers.

PINEAPPLE IN THE SHELL
WITH MANGO SAUCE

SERVES 20 (SEE PAGE 251)   CAROLINE WALDEGRAVE

3 large pineapples
15 fresh dates (optional)

For the sauce:
5 passion fruit
3 large ripe mangoes

Cut the top and bottom off each pineapple so that you are left with a cylinder of fruit. Do not throw away the leafy top. With a sharp knife cut round the inside skin, working from one end and then the other, so that you can push the fruit out in 1 piece. Try not to pierce or tear the skin.

Slice each pineapple. Remove the core with a small pastry cutter, and cut the flesh into cubes. Cut the dates in half, if using, and remove their stones. Stand the pineapple shells in two shallow dishes, combine the cubes of pineapple and halved dates, put the fruit back in the shells and replace the tops. Do not refrigerate because the smell of the pineapple will taint all the other food.

To make the mango sauce, cut the passion fruit in half and scoop out the flesh with a teaspoon. Skin and stone the mangoes. Process the mango and passion fruit flesh and 5 tablespoons of water in a food processor or liquidiser. (If you are using a liquidiser, the passion fruit should be sieved before liquidising.) Strain into a sauceboat and serve with the pineapple.

YOGHURT SUNDAES

SERVES 20 (SEE PAGE 251)   LYN HALL

Dried fruit has a more intense flavour than its fresh counterpart, and gives this generously to a steeping liquor. Lined up in rows on the buffet table in pretty, sparkling goblets, creamy and cold, this dessert will be a delectable finale to your party.

3 tablespoons allspice berries
5 sticks cinnamon, 6 inches (15 cm) long, broken into smaller pieces
1 lb 12 oz (800 g) mixed dried fruit, such as figs, peaches, pears, apples
2 pints 10 fl oz (1·4 litres) red grape juice, with no added sugar
1 oz (25 g) fresh ginger root, peeled and sliced into rounds
Rind of 2 lemons
2 lb 4 oz (1 kg) thick Greek-style natural yoghurt
4 fl oz (100 ml) Kirsch
6 egg whites
1½ oz (40 g) caster sugar
Ground cinnamon
10 sticks cinnamon, 2 inches (5 cm) long, split lengthways
20 small mint leaves

Tie up the allspice berries and broken cinnamon sticks loosely in a piece of muslin, and crush them with a rolling pin. Place the dried fruit, grape juice, ginger and lemon rind in a pan (not an iron one or the ingredients may turn blue) with the muslin bag of crushed spices, and bring to the boil. Remove the pan from the heat, transfer the mixture to a glass bowl and allow it to soak overnight in a cool place.

Remove and discard the bag of spices. Strain the juice into a wide pan and reduce it to 1 pint (570 ml) by fast boiling. Cool and chill. Meanwhile chop the fruit neatly, and divide it equally between 20 glasses.

Pour the chilled juice and Kirsch over the fruit. Beat the egg whites until thick and creamy. Add a tablespoon of the caster sugar and beat until stiff. Quickly whisk in all the remaining sugar. Whisk a little of the beaten egg white into the yoghurt, then lightly fold in the remaining egg white.

Pour the yoghurt mixture over the fruit in the glasses, and sprinkle with ground cinnamon.

Garnish each glass with a halved cinnamon stick and a mint leaf, and chill before serving.

PINEAPPLE SORBET

Sorbet à l'Ananas

SERVES 20 (SEE PAGE 251)   CHRISTOPHE BUEY

A simple 'tangy' sorbet made with pineapple, orange, egg white and a little Grand Marnier. No sugar is added!

4 large pineapples
4 large oranges
4 dessertspoons Grand Marnier
8 egg whites

Set the freezer to its lowest temperature. Peel and core the pineapples. Liquidise the pineapple flesh, together with the rind and flesh (but not the pith) of the oranges, then add the Grand Marnier. Freeze the mixture for 30 minutes or until it is nearly frozen. Whisk the egg whites until they are stiff, fold them into the frozen but still creamy pineapple and orange. Deep-freeze the sorbet for 3 hours until it is solid. 30 minutes before serving, place it in the refrigerator to soften it slightly.

BIOGRAPHIES

Raymond Blanc was born and brought up in rural France. At 20 years old he decided to make a career in food, in spite of his lack of formal training. He worked first as a waiter, then as a restaurant manager, but his secret ambition was to become a chef. He came to England in the seventies to manage the restaurant *Rose Revived*. He fell in love with the restaurant and also fell in love with and married the owner's daughter. After a year in Germany, they returned to the *Rose Revived*. This time, with much inward trepidation, he took over the kitchen as chef. As he says, 'I crowned myself!' The restaurant was a success, and in 1977 he started his Oxford restaurant *Les Quat' Saisons*, then in 1984 opened *Le Manoir aux Quat' Saisons*, which already has two Michelin stars. He is renowned for the lightness and fresh taste of his food and for its superb presentation. He and his wife, Jenny, have three children and live in Oxford.

Christophe Buey is French, and diploma holder of the Lausanne Hotel School. After working in traditional restaurants such as the *Four Seasons* in New York and being trained to teach at L'Ecole du Cordon Bleu de Paris, he created, with Sabine de Mirbeck, l'Ecole de Cuisine Française, a French cookery school in Litlington, Sussex. He is head teacher there and his courses on French cuisine include a special week each term when healthy food is emphasised. His particular interest is in adapting French traditional recipes to a healthier cuisine for the eighties. He says that this does not preclude 'the occasional blow out on cream, sugar and butter!'

Antonio Carluccio was born in Italy and worked first as a journalist, then as an international wine merchant. He now runs *The Neal Street Restaurant* in London. Although he has lived and worked all over the world, he still believes passionately in the delights and pleasures of Italian food with its special emphasis on fresh, colourful vegetables and strong, clean tastes. He loves inventing new recipes and is a tireless collector of funghi which he hunts – even in the London suburbs! He has contributed to cookery books and cookery columns, and his own forthcoming cookery book reflects his belief that the best food is simple home cooking. He is married to Priscilla Conran, lives in London and has three step-children.

Evelyn Findlater has been an enthusiastic cook of healthy food for about 10 years, dating back to the time when she was a mature student with very little money at a teacher training college. Her experiments were so successful that she began giving recipes to friends and colleagues. Eventually she set up her own wholefood shop and café in North Devon and by popular demand began teaching cookery. She regards her greatest personal triumph as being the successful courses she has run for school meals supervisors, which proved to them that even school food can be healthy and delicious. She has a special interest in creating 'plenty out of little' and most of her recipes are notable for their imaginative use of economical ingredients. She has published several books, including *The Wholefood Cookery Course*, and has presented a local television series on cookery. Her four children range from a 21-year-old son to the 3-year-old daughter of her second marriage.

Nick Gill at 28 is one of the youngest of Britain's top chefs. On leaving school he considered becoming a magician, but then decided to devote his sense of showmanship to food instead, and at 15 went to the Savoy to train under the great chef Trompetto. Later he moved to Paris for three years and during this time persuaded *Maxim's* to employ him as a *chef partie*, an almost unheard-of feat for an Englishman. Once back in Britain, he joined with Tim Hart to open the luxury hotel, Hambleton Hall, in Rutland. Here he created a new and imaginative approach to English cooking, which reflected his style in having, as he says, a 'balance of textures, colours, flavours and lightness'. This, and his exceptional flair in the presentation of his dishes, has won Hambleton Hall various accolades including a Michelin Rosette for 1982/3. Nick believes that healthier eating must stem from 'a lighter, more subtle approach to cooking, where each ingredient is allowed to speak for itself. It is up to us to demand the best ingredients, and prepare them simply and carefully'.

Lyn Hall worked as a model and in advertising before turning to cookery in the mid-seventies. She was Chef at Blake's Hotel in 1975 and opened her cookery school, La Petite Cuisine, in Richmond shortly afterwards. She is especially interested in classical French cooking, but is also fascinated by modern trends in food and its presentation. She has a positive attitude to health, eating, and fitness; daily exercising is part of her routine. She believes that you are what you eat, and says 'I try to eat intelligently and healthily. On the other hand, I can easily succumb to something unusual and lovely from time to time, like a beautiful pastry!' Her business partner, *Anton Mosimann*, is one of the best-known chefs in Britain. Born in Switzerland, he learnt his craft in distinguished hotels and restaurants all over Europe. Since 1975 he has worked at the Dorchester Hotel in London where he is now Maitre Chef des Cuisines. The highly successful *Terrace Restaurant* at the Dorchester has been his own special project. He believes in light food which is based on top quality ingredients, a philosophy he has expounded in several books. He plays squash, jogs, and is married with two sons.

Carole Handslip trained in Home Economics for two years, then worked as an air stewardess with BOAC, but her interest in food soon led her back to cookery demonstrating and then to teaching at the Cordon Bleu Schools in London and Berkshire. She has prepared food for photography, and is the author of many successful cookery books published for Sainsbury's. She loves devising and preparing recipes for cakes and puddings, and has made a speciality of dishes which use far less than the conventional amount of fat and sugar. Her husband runs his own travel business and they have a teenage son and daughter who are appreciative and critical first testers of her recipes.

Madhur Jaffrey was born in India and first came to England as a young drama student who had never done cooking at all. Living in lodgings in North London, she so missed home cooking that she wrote to her mother begging for instructions on how to make the delicious food she remembered from childhood. Following her mother's carefully composed replies was the beginning of a life-long commitment to cooking Indian food, writing about it and passing on her own expertise to others. Her *Invitation to Indian Cooking* is the classic reference book on the subject, but she reached an even wider audience with her BBC TV series *Madhur Jaffrey's Indian Cookery* and its accompanying best-selling book. Simultaneously she has maintained her career in acting and has appeared in many films, including *Diary of a Princess* with James Mason and *Heat and Dust* with Julie Christie. Madhur travels widely, has three grown-up daughters and now lives in New York with her violinist husband, Sanford Allen.

Leslie Kenton has been Health and Beauty Editor for *Harpers and Queen* for 12 years. Her unorthodox approach to 'beauty' initially raised many eyebrows, as she insisted on treating food, fitness and beauty as equally important aspects of the same desirable approach to life. Her many books include *Raw Energy* (which she wrote with her daughter, Susannah) and *Ultrahealth*, which emphasise the value of the raw food diet she enjoys herself. She is also interested in physical fitness and relaxation techniques and in her personal life is a keen exponent of both, perhaps proving the truth of her own belief that it *is* possible to 'stay healthy in an unhealthy world'. She is the daughter of the American jazz musician Stan Kenton, lives for much of the year in Pembrokeshire and has four children.

Elisabeth Lambert Ortiz has worked as a writer and journalist all her life, and her output includes novels, plays and poetry as well as a number of distinguished cookery books. She is fascinated by the long history of food and cooking all over the world, but she is especially well known for her work on Latin American cuisine. Her *Book of Latin American Cooking* is widely regarded as the classic work on the subject and is notable for its racy accounts of meals cooked and eaten all over the South American continent. She says she still eats in the sensible and ungimmicky way she learnt from her mother: 'lots of green vegetables and fresh fruit with some fish and poultry'. She is married to the Mexican journalist Cesar Ortiz-Tinoco. They live in London with their demanding cat, Polly, who also likes to eat healthily, an attitude which includes showing complete disdain for tinned foods.

Paul Laurenson and *Ethel Minogue* began their careers as law lecturer and costume historian respectively. A love of French home cooking eventually led to their opening *Twenty Two*, a restaurant which they ran from their own home in Cambridge. They always featured vegetarian dishes on their menus and made a speciality of unusual salads which included edible plants not commonly found in restaurant salads. They devised the salads which were photographed and described in Joy Larkcom's book *The Salad Garden*. They now run a restaurant in Islington, North London.

Dinah Morrison worked originally as a secretary – her former bosses include Sir Francis Chichester and Sir Terence Conran. She went on to become a food stylist for cookery books and magazines, and now contributes regular articles to national newspapers and magazines, including *The Sunday Times*. She says her attitude to healthy eating is 'unfaddy', but she believes in keeping a careful eye on the amounts of fat, sugar she and her family eat. She is married and has three grown-up children. Her dog and her horse help her to enjoy the pleasures of country life in Kent where she is also an enthusiastic vegetable gardener.

Michael Quinn was until recently the Head Chef at the Ritz Hotel in London, and the first Englishman to take over this bastion of French cuisine from a long line of French chefs. He was born in Yorkshire and from the age of 14 wanted to become a famous chef. He worked all over the country learning his craft, and established his reputation as one of Britain's top chefs at the country house hotel Gravetye Manor in Sussex. He is a founder member of the Country Chefs Seven, a group of seven outstanding British chefs who are keen to support higher standards of cooking in Britain, and who meet during the year to share and discuss developing trends and ideas in food. Michael travels around the world cooking, judging and demonstrating. He believes that food 'plays a very important part in life as a way of cementing friendships, and, for the cook, offers freedom of expression. But it is equally important to eat sensibly in order to look after one's physical and mental state'. He now lives in Warwickshire with his wife and three children and is Head Chef at Ettington Park Hotel near Stratford-upon-Avon. He received the MBE in the Queen's Birthday Honours List in June 1985.

Claudia Roden was born in Egypt and began her career as a painter, but the publication of her classic *Book of Middle Eastern Food* quickly established her as one of our most talented cookery writers. She followed this book with *Coffee* and *Picnic* and has contributed to many others. All her books are more than mere collections of recipes – they are full of observations on the history and social customs surrounding food. Middle Eastern food is one of the world's healthiest cuisines with its emphasis on pulses, fresh vegetables and making a little meat or fish go a long way. Claudia believes that Middle Eastern food could be a pattern for all of us as it is tasty and enjoyable as well as healthy. She lives in London and runs cookery courses from her own home. She has three grown-up children.

Jenny Rogers started her career as a teacher where her special interest was adult education, a subject on which she has written several books. She first joined the BBC as an Education Officer, then moved to television about 10 years ago. Cookery is both an absorbing personal interest and a professional concern: she produced the first series of *Delia Smith's Cookery Course* and also *Madhur Jaffrey's Indian Cookery*. Her husband runs a busy department for BBC Radio and they have two young sons.

Shirley Rilla and *Jill Cox*. *Shirley Rilla* began her career as a public relations consultant to various national food companies. *Jill Cox* is a food and drink journalist who writes regularly for various newspapers and magazines. Shirley and Jill now run their own gourmet catering and hamper company in London. Shirley has travelled widely with her film director husband, Wolf Rilla, and has a special interest in tropical food. They have one teenage son. Jill is married to David Cox, a publicist, and has a teenage son and daughter. Shirley and Jill believe strongly that food should be enjoyable and 'not just body fuel'. They also think that changing to a more 'healthy' way of eating is an urgent necessity which need not mean a life of denial and boredom. Both have found that changing to a healthier regime in home cooking has not only been accepted but also enjoyed by their families.

Caroline Waldegrave has run Leith's School of Food and Wine in London for 10 years, and is co-author with Prue Leith of *Leith's Cookery Course*. She has made a speciality of devising food which is beautifully presented and which also uses little fat, sugar or salt. She believes in an 'uncranky' approach in which simple fresh food speaks for itself. Her husband, William, is a Member of Parliament and they have three young children. Her four-year-old daughter, Kate, already has well formed views of her own about food and has been an exacting critic of all the children's recipes Caroline has devised for this book.

FURTHER READING

BRIGGS, David and WAHLQVIST, Mark *Food facts: the complete no-fads – plain facts guide to healthy eating* Penguin, 1984.

CANNON, Geoffrey and EINZIG, Hetty *Dieting makes you fat: a guide to energy, fitness and health* Century, 1983.

FINDLATER, Evelyn *Wholefood cookery course* Muller, cased and paperback 1984.

HANDSLIP, Carole *The Sainsbury book of wholefood cooking* Cathay Books for J. Sainsbury, 1981.

JAFFREY, Madhur *Invitation to Indian cookery* Cape, 1976.

JAFFREY, Madhur *Madhur Jaffrey's Indian cookery* BBC Publications, cased and paperback 1982.

KENTON, Leslie and Susannah *Raw energy: eat your way to radiant health* Century, 1984.

LARKCOM, Joy *The salad garden* Windward, 1984.

MOSIMANN, Anton *Cuisine naturelle* Macmillan, 1985.

LEITH, Prue and WALDEGRAVE, Caroline *Leith's cookery course* 3 vols. Fontana, 1979–80; 3 vols. in 1 Deutsch, 1980.

ORTIZ, Elisabeth Lambert *The book of Latin American cooking* (A Jill Norman book). R. Hale, 1984.

RODEN, Claudia *A new book of Middle Eastern food* Viking, 1985.

SPENCER, Colin *Gourmet cooking for vegetarians* Deutsch, 1978; R. Clark, paperback 1980.

STOBART, Tom *Herbs, spices and flavourings* Penguin, 1977.

THOMAS, Anna *The vegetarian epicure* Penguin, 1973.

TUDGE, Colin *Future cook: a taste of things to come* Mitchell Beazley, 1980.

TUDGE, Colin *The food connection: the BBC guide to healthy eating* BBC Publications, 1985.

WALKER, Caroline and CANNON, Geoffrey *The food scandal: what's wrong with the British diet and how to put it right* Century, 1984.

Healthy eating Pelham Books for the Open University and the Health Education Council, 1985.

USEFUL MAIL-ORDER ADDRESSES

Kitchen equipment catalogues can be obtained from:
DIVERTIMENTI, 68 Marylebone Lane, London W1. (£1.50 p. & p.)
HABITAT DESIGNS LTD – newsagents, or any branch of Habitat.

Herb plant suppliers:
HOLLINGTON NURSERIES, Woolton Hill, Newbury, Berkshire RG15 9XT

Specialist salad and vegetable seed suppliers:
SUFFOLK HERBS, Sawyers Farm, Little Cornard, Sudbury, Suffolk.
CHILTERN SEEDS, Bortree Stile, Ulverston, Cumbria LA12 7PB
HENRY DOUBLEDAY, Bocking, Braintree, Essex OM7 6RN

INDEX

Page numbers in italics indicate a colour illustration.